D0794137
DISCARDED
The Usborne Internet-linked
912 TUR
1100491
Turnbull, Stephanie
Fraser Valley Elementary School
Fraser Valley Elementary Media Cente
125 Eastom Av. / PO Box 128
Fraser, CO 80442 / 970-726-8033

THE USBORNE

INTERNET-LINKED

ESSENTIAL ATLAS OF THE WORLD

Stephanie Turnbull

Designers: Stephen Moncrieff and Helen Wood

Consultant cartographic editor: Craig Asquith

Cartography by European Map Graphics Ltd

Map design by Laura Fearn and Keith Newell

CONTENTS

4 Internet links
6 Maps and atlases
8 Dividing lines
10 How maps are made
12 Thematic maps
14 How to use the maps

16 World – political
18 World – physical

20 North America
22 Canada and Alaska
24 United States of America
26 Central America and the Caribbean

28 South America
30 Northern South America
32 Southern South America

34 Australasia and Oceania
36 Oceania
38 Australia and New Zealand

40 Asia
42 Southern Southeast Asia
44 Northern Southeast Asia
46 China, Korea and Japan
48 India and Central Asia
50 Western Asia
52 Northern Eurasia

54 Europe
56 Eastern Europe
58 Central and Northern Europe
60 Western Europe
62 Southern Europe

64 Africa
66 Northeast Africa
68 Northwest Africa
70 Central Africa
72 Southern Africa

74 The Arctic

76 Antarctica

78 World records
80 Time zones
81 Types of governments
82 Gazetteer of states

96 Useful websites
98 Map index
112 General index and acknowledgements

This page: African elephants graze on plains south of the Sahara Desert.

Title page: Evening sunlight shines on Mount Rainier, in Washington, northwestern U.S.A.

Endpapers: This picture of the world at night has been made by combining many satellite images.

INTERNET LINKS

This book contains descriptions of many interesting websites where you can find out more about maps and places around the world. For links to these sites, go to the Usborne Quicklinks Website at **www.usborne-quicklinks.com** and enter the keywords "essential atlas". There you will find links to take you to all the sites.

Site availability

The links on the Usborne Quicklinks Website will be reviewed and updated regularly. If any sites become unavailable, we will, if possible, replace them with suitable alternatives.

Occasionally, you may get a message saying that a website is unavailable. This may be temporary, so try again a few hours later, or even the next day.

Internet links

For links to all the websites described in this book, go to **www.usborne-quicklinks.com** and enter the keywords "essential atlas".

Help

For general help and advice on using the Internet, go to the Usborne Quicklinks Website and click on "Net Help".

To find out more about using your web browser, click on your browser's Help menu and choose "Contents and Index". You'll find a searchable dictionary containing tips on how to find your way around the Internet easily.

What you need

The websites described in this book can be accessed using a standard home computer and a web browser (the software that enables you to display information from the Internet). Here's a list of the basic requirements:

- A PC with Microsoft® Windows® 98 or a later version, or a Macintosh computer with System 9.0 or later
- 64Mb RAM
- A web browser such as Microsoft® Internet Explorer 5, or Netscape® 6, or later versions
- Connection to the Internet via a modem (preferably 56kbps) or a faster digital or cable line
- An account with an Internet Service Provider (ISP)
- A sound card to hear sound files

Computer not essential

If you don't have use of the Internet, don't worry. This atlas is a complete, self-contained reference book on its own.

Extras

Some websites need additional free programs, called plug-ins, to play sounds, or to show videos, animations or 3-D images. If you go to a site and you do not have the necessary plug-in, a message should come up on the screen.

There is usually a button on the site that you can click on to download the plug-in. Alternatively, go to Usborne Quicklinks and click on "Net Help". There you can find links to download plug-ins. Here is a list of plug-ins that you might need:

- **QuickTime** – lets you play video clips.
- **RealOne™ Player** – lets you play video clips and sound files.
- **Flash™** – lets you play animations.
- **Shockwave®** – lets you play animations and enjoy interactive sites.

Computer viruses

A computer virus is a program that can damage your computer. A virus can get into your computer when you download programs from the Internet, or in an attachment (an extra file) that arrives with an email. We strongly recommend that you buy anti-virus software to protect your computer and that you update the software regularly. You can buy anti-virus software at computer stores or download it from the Internet. To find out more about viruses, go to Usborne Quicklinks and click on "Net Help".

Macintosh and QuickTime are trademarks of Apple computer, Inc., registered in the U.S.A. and other countries.

RealOne Player is a trademark of RealNetworks, Inc., registered in the U.S.A. and other countries.

Flash and Shockwave are trademarks of Macromedia, Inc., registered in the U.S.A. and other countries.

Internet safety

When using the Internet, make sure you follow these simple safety rules.

- Ask your parent's or guardian's permission before you connect to the Internet. They can then stay nearby if they think they should do so.
- If you write a message in a website guest book or on a website message board, do not include your email address, real name, address or telephone number.
- If a website asks you to log in or register by typing your name or email address, ask the permission of an adult first.
- If you receive email from someone you don't know, tell an adult and do not reply to the email.
- Never arrange to meet anyone you have talked to on the Internet.

Note for parents

The websites described in this book are regularly checked and reviewed by Usborne editors and the links in Usborne Quicklinks are updated. However, the content of a website may change at any time and Usborne Publishing is not responsible for the content of any website other than its own.

We recommend that children are supervised while on the Internet, that they do not use Internet chat rooms and that you use Internet filtering software to block unsuitable material. Please ensure that your children follow the safety guidelines above. For more information, go to the Net Help area on the Usborne Quicklinks Website at **www.usborne-quicklinks.com**

MAPS AND ATLASES

An atlas is a collection of maps, along with useful information about the areas shown. The maps in this atlas cover the whole world and are grouped by continent.

What maps show

A map is an image that represents an area of the Earth's surface, usually from above. Unlike a photograph, which shows exactly what an area looks like, a map can show features of the area in a clear, simplified way. It can also give different information, such as place names. Symbols are often used to mark features such as volcanoes and waterfalls.

Which way is up?

Although the Earth doesn't have a top and a bottom, north is usually at the top of maps. But it is sometimes more convenient to reposition a map, so north might not necessarily be at the top. Some maps have a compass symbol that indicates where north lies.

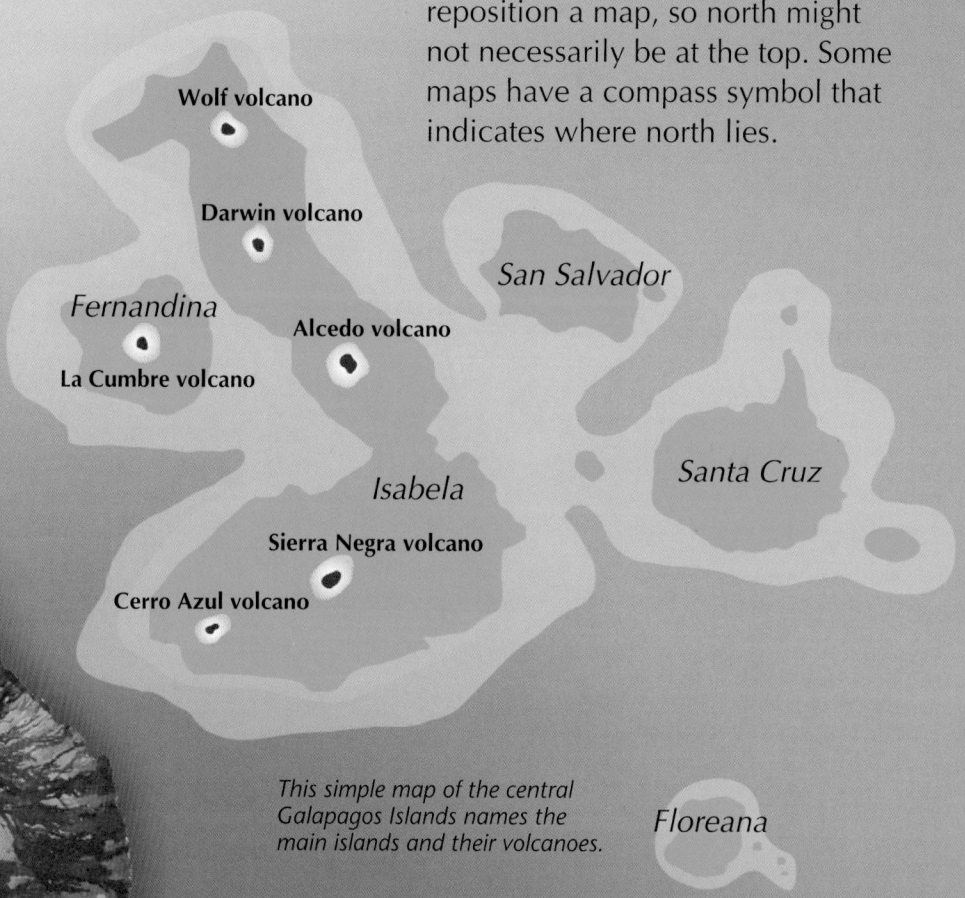

This simple map of the central Galapagos Islands names the main islands and their volcanoes.

This is a satellite image of part of the Galapagos Islands. Using the map on this page, can you identify the islands shown in the satellite photo?

Physical and political

Physical maps indicate natural features such as mountains, deserts, rivers and lakes. Political maps focus on the division of the Earth's surface into different countries. Look on pages 16–17 for a political map of the world, and on pages 18–19 for a physical map. Most of the maps in this atlas show physical features as well as country borders, cities and towns.

Using satellites

Today, scientists can make more accurate maps of the world than ever before, using information from artificial satellites in space. These devices travel around, or orbit, the Earth, and send back pictures of its surface. Satellite images provide detailed views of the Earth, and are often artificially shaded to highlight certain features, for example forests or deserts, so they are easier to see. They are used for a variety of purposes, such as monitoring weather conditions and natural hazards.

This illustration shows a satellite that monitors weather conditions on Earth. It collects data using powerful radar.

Map scales

The size of a map in relation to the area it shows is called its scale. Some maps have a scale bar, which is a rule with measurements. It tells you how many miles or km are represented by a certain distance on the map. Other maps show these relative distances just as numbers. For example, the figure 1:100 means that 1cm on the map represents 100cm on the Earth's surface.

The scale of a map depends on its purpose. A map showing the whole world is on a very small scale, but a town plan is on a much larger scale so that features such as roads can be shown clearly.

Internet links

For links to the following websites, go to **www.usborne-quicklinks.com**

Website 1 Find physical and political maps of different countries.

Website 2 Look at detailed satellite pictures of any part of the world.

1:80,000,000

0 1,000 2,000 3,000km

0 1,000 2,000 miles

This map of Europe is on a small scale so that it all fits onto one small map.

1:7,000,000

0 100 200 300km

0 100 200 miles

This map of Denmark is on a larger scale to show more detail.

DIVIDING LINES

The Earth is divided up with imaginary lines that help us measure distances and find where places are. There are two sets of lines, called latitude and longitude.

Latitude lines

Lines of latitude run around the globe. They are parallel to each other and get shorter the closer they are to the two poles. The latitude line that runs around the middle of the Earth is called the Equator. It is the most important line of latitude as all other lines are measured north or south of it.

Longitude lines

Lines of longitude run from the North Pole to the South Pole. All the lines are the same length, and they all meet at the North and South Poles.

The most important line of longitude is the Prime Meridian Line, which runs through Greenwich, in England. All other lines of longitude are measured east or west of this line.

Latitude lines

Longitude lines

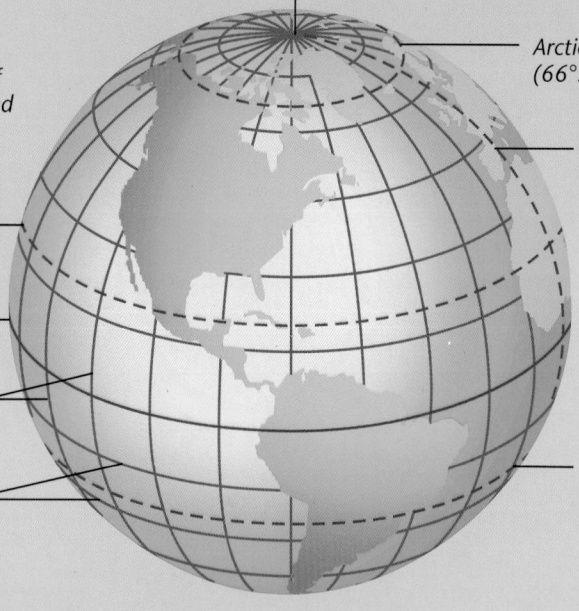

This drawing of the Earth shows some of the main latitude and longitude lines.

This arctic fox lives in northern Canada, very near the Arctic Circle line of latitude.

Other lines

The Equator is not the only named line of latitude. The Tropic of Cancer is a line north of the Equator. The Tropic of Capricorn is at the same distance south of the Equator. Between these lines are the hottest, wettest parts of the world. This region is called the tropics.

The Arctic Circle is a latitude line far north of the Equator. The area north of this includes the North Pole and is called the Arctic. On the other side of the globe is the Antarctic Circle. The area south of this includes the South Pole and is known as the Antarctic.

Internet link

For a link to a website where you can find out more about the Earth's lines of latitude and longitude, and test your knowledge with a great latitude and longitude quiz, go to **www.usborne-quicklinks.com**

Using the lines

Lines of latitude and longitude are measured in degrees (°). The positions of places are described according to which lines of latitude and longitude are nearest to them. For example, a place with a location of 50°S and 100°E has a latitude 50 degrees south of the Equator, and a longitude 100 degrees east of the Prime Meridian Line.

Exact locations

The distance between degrees is divided up to give even more precise measurements. Each degree is divided into 60 minutes (′), and each minute is divided into 60 seconds (″). The subdivisions allow us to locate any place on Earth. For example, the city of New York, U.S.A., is at 40°42′51″N and 74°00′23″W.

The steamy rainforests of Malaysia lie near the Equator. Many apes, like the one shown here, live in these rainforests.

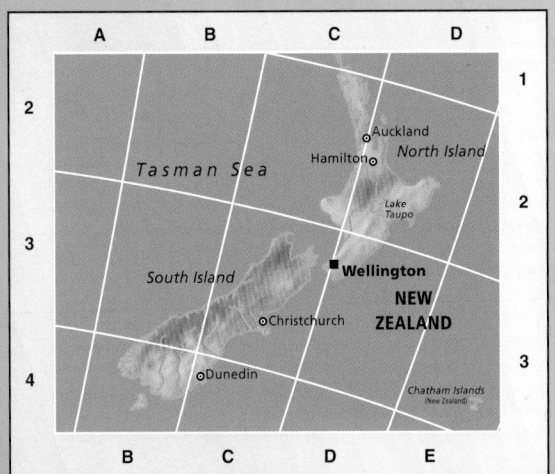

This is a map of New Zealand, with a grid formed by lines of latitude and longitude.

Using a grid

Lines of latitude and longitude form grids on maps. The maps in this book look similar to the one on the left. The columns that run from top to bottom are formed by lines of longitude and marked with letters. The rows running across the page are formed by lines of latitude and are numbered.

All the places listed in the map index on page 98 have a letter and a number reference that tell you where to find them on a particular page. For example, on the map on the left, the city of Christchurch would have a grid reference of C3.

HOW MAPS ARE MADE

The process of making maps is called cartography. Map-makers, or cartographers, compile each map by gathering information about the area and representing it as an image as accurately as possible.

Internet link

For a link to a website where you can see examples of all kinds of different map projections, including cylindrical, conical and azimuthal projections, go to **www.usborne-quicklinks.com**

Creating maps

Many sources are used to create maps. These include satellite images and aerial photographs. Cartographers often visit the area to be mapped, where they take many extra measurements.

In addition, cartographers use statistics, such as population figures, from censuses and other documents. As the maps are being made, many people check them to make sure they are accurate and up to date.

Map projections

Cartographers can't draw maps that show the world exactly as it is, because it is impossible to show a curved surface on a flat map without distorting (stretching or squashing) some areas. A representation of the Earth on a map is called a projection. Projections are worked out using complex mathematics.

There are three basic types of projections – cylindrical, conical and azimuthal, but there are also variations on these. They all distort the Earth's surface in some way, either by altering the shapes or sizes of areas of land or the distance between places.

A cartographer uses an electronic distance measurer to check the measurements of an area of land.

Cylindrical projections

A cylindrical projection is similar to the image created by wrapping a piece of paper around a globe to form a cylinder and then shining a light inside the globe. The shapes of countries would be projected onto the paper. Near the middle they would be accurate, but farther away they would be distorted.

Cartographers often alter the basic cylindrical projection to make the distortion less obvious in certain areas, but they can never make a map that is completely accurate.

This picture of a piece of paper wrapped around a globe illustrates how a cylindrical projection is made.

Below is a type of cylindrical projection called the Mercator projection, which was invented in 1596 by a cartographer named Gerardus Mercator. It makes countries the right shape, but makes those near the poles too big.

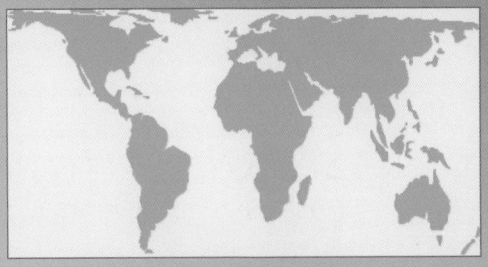

This cylindrical projection makes countries the right size in relation to each other, but some parts are too long. The projection was created in 1973 by Arno Peters. It is called the Peters Projection.

Conical projections

A conical projection is similar to the image you would get if you wrapped a cone of paper around part of a globe, then shone a light inside the globe. Where the cone touches the globe, the projection will be most accurate.

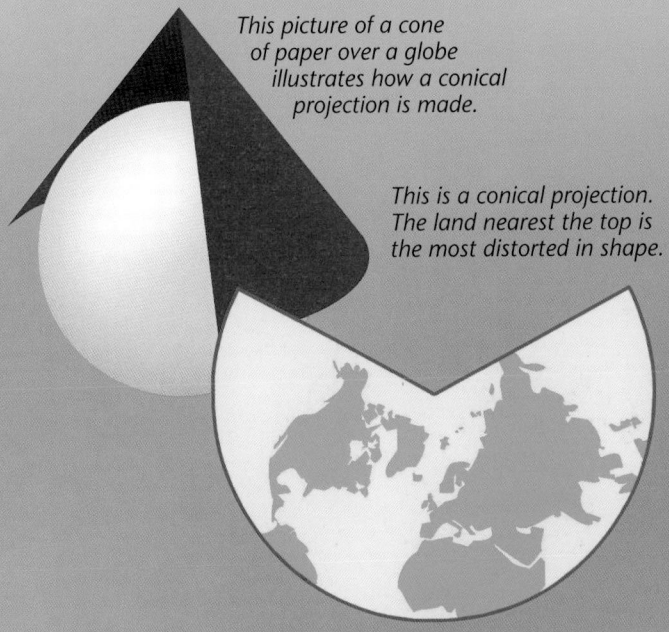

This picture of a cone of paper over a globe illustrates how a conical projection is made.

This is a conical projection. The land nearest the top is the most distorted in shape.

Azimuthal projections

An azimuthal projection is like an image made by holding paper in front of a globe, and shining a light through it. Land projected onto the middle of the paper would be accurate, but areas farther away would be distorted.

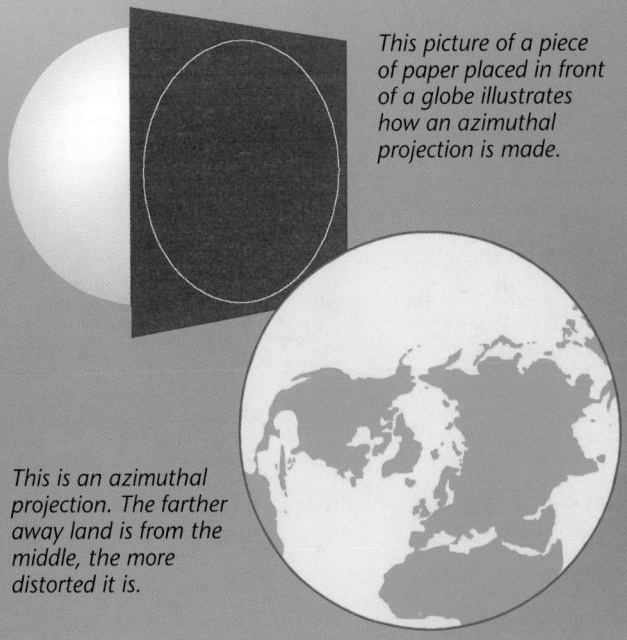

This picture of a piece of paper placed in front of a globe illustrates how an azimuthal projection is made.

This is an azimuthal projection. The farther away land is from the middle, the more distorted it is.

THEMATIC MAPS

Maps that represent information on particular themes, like the ones on these pages, are known as thematic maps. They help you to identify patterns and make comparisons between the features of different areas.

Earth's resources

The Earth contains all kinds of useful resources. Rocks and minerals can be used as building materials, and fuels such as coal, oil and gas contain energy that can be turned into heat and electricity.

Countries with large amounts of natural resources can become very rich. For example, Saudi Arabia, in western Asia, has large oil and gas reserves, which it exports all over the world.

This is an oil field, where oil is extracted from the ground using pumps. It is then piped to refineries and turned into products such as motor fuel.

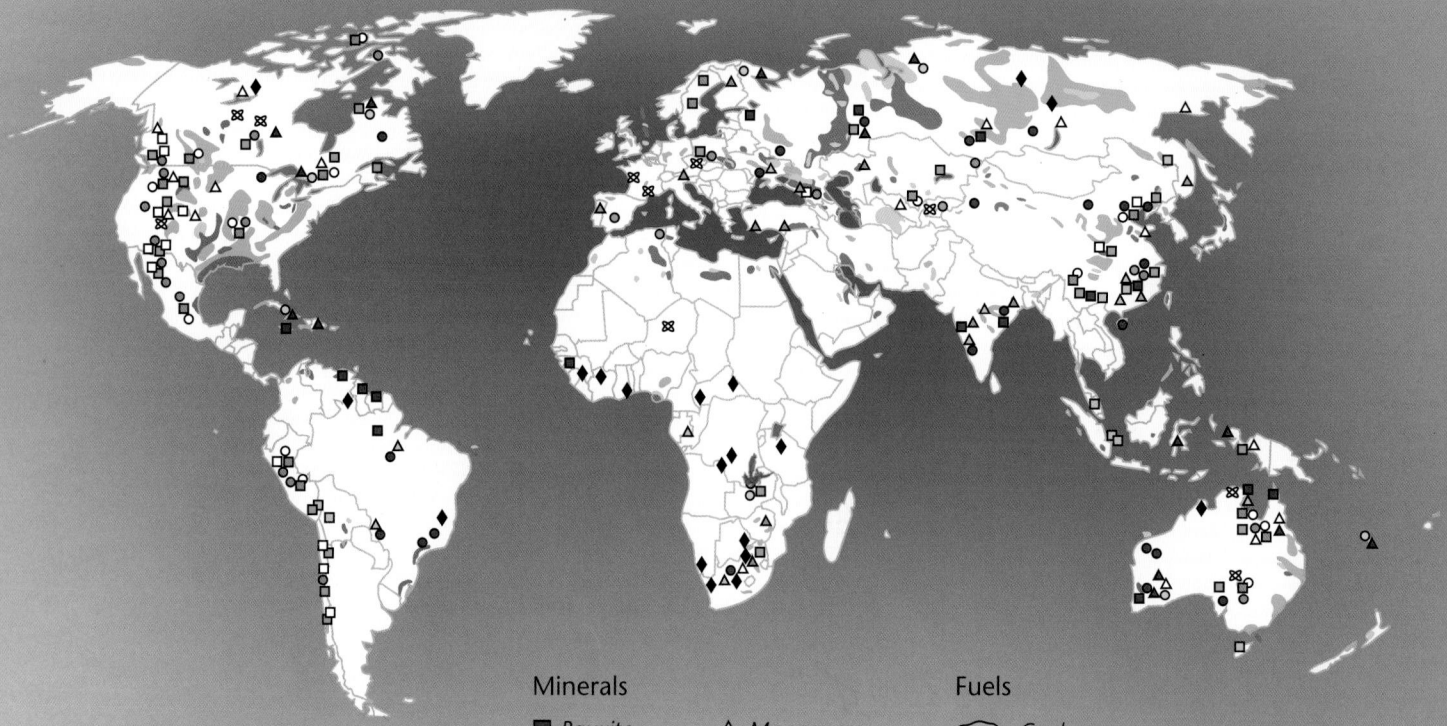

Minerals

- *Bauxite*
- *Chromium*
- *Cobalt*
- *Copper*
- *Diamonds*
- *Gold*
- *Iron*
- *Lead*
- *Manganese*
- *Mercury*
- *Molybdenum*
- *Nickel*
- *Silver*
- *Tin*
- *Tungsten*
- *Zinc*

Fuels

- *Coal*
- *Natural gas*
- *Oil*
- *Uranium*

This map shows the main areas of the world where minerals and natural fuels are found. Over half of the world's oil, gas and coal comes from Asia.

Different climates

The long-term or typical pattern of weather in a particular area is known as its climate. Climates vary across the world and depend largely on each area's latitude. The hottest parts of the world are those closest to the Equator.

Climate is also affected by other factors, such as wind and the height of the land. Oceans influence climate too – places near the sea normally have a milder, wetter climate than areas farther inland.

On this map, land is divided into five climate types. Dry areas are generally hot, but temperatures there can fall very low too. Some dry places, such as the Gobi Desert in eastern Asia, are extremely cold in winter.

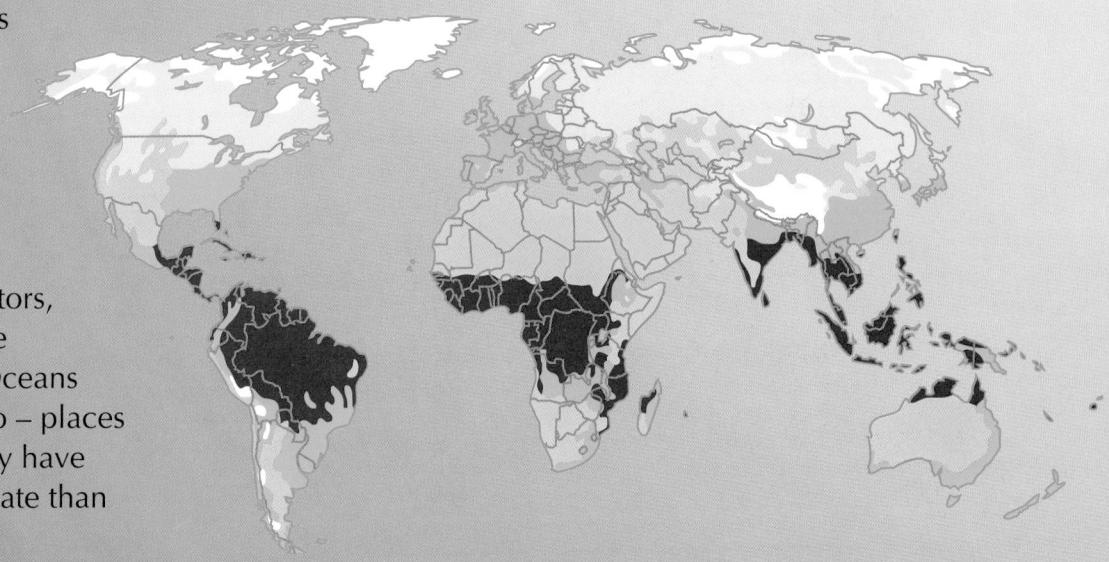

World population

There are more than six billion people in the world, and the population is still growing. Experts think it may reach more than nine billion by 2050. The number of people living in a given area is known as its population density. Europe and Asia are the most densely populated continents in the world. About a third of the world's population lives in China and India alone.

Internet link

For a link to a website where you can discover how many people there were on Earth when you were born, and find out about the effects of population growth, go to **www.usborne-quicklinks.com**

This map shows the average population density by country. The shading indicates the number of people per sq km (0.386 sq miles).

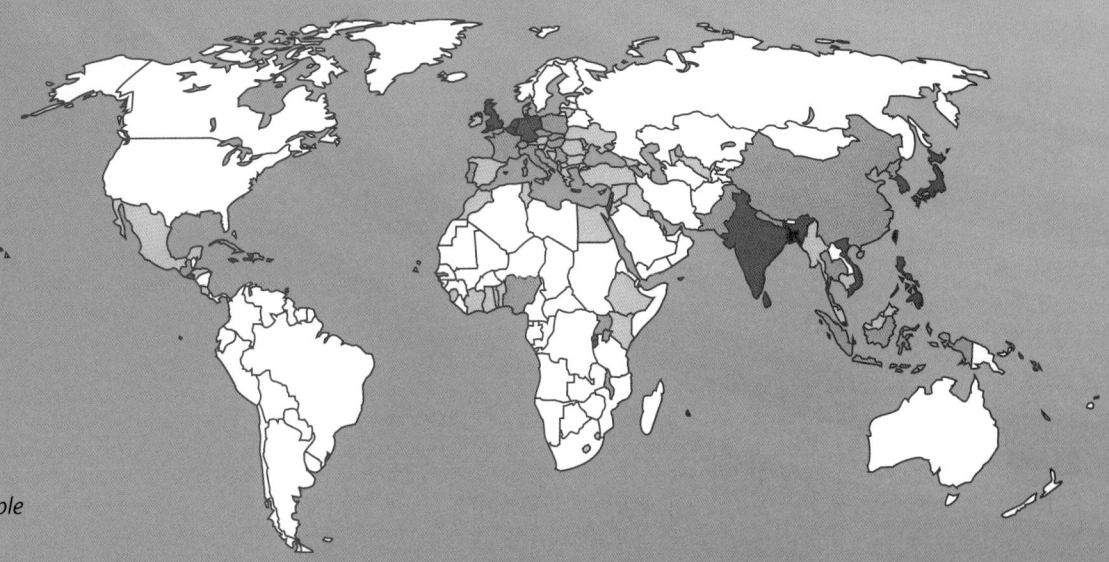

HOW TO USE THE MAPS

Each continent section in this atlas begins with a political map showing the whole continent. The rest of the maps are larger scale maps showing the various parts of the continent in more detail.

Political maps

The shading on the political maps in this atlas is there to help you see clearly the different countries that make up each continent. The main purpose of these maps is to show country borders and capital cities. Alongside them there are facts and figures about the continents and their features.

This is a section of the political map of South America. You can see the whole map on pages 28–29.

Environmental maps

The majority of the maps in this atlas are environmental maps, like the one on the right. The shading on these maps shows different types of land, or environments, such as desert, mountain or wetland.

The main key on the opposite page shows what the different shading means. It also shows the symbols used to represent towns, cities and other features. There is a smaller key on each environmental map repeating the most important information from this key.

Finding places

To find a particular place or feature on the environmental maps, look up its name in the index on pages 98–111. Its page number and grid reference is given next to the name. You can find out how to use the grid on page 9.

The map on the right is part of the environmental map of the U.S.A. The numbered labels at the top explain some important features of these maps.

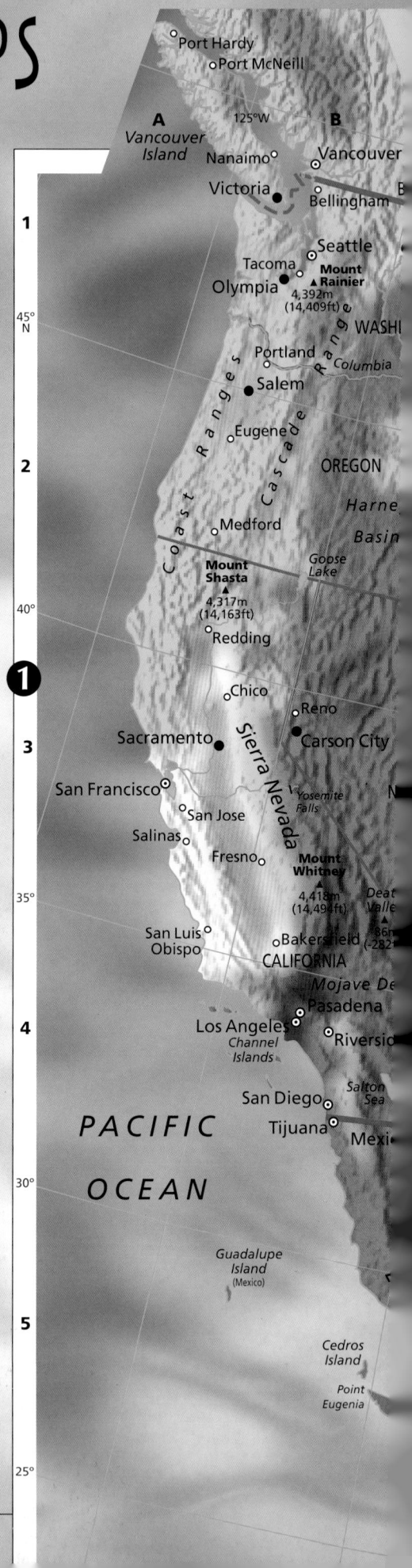

❶ *The letters and numbers in the border help you to find a place you have looked up in the index.*

❷ *Lines of latitude and longitude are shown as thin blue lines.*

❸ *The names of countries are shown in large, bold type with capital letters.*

❹ *The thick purple lines are country boundaries.*
❺ *The thinner purple lines are boundaries of internal regions within a country.*

Main key

Land cover:

- *Boreal forest*
- *Temperate forest*
- *Tropical forest*
- *Temperate grassland*
- *Savanna*
- *Semi-desert and scrub*
- *Hot desert*
- *Wetland*
- *Mountain (Only high mountains are marked.)*
- *Tundra*
- *Ice*
- *Cultivation*
- *Urban*

Cities and towns:

- *National capital*
- *Internal capital*
- *Major city or town*
- *Other town*

Boundaries:

- *International boundary*
- *International boundary through water*
- *Internal boundary*
- *Internal boundary through water*

Water features:

- *Sea*
- *Lake or reservoir*
- *Seasonal lake*
- *Dry lake/salt pan*
- *River*
- *Seasonal river*
- *Waterfall/dam*

Other features:

- 2,490m (7,988ft) *Height above or below sea level (Only a selection of elevation points are given. Places below sea level have a minus sign in front of the height.)*
- *Ruin or other place of interest*
- *Ancient wall*

Scale:

This tells you the size of the map in relation to the area it represents. For example:

1:12,000,000

0 200 400km

0 100 200 300 miles

GREENLAND
(Denmark)
Arctic Circle
ALASKA
(U.S.A.)
CANADA
UNITED STATES OF AMERICA
ICELAND
NORWAY
DENMARK
UNITED KINGDOM
IRELAND
NETH.
BELG.
LUX.
SWITZ.
FRANCE
SPAIN
PORTUGAL
Azores
(Portugal)
TUNISIA
MOROCCO
Canary Islands
(Spain)
ALGERIA
WESTERN SAHARA
(Morocco)
MAURITANIA
MALI
NIGER
CAPE VERDE
SENEGAL
THE GAMBIA
GUINEA-BISSAU
BURKINA FASO
GUINEA
BENIN
TOGO
SIERRA LEONE
IVORY COAST
NIGERIA
LIBERIA
GHANA
EQUATORIAL GUINEA
SAO TOME AND PRINCIPE
Tropic of Cancer
Hawaiian Islands
(U.S.A.)
MEXICO
THE BAHAMAS
CUBA
DOMINICAN REPUBLIC
HAITI
JAMAICA
BELIZE
HONDURAS
GUATEMALA
EL SALVADOR
NICARAGUA
Caribbean Sea
DOMINICA
TRINIDAD AND TOBAGO
COSTA RICA
PANAMA
VENEZUELA
GUYANA
SURINAM
FRENCH GUIANA
(France)
COLOMBIA
ECUADOR
Galapagos Islands
(Ecuador)
Equator
PACIFIC OCEAN
ATLANTIC OCEAN
KIRIBATI
Cook Islands
(New Zealand)
French Polynesia
(France)
Pitcairn Islands
(U.K.)
Tropic of Capricorn
PERU
BRAZIL
BOLIVIA
PARAGUAY
CHILE
URUGUAY
ARGENTINA
1:80,000,000
0 1,000 2,000 3,000 4,000 5,000km
0 1,000 2,000 3,000 miles
Falkland Islands
(U.K.)
South Georgia
(U.K.)
Antarctic Circle
Weddell Sea
160° 140° 120° 100° 80° 60° 40° 20° W 0°
80° 60° 40° 20° N 20° S

Copyright © Usborne Publishing Ltd.

160°
140°
120°
100°
80°
60°
40°
20° W
0°
80°
Ellesmere Island
Beaufort Sea
Victoria Island
Queen Elizabeth Islands
Greenland
Greenland Sea
Baffin Bay
Baffin Island
Iceland
Arctic Circle
Alaska
Yukon
Mount McKinley
6,194m
(20,321ft)
60°
Hudson Bay
Labrador Sea
British Isles
North Sea
Aleutian Islands
Gulf of Alaska
Rocky Mountains
Great Plains
NORTH AMERICA
Great Lakes
Newfoundland
Appalachian Mountains
40°
Azores
Mississippi
Canary Islands
Atlas Mountai
Tropic of Cancer
Gulf of Mexico
Cuba
West Indies
20° N
Greater Antilles
Hawaiian Islands
Caribbean Sea
Lesser Antilles
Cape Verde Islands
Guiana Highlands
0° Equator
Galapagos Islands
Amazon Basin
Amazon
ATLANTIC OCEAN
PACIFIC OCEAN
Polynesia
Selvas
SOUTH AMERICA
Tahiti
20° S
Tropic of Capricorn
Andes
Atacama Desert
Easter Island
Aconcagua
6,959m
(22,831ft)
Pampas
40°
1:80,000,000
0 1,000 2,000 3,000 4,000 5,000km
0 1,000 2,000 3,000 miles
Patagonia
Falkland Islands
Cape Horn
South Georgia
60°
Antarctic Circle
Antarctic Peninsula
Weddell Sea
80°
160°
140°
120°
100°
80°
60°
40°
20° W
0°

Copyright © Usborne Publishing Ltd.

NORTH AMERICA

The name "North America" can be used to mean several different things. In this atlas, North America includes Greenland, Canada, the U.S.A., the Caribbean, and the countries of Central America, which run along the narrow strip of land between the U.S.A. and South America. The continent has over 20 countries, including Canada, the second-largest country in the world.

These are columns of rock called hoodoos in Bryce Canyon National Park, U.S.A.

Copyright © Usborne Publishing Ltd.

The shading on this map is there to help you see clearly the different countries that make up the continent.

Internet link

For a link to a website where you can find out about the history and geography of each U.S. state, go to **www.usborne-quicklinks.com**

Ellesmere Island
GREENLAND (Denmark)
Arctic Circle
Queen Elizabeth Islands
Baffin Island
Godthab
Hudson Bay
Newfoundland
St. Lawrence
Montreal
Ottawa
Great Lakes
Chicago
New York
Washington D.C.
ATLANTIC OCEAN
OF AMERICA
Mississippi
Tropic of Cancer
Houston
THE BAHAMAS
Gulf of Mexico
Havana
CUBA
Puerto Rico (U.S.A.)
Guadeloupe (France)
DOMINICA
Martinique (France)
HAITI
DOMINICAN REPUBLIC
BARBADOS
JAMAICA
TRINIDAD AND TOBAGO
BELIZE
Caribbean Sea
GUATEMALA
HONDURAS
EL SALVADOR
NICARAGUA
COSTA RICA
PANAMA

Facts

Total land area 22,656,190 sq km (8,745,289 sq miles)
Total population 487 million
Biggest city Mexico City, Mexico
Biggest country Canada *9,970,610 sq km (3,849,653 sq miles)*
Smallest country Saint Kitts and Nevis *269 sq km (104 sq miles)*

Highest mountain Mount McKinley, Alaska, U.S.A. *6,194m (20,321ft)*
Longest river Mississippi/Missouri, U.S.A. *6,019km (3,741 miles)*
Biggest lake Lake Superior, between the U.S.A. and Canada *82,414 sq km (31,820 sq miles)*
Highest waterfall Yosemite Falls, on the Yosemite Creek, California, U.S.A. *739m (2,425ft)*
Biggest desert Great Basin Desert, U.S.A. *492,000 sq km (190,000 sq miles)*
Biggest island Greenland *2,175,600 sq km (840,000 sq miles)*

Main mineral deposits Silver, gold, copper, lead, zinc, graphite, molybdenum, nickel
Main fuel deposits Oil, coal, natural gas, uranium

The bald eagle is the national bird of the U.S.A. It is not really bald, but has white feathers on its head.

Canada and Alaska
Boreal forest
Temperate forest
Tropical forest
Temperate grassland
Savanna
Semi-desert and scrub
Hot desert
Wetland
Mountain
Tundra
Ice
Cultivation
Urban
National capital
Internal capital
Major city or town
Other town
International boundary
Internal boundary
2,490m (7,988ft) Height above or below sea level
See also main key on page 15.
1:16,000,000
0 200 400 600km
0 100 200 300 400 miles
RUSSIA
Arctic Circle
Chukchi Sea
Bering Strait
St. Lawrence Island
Bering Sea
Teller
Seward Peninsula
Wainwright
Point Barrow
ARCTIC OCEAN
Queen Elizabeth
Parry
Prudhoe Bay
Brooks Range
Beaufort Sea
McClure Strait
Melville Island
Banks Island
Viscount Melville Sound
McClintock Channel
Nunivak Island
Yukon
Bethel
ALASKA (U.S.A.)
Mount McKinley 6,194m (20,321ft)
Alaska Range
Fairbanks
Mackenzie Bay
Inuvik
Amundsen Gulf
Victoria Island
Bristol Bay
Iliamna Lake
Alaska Peninsula
Anchorage
Seward
Dawson
Mackenzie Mountains
Mackenzie
Great Bear Lake
Kodiak Island
Gulf of Alaska
YUKON TERRITORY
Mount Logan 5,959m (19,551ft)
Whitehorse
NORTHWEST TERRITORIES
PACIFIC OCEAN
Juneau
Watson Lake
Yellowknife
Dubawnt Lake
Alexander Archipelago
Dease Lake
Fort Providence
Great Slave Lake
Coast Mountains
ROCKY MOUNTAINS
Fort Nelson
Fort Chipewyan
Fort Vermilion
Lake Athabasca
Prince Rupert
BRITISH COLUMBIA
Fort St. John
Wollaston Lake
Queen Charlotte Islands
Peace River
Fort McMurray
Reindeer Lake
ALBERTA
Grande Prairie
Prince George
Athabasca
Mount Robson 3,954m (12,972ft)
Whitecourt
CAN
Flin Flon
Port Hardy
Williams Lake
Hinton
Edmonton
Cedar Lake
Vancouver Island
Port McNeill
Lloydminster
Red Deer
Prince Albert
Kamloops
Saskatoon
Nanaimo
Vancouver
Revelstoke
Calgary
Lake Winnipegosis
Victoria
Kelowna
SASKATCHEWAN
Bellingham
Moose Jaw
Regina
Lethbridge
Seattle
Swift Current
Olympia
Mount Rainier 4,392m (14,409ft)
WASHINGTON
Estevan
Missouri
Salem
Columbia
Helena
MONTANA
NORTH
Bismarck
Coast Ranges
Cascade Ranges
UNITED STATES OF
OREGON
IDAHO
Boise
Grand Teton 4,197m (13,770ft)
SOUTH
Pierre
WYOMING
CALIFORNIA
NEVADA
B
C
D
E
F
G
H
J
170°W
160°
150°
140°
130°
120°
110°
60° N
50°
40°
3
4
5
130°W
120°
110°

Copyright © Usborne Publishing Ltd.

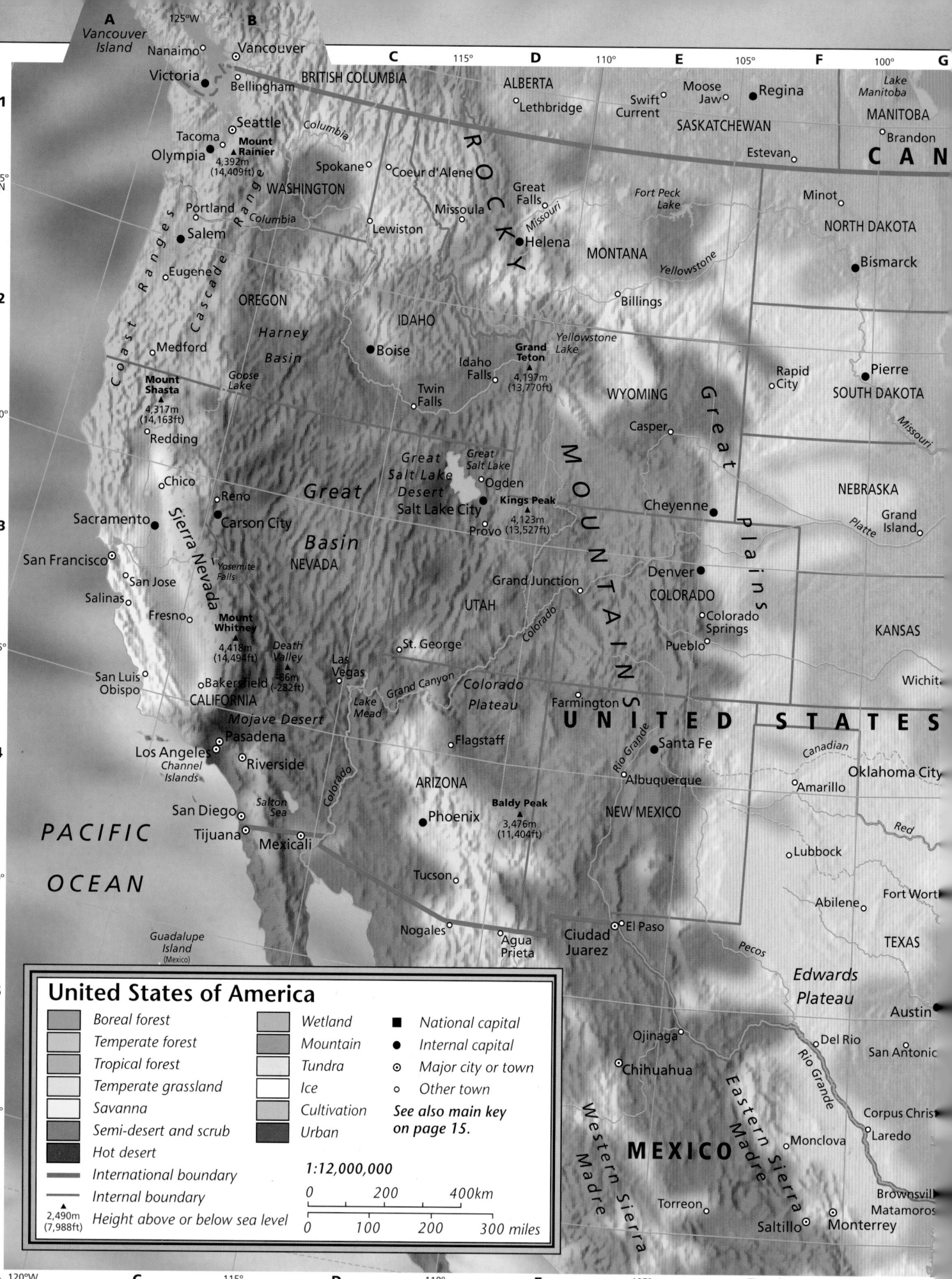

Copyright © Usborne Publishing Ltd.

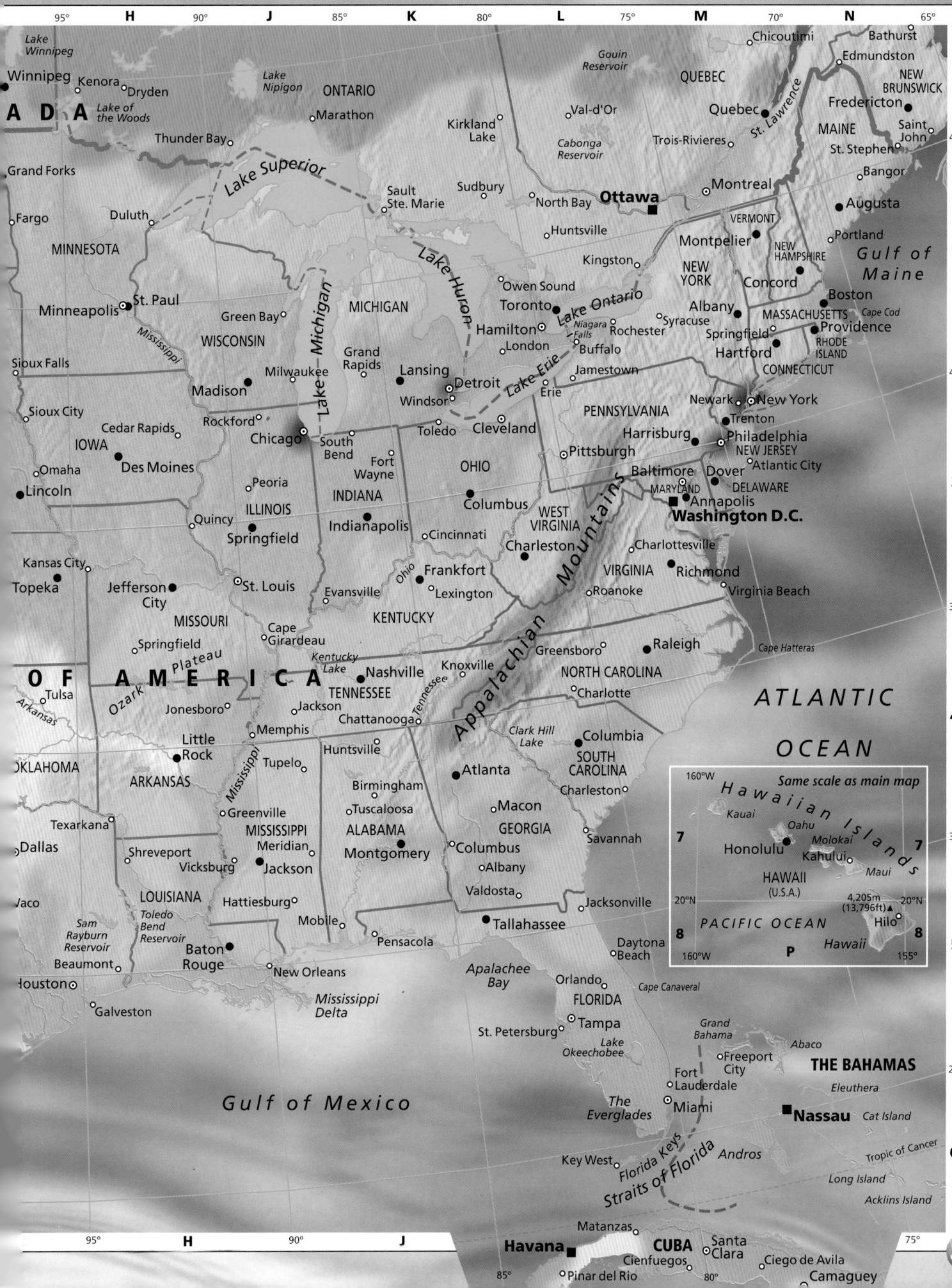
95° H 90° J 85° K 80° L 75° M 70° N 65°
1
2
3
4
5
6
45° N
40°
35°
30°
25°
Lake Winnipeg
Winnipeg
Kenora
Dryden
Lake of the Woods
Lake Nipigon
ONTARIO
Marathon
Thunder Bay
Kirkland Lake
Gouin Reservoir
Val-d'Or
Cabonga Reservoir
QUEBEC
Chicoutimi
Bathurst
Edmundston
NEW BRUNSWICK
Quebec
St. Lawrence
Fredericton
MAINE
Saint John
St. Stephen
Trois-Rivières
Bangor
Grand Forks
Lake Superior
Sault Ste. Marie
Sudbury
North Bay
Ottawa
Montreal
Augusta
Fargo
Duluth
Huntsville
VERMONT
Montpelier
Portland
MINNESOTA
Kingston
NEW HAMPSHIRE
Gulf of Maine
Lake Huron
Owen Sound
NEW YORK
Concord
Boston
Minneapolis
St. Paul
Green Bay
MICHIGAN
Toronto
Lake Ontario
Albany
MASSACHUSETTS
Cape Cod
Mississippi
WISCONSIN
Lake Michigan
Hamilton
Niagara Falls
Rochester
Syracuse
Springfield
Providence
RHODE ISLAND
Sioux Falls
Grand Rapids
London
Buffalo
Hartford
Milwaukee
Lansing
Lake Erie
Jamestown
CONNECTICUT
Madison
Detroit
Erie
Sioux City
Windsor
Newark
New York
Rockford
PENNSYLVANIA
Trenton
Cedar Rapids
Chicago
Toledo
Cleveland
Harrisburg
Philadelphia
IOWA
South Bend
Pittsburgh
NEW JERSEY
Omaha
Des Moines
Fort Wayne
OHIO
Baltimore
Dover
Atlantic City
Lincoln
Peoria
MARYLAND
DELAWARE
INDIANA
Columbus
Annapolis
ILLINOIS
WEST VIRGINIA
Washington D.C.
Quincy
Indianapolis
Springfield
Cincinnati
Appalachian Mountains
Charleston
Charlottesville
Kansas City
Ohio
Frankfort
VIRGINIA
Richmond
Topeka
Jefferson City
St. Louis
Evansville
Lexington
Roanoke
Virginia Beach
MISSOURI
KENTUCKY
Cape Girardeau
Springfield
Greensboro
Raleigh
Cape Hatteras
Kentucky Lake
Ozark Plateau
Nashville
Knoxville
NORTH CAROLINA
Tulsa
TENNESSEE
Charlotte
Arkansas
Jonesboro
Jackson
Tennessee
Chattanooga
ATLANTIC OCEAN
Memphis
Clark Hill Lake
Columbia
Little Rock
Huntsville
SOUTH CAROLINA
OKLAHOMA
Tupelo
Atlanta
ARKANSAS
Mississippi
Birmingham
Charleston
Greenville
Tuscaloosa
Macon
Texarkana
MISSISSIPPI
ALABAMA
GEORGIA
Dallas
Meridian
Montgomery
Savannah
Shreveport
Vicksburg
Jackson
Columbus
Albany
Valdosta
LOUISIANA
Hattiesburg
Jacksonville
Waco
Sam Rayburn Reservoir
Toledo Bend Reservoir
Mobile
Tallahassee
Pensacola
Baton Rouge
Daytona Beach
Beaumont
New Orleans
Apalachee Bay
Orlando
Houston
Cape Canaveral
Mississippi Delta
FLORIDA
Galveston
Tampa
St. Petersburg
Grand Bahama
Lake Okeechobee
Abaco
Freeport City
THE BAHAMAS
Fort Lauderdale
Eleuthera
Gulf of Mexico
The Everglades
Miami
Nassau
Cat Island
Key West
Florida Keys
Andros
Tropic of Cancer
Straits of Florida
Long Island
Acklins Island
Matanzas
Havana
CUBA
Santa Clara
Cienfuegos
Ciego de Avila
Pinar del Rio
Camaguey
Same scale as main map
Hawaiian Islands
Kauai
Oahu
Molokai
Honolulu
Kahului
Maui
HAWAII (U.S.A.)
4,205m (13,796ft)
Hilo
PACIFIC OCEAN
Hawaii
160°W
20°N
155°
7
8
P

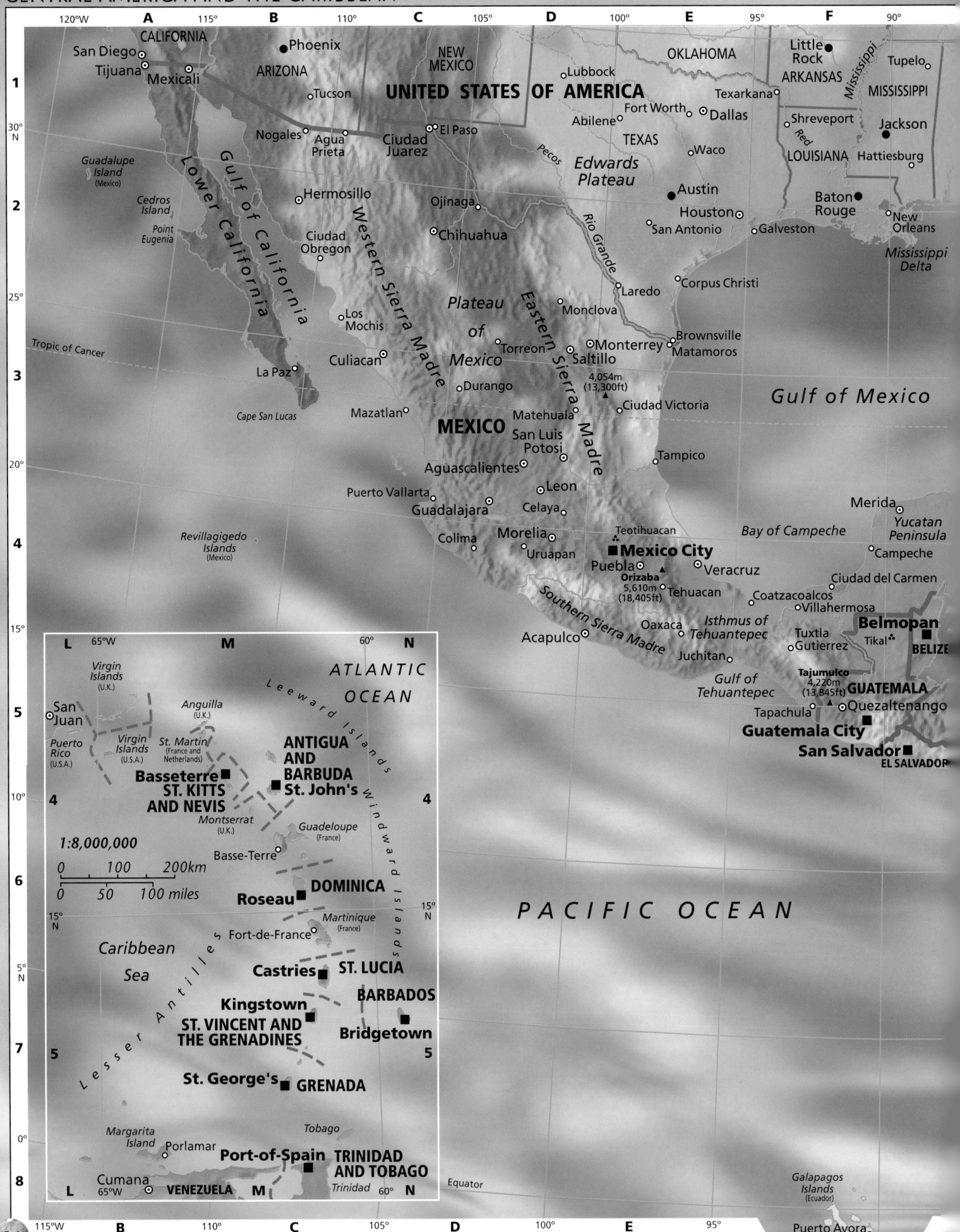
UNITED STATES OF AMERICA
CALIFORNIA
ARIZONA
NEW MEXICO
OKLAHOMA
TEXAS
ARKANSAS
LOUISIANA
MISSISSIPPI
San Diego
Tijuana
Mexicali
Phoenix
Tucson
Nogales
Agua Prieta
Ciudad Juarez
El Paso
Lubbock
Abilene
Fort Worth
Dallas
Texarkana
Little Rock
Tupelo
Shreveport
Jackson
Hattiesburg
Waco
Austin
Houston
San Antonio
Galveston
Baton Rouge
New Orleans
Mississippi Delta
Mississippi
Red
Pecos
Edwards Plateau
Rio Grande
Guadalupe Island (Mexico)
Cedros Island
Point Eugenia
Lower California
Gulf of California
Hermosillo
Ojinaga
Ciudad Obregon
Chihuahua
Western Sierra Madre
Eastern Sierra Madre
Plateau of Mexico
Laredo
Corpus Christi
Monclova
Los Mochis
Torreon
Monterrey
Saltillo
Brownsville
Matamoros
Tropic of Cancer
Culiacan
La Paz
Durango
4,054m (13,300ft)
Ciudad Victoria
Gulf of Mexico
Cape San Lucas
Mazatlan
Matehuala
MEXICO
San Luis Potosi
Tampico
Aguascalientes
Leon
Puerto Vallarta
Guadalajara
Celaya
Merida
Yucatan Peninsula
Bay of Campeche
Revillagigedo Islands (Mexico)
Colima
Morelia
Teotihuacan
Mexico City
Uruapan
Puebla
Veracruz
Campeche
Orizaba 5,610m (18,405ft)
Tehuacan
Ciudad del Carmen
Coatzacoalcos
Villahermosa
Southern Sierra Madre
Oaxaca
Isthmus of Tehuantepec
Belmopan
Acapulco
Tuxtla Gutierrez
Tikal
BELIZE
Juchitan
Gulf of Tehuantepec
Tajumulco 4,220m (13,845ft)
GUATEMALA
Tapachula
Quezaltenango
Guatemala City
San Salvador
EL SALVADOR
PACIFIC OCEAN
Equator
Galapagos Islands (Ecuador)
Puerto Ayora
ATLANTIC OCEAN
Virgin Islands (U.K.)
San Juan
Puerto Rico (U.S.A.)
Virgin Islands (U.S.A.)
Anguilla (U.K.)
St. Martin (France and Netherlands)
Leeward Islands
ANTIGUA AND BARBUDA
St. John's
Basseterre
ST. KITTS AND NEVIS
Montserrat (U.K.)
Guadeloupe (France)
Basse-Terre
1:8,000,000
0 100 200km
0 50 100 miles
Windward Islands
DOMINICA
Roseau
Martinique (France)
Fort-de-France
Caribbean Sea
Lesser Antilles
Castries
ST. LUCIA
BARBADOS
Kingstown
ST. VINCENT AND THE GRENADINES
Bridgetown
St. George's
GRENADA
Margarita Island
Porlamar
Tobago
Port-of-Spain
TRINIDAD AND TOBAGO
Trinidad
Cumana
VENEZUELA

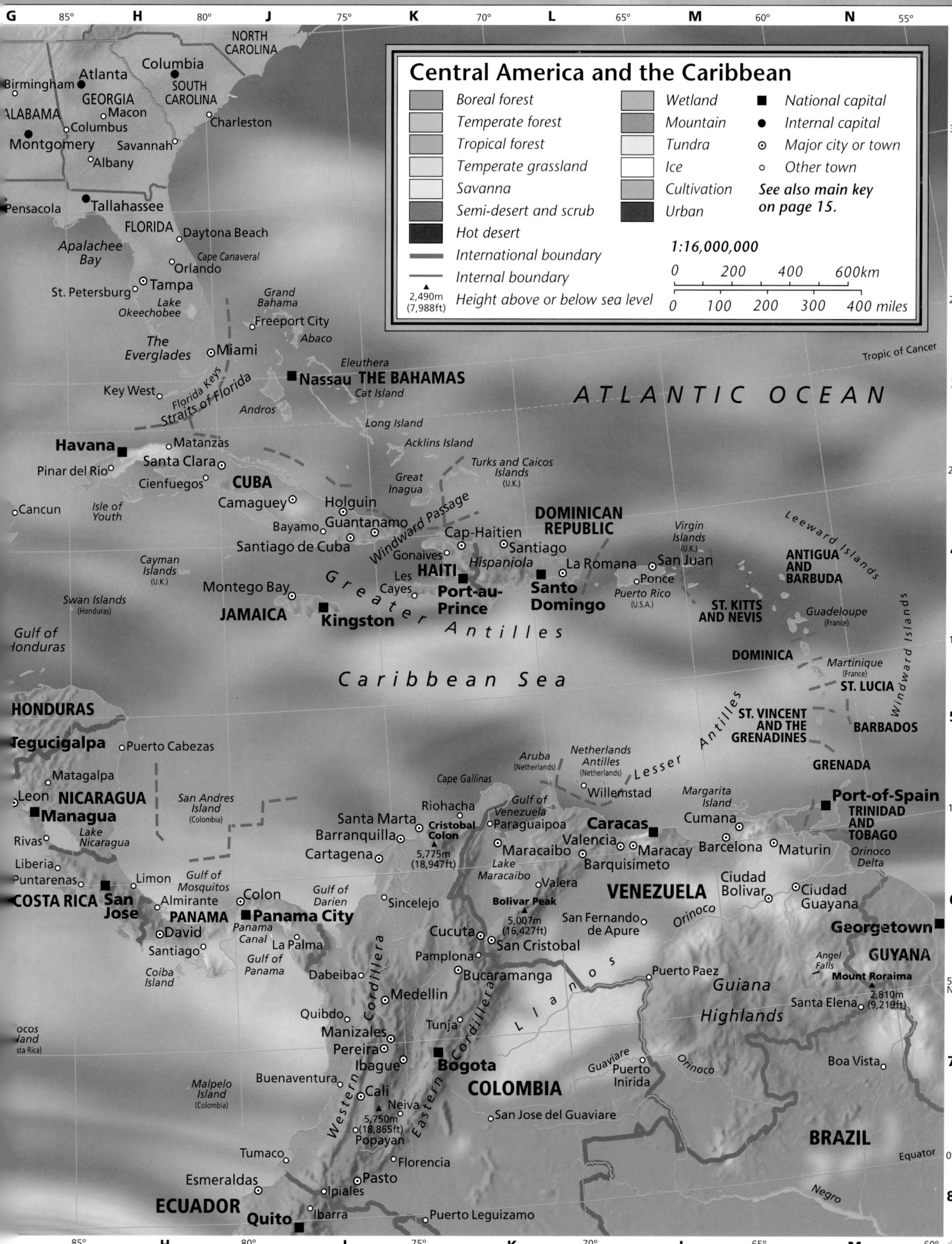

Copyright © Usborne Publishing Ltd.

SOUTH AMERICA

South America is made up of 12 independent countries, along with French Guiana, which belongs to France. The continent's biggest and most industrialized country is Brazil, which covers about half of the total land. Brazil is also home to half of South America's population.

This is a guanaco. Guanacos are members of the camel family that live in South America. Guanaco hair is used to make textiles.

The shading on this map is there to help you see clearly the different countries that make up the continent.

Internet link

For a link to a website where you can discover the sights and sounds of the Amazon rainforest, go to **www.usborne-quicklinks.com**

This is a red-eyed tree frog. These frogs live in rainforests in South and Central America.

Facts

Total land area 17,866,130 sq km (6,898,113 sq miles)
Total population 346 million
Biggest city Sao Paulo, Brazil
Biggest country Brazil *8,547,400 sq km (3,300,151 sq miles)*
Smallest country Surinam *163,270 sq km (63,039 sq miles)*

Highest mountain Aconcagua, Argentina *6,959m (22,831ft)*
Longest river Amazon, mainly in Brazil *6,440km (4,000 miles)*
Biggest lake Lake Maracaibo, Venezuela *13,312 sq km (5,140 sq miles)*
Highest waterfall Angel Falls, on the Churun River, Venezuela *979m (3,212ft)*
Biggest desert Patagonian Desert, Argentina *673,000 sq km (260,000 sq miles)*
Biggest island Tierra del Fuego *46,360 sq km (17,900 sq miles)*

Main mineral deposits Copper, tin, molybdenum, bauxite, emeralds
Main fuel deposits Oil, coal

Copyright © Usborne Publishing Ltd.

Cape Gallinas
Aruba (Netherlands)
Netherlands Antilles (Netherlands)
Lesser Antilles
GRENADA
TRINIDAD AND TOBAGO
Tortuga Island
Margarita Island
Willemstad
Gulf of Venezuela
Riohacha
Santa Marta
Cristobal Colon
5,775m (18,947ft)
Paraguaipoa
Coro
Barranquilla
Maracaibo
Maracay
Caracas
Cumana
Guiria
Port-of-Spain
Liberia
Puntarenas
Limon
San Jose
COSTA RICA
Cartagena
Lagunillas
Barquisimeto
Valencia
Barcelona
Maturin
Gulf of Mosquitos
Colon
Gulf of Darien
Sincelejo
Lake Maracaibo
Valera
Araure
Zaraza
Tucupita
Orinoco Delta
Almirante
Panama City
Panama Canal
Magangue
Bolivar Peak
5,007m (16,427ft)
Barinas
Ciudad Bolivar
David
Santiago
Penonome
La Palma
Puerto Armuelles
PANAMA
Gulf of Panama
Turbo
Caceres
Cucuta
VENEZUELA
Ciudad Guayana
Coiba Island
Pamplona
San Cristobal
San Fernando de Apure
Caicara
Orinoco
Dabeiba
Bucaramanga
Medellin
Cravo Norte
Llanos
Puerto Paez
Angel Falls
Nuqui
Quibdo
Duitama
Tunja
Guiana Highlands
Mount Roraima 2,810m (9,219ft)
Pereira
Manizales
Western Cordillera
Eastern Cordillera
Bogota
Santa Elena
Malpelo Island (Colombia)
Buenaventura
Buga
Ibague
Cali
Guaviare
Puerto Inirida
COLOMBIA
Neiva
5,750m (18,865ft)
Boa Vista
Popayan
San Jose del Guaviare
Tumaco
Florencia
Esmeraldas
Cape San Francisco
Ipiales
Pasto
Ibarra
Equator
Quito
Santo Domingo de los Colorados
Nueva Loja
Puerto Leguizamo
Negro
Manta
Quevedo
La Chorrera
ECUADOR
Ambato
6,310m (20,702ft)
Babahoyo
Montalvo
Japura
La Libertad
Guayaquil
Gulf of Guayaquil
Cuenca
Tumbes
Machala
Amazon
Iquitos
Amazon
Loja
Leticia
Talara
Zumba
Atalaia do Norte
Maranon
Sullana
Piura
Chulucanas
Selvas
Cape Negro
Yurimaguas
Ucayali
Moyobamba
Jurua
Central Cordillera
PERU
Chiclayo
Madeira
Cajamarca
Purus
Pacasmayo
Cruzeiro do Sul
Pucallpa
Trujillo
Huacrachuco
Chimbote
Porto Velho
Mount Huascaran 6,746m (22,132ft)
Huanuco
Rio Branco
Cerro de Pasco
PACIFIC OCEAN
Riberalta
La Oroya
Cobija
Lima
Huancayo
Western Cordillera
ANDES
Eastern Cordillera
Puerto Maldonado
Mala
Quillabamba
Machu Picchu
Chincha Alta
Ayacucho
Magdalena
Cusco
Ica
Sicuani
Rurrenabaque
Nazca
Trinidad
Mount Coropuna 6,425m (21,079ft)
Juliaca
Lake Titicaca
Concepcion
Chala
Puno
La Paz
Arequipa
BOLIVIA
Mollendo
Mount Illimani 6,402m (21,004ft)
Cochabamba
San Jose de Chiquito
Tacna
Oruro
Santa Cruz
Gulf of Arica
Arica
Lake Poopo
Challapata
Sucre
CHILE
Potosi
Charagua
Camiri
Same scale as main map
Galapagos Islands (Ecuador)
Equator
San Salvador
Fernandina
Santa Cruz
Isabela
Puerto Ayora
San Cristobal
PACIFIC OCEAN

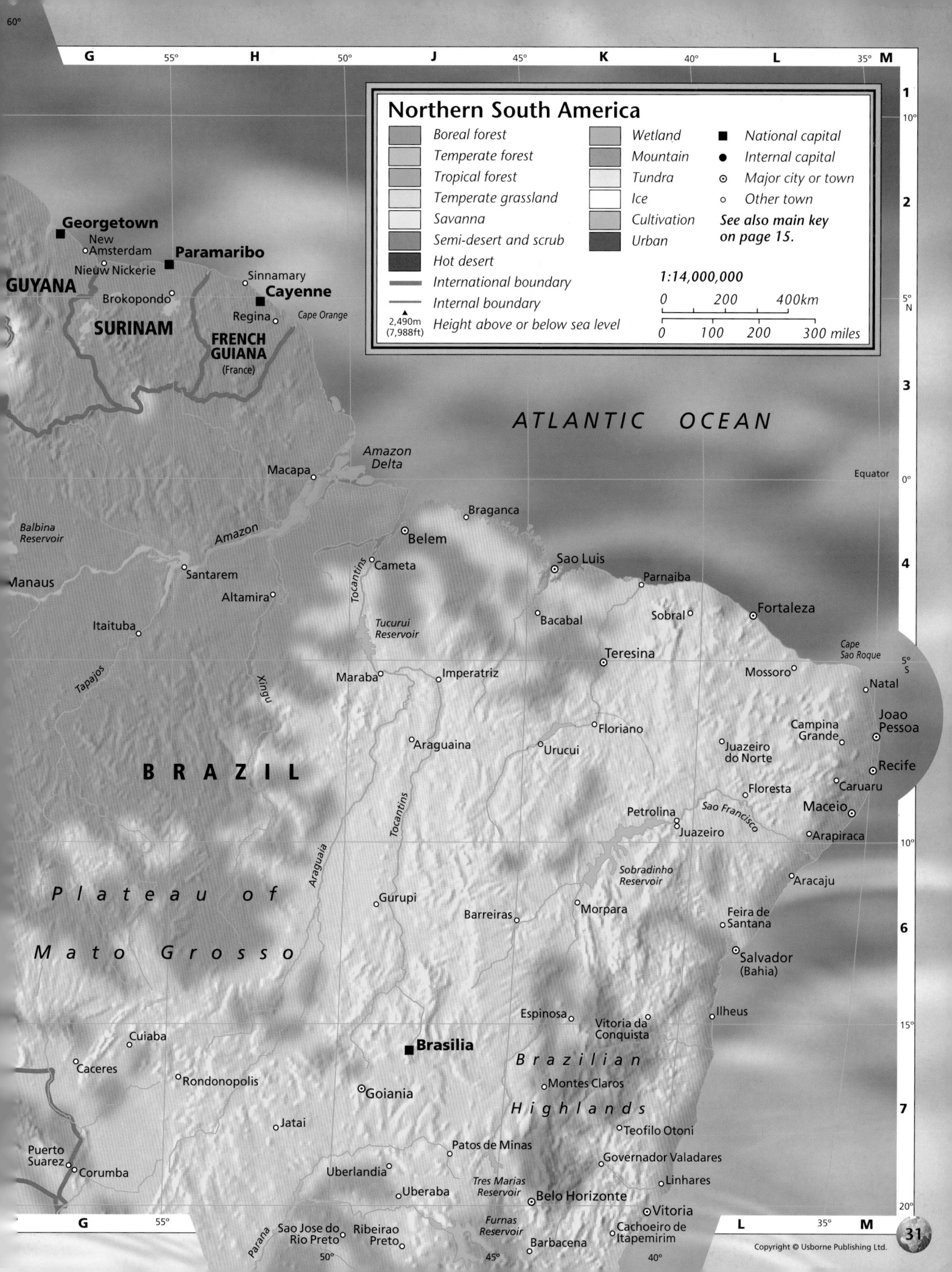

Copyright © Usborne Publishing Ltd.

SOUTHERN SOUTH AMERICA
D 70°W
E
65°
F
60°
G
55°
H
50°
J
45°
K
40°
L
1
2
3
4
5
6
10° S
15°
20°
25°
30°
35°
Plateau of Mato Grosso
BRAZIL
Brazilian Highlands
PERU
BOLIVIA
PARAGUAY
URUGUAY
CHILE
ANDES
Gran Chaco
Atacama Desert
Tropic of Capricorn
Rio Branco
Riberalta
Cobija
Puerto Maldonado
Magdalena
Rurrenabaque
Trinidad
Juliaca
Puno
Lake Titicaca
La Paz
Mount Illimani 6,402m (21,004ft)
Cochabamba
Oruro
Tacna
Arica
Lake Poopo
Challapata
Sucre
Potosi
Charagua
Camiri
Iquique
Pica
Uyuni
Ollague
Tupiza
Tarija
Calama
San Pedro de Atacama
Tartagal
Antofagasta
San Salvador de Jujuy
Salta
Taltal
Chanaral
Mount Ojos del Salado 6,908m (22,664ft)
Copiapo
Vallenar
Catamarca
La Rioja
Coquimbo
Ovalle
Illapel
San Juan
Aconcagua 6,959m (22,831ft)
Valparaiso
Santiago
Rancagua
Mendoza
Merlo
San Luis
Villa Mercedes
Cordoba
San Francisco
Villa Maria
Rio Cuarto
Rufino
Santa Fe
Rosario
Venado Tuerto
Chacabuco
Buenos
Concordia
Salto
Tacuarembo
Paysandu
Rivera
Gualeguaychu
San Nicolas de los Arroyos
Durazno
Minas
Bage
Pelotas
Melo
Rio Grande
Mirim Lake
Patos Lagoon
Porto Alegre
Santa Maria
Uruguaiana
Reconquista
Caxias do Sul
Criciuma
Passo Fundo
Florianopolis
Itajai
Curitiba
Paranagua
Guarapuava
Cascavel
Foz do Iguacu
Iguacu Falls
Ciudad del Este
Villarrica
Formosa
Eldorado
Encarnacion
Posadas
Corrientes
Santiago del Estero
Salado
Pilcomayo
Paraguay
Parana
Asuncion
Concepcion
Pedro Juan Caballero
Ponta Pora
Dourados
Campo Grande
Sao Jose do Rio Preto
Ribeirao Preto
Presidente Prudente
Araraquara
Marilia
Londrina
Campinas
Itapetininga
Sao Paulo
Pocos de Caldas
Mount Agulhas Negras 2,787m (9,144ft)
Nova Iguacu
Rio de Janeiro
Macae
Juiz de Fora
Campos
Barbacena
Cachoeiro de Itapemirim
Vitoria
Furnas Reservoir
Belo Horizonte
Tres Marias Reservoir
Uberaba
Uberlandia
Patos de Minas
Governador Valadares
Linhares
Teofilo Otoni
Montes Claros
Jatai
Goiania
Brasilia
Caceres
Cuiaba
Rondonopolis
Gurupi
Araguaia
Tocantins
Barreiras
Morpara
Sobradinho Reservoir
Feira de Santana
Espinosa
Ilheus
Vitoria da Conquista

Copyright © Usborne Publishing Ltd.

AUSTRALASIA AND OCEANIA

Australasia is made up of Australia, New Zealand and Papua New Guinea. Oceania is a collection of over 20,000 islands stretching out into the Pacific Ocean.

This small island belongs to Papua New Guinea.

PACIFIC OCEAN

The shading on this map is there to help you see clearly the different countries that make up the continent.

Line Islands

Equator

Tokelau
(New Zealand)

American Samoa
(U.S.A.)

Marquesas Islands

French Polynesia
(France)

Niue
(New Zealand)

Society Islands

Cook Islands
(New Zealand)

Pitcairn Islands
(U.K.)

Tropic of Capricorn

Internet link

For a link to a website where you can take a virtual tour of New Zealand and find out all about its sights, cities and landscape, go to **www.usborne-quicklinks.com**

Facts

Total land area 8,564,400 sq km (3,306,715 sq miles)
Total population 31 million
Biggest city Sydney, Australia
Biggest country Australia *7,686,850 sq km (2,967,124 sq miles)*
Smallest country Nauru *21 sq km (8 sq miles)*

Highest mountain Mount Wilhelm, Papua New Guinea *4,509m (14,793ft)*
Longest river Murray/Darling River, Australia *3,718km (2,310 miles)*
Biggest lake Lake Eyre, Australia *9,000 sq km (3,470 sq miles)*
Highest waterfall Sutherland Falls, on the Arthur River, New Zealand *580m (1,904ft)*
Biggest desert Great Victoria Desert, Australia *388,500 sq km (150,000 sq miles)*
Biggest island New Guinea *800,000 sq km (309,000 sq miles)* (Australia is counted as a continental land mass and not as an island.)

Main mineral deposits Iron, nickel, precious stones, lead, bauxite
Main fuel deposits Oil, coal, uranium

The Moorish idol fish is found in shallow waters throughout the Pacific. It has very bold stripes and a long, distinctive snout.

Copyright © Usborne Publishing Ltd.

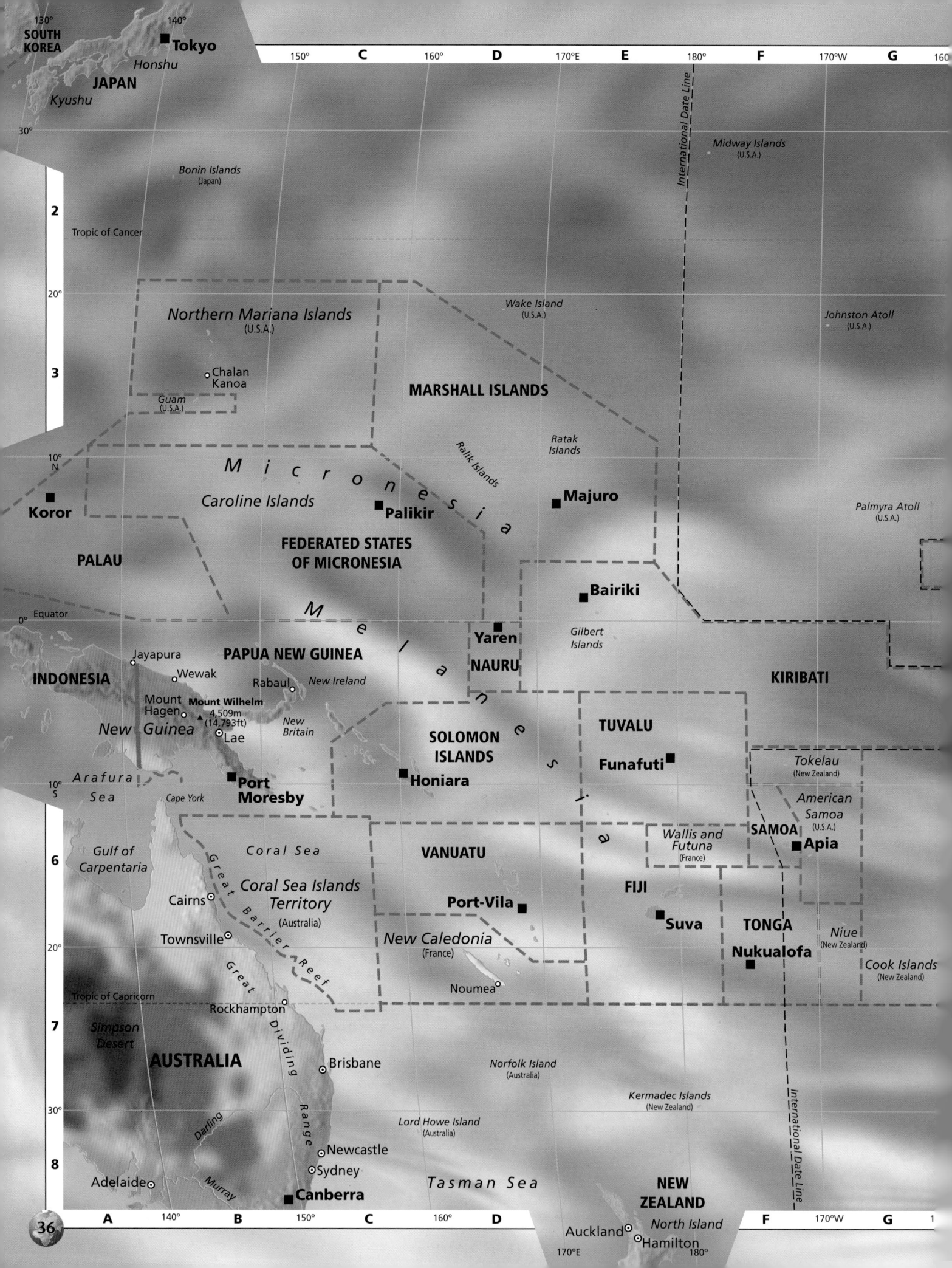
SOUTH KOREA
Tokyo
Honshu
JAPAN
Kyushu
Bonin Islands
(Japan)
Tropic of Cancer
Northern Mariana Islands
(U.S.A.)
Chalan Kanoa
Guam
(U.S.A.)
Wake Island
(U.S.A.)
Midway Islands
(U.S.A.)
Johnston Atoll
(U.S.A.)
International Date Line
MARSHALL ISLANDS
Ratak Islands
Ralik Islands
Majuro
Micronesia
Caroline Islands
Palikir
Koror
PALAU
FEDERATED STATES OF MICRONESIA
Palmyra Atoll
(U.S.A.)
Bairiki
Gilbert Islands
Equator
Melanesia
Yaren
NAURU
KIRIBATI
Jayapura
PAPUA NEW GUINEA
INDONESIA
Wewak
Rabaul
New Ireland
Mount Hagen
Mount Wilhelm
4,509m
(14,793ft)
New Guinea
Lae
New Britain
SOLOMON ISLANDS
Honiara
TUVALU
Funafuti
Tokelau
(New Zealand)
Arafura Sea
Port Moresby
Cape York
American Samoa
(U.S.A.)
SAMOA
Apia
Wallis and Futuna
(France)
Gulf of Carpentaria
Coral Sea
VANUATU
Great Barrier Reef
Coral Sea Islands Territory
(Australia)
Cairns
Port-Vila
FIJI
Suva
TONGA
Nukualofa
Niue
(New Zealand)
Townsville
New Caledonia
(France)
Cook Islands
(New Zealand)
Noumea
Great Dividing Range
Tropic of Capricorn
Rockhampton
Simpson Desert
AUSTRALIA
Brisbane
Norfolk Island
(Australia)
Kermadec Islands
(New Zealand)
Lord Howe Island
(Australia)
Darling
Newcastle
Sydney
Adelaide
Murray
Canberra
Tasman Sea
NEW ZEALAND
Auckland
North Island
Hamilton
130°
140°
150°
160°
170°E
180°
170°W
160
30°
20°
10° N
0°
10° S
20°
30°
A
B
C
D
E
F
G
1
2
3
6
7
8

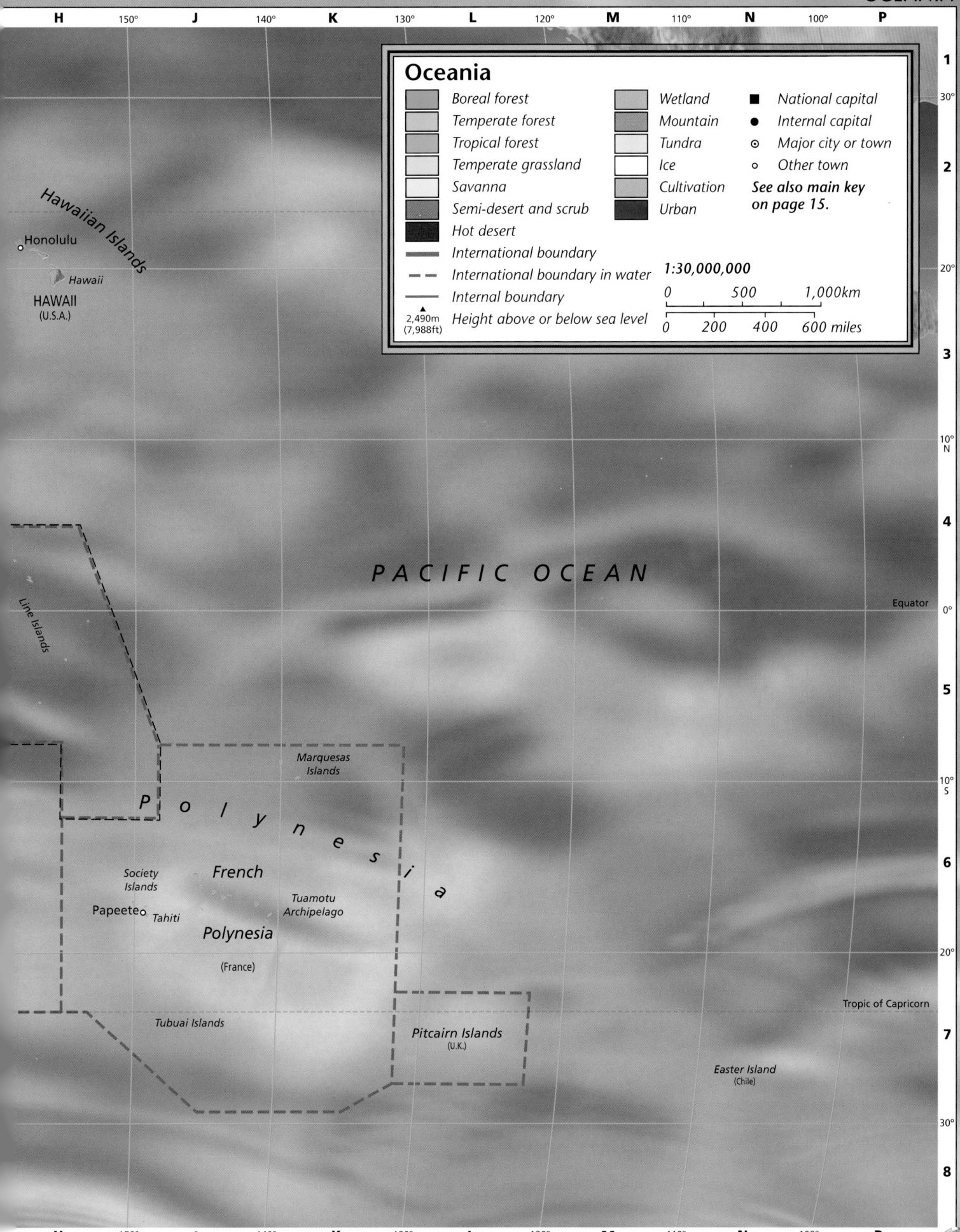

Copyright © Usborne Publishing Ltd.

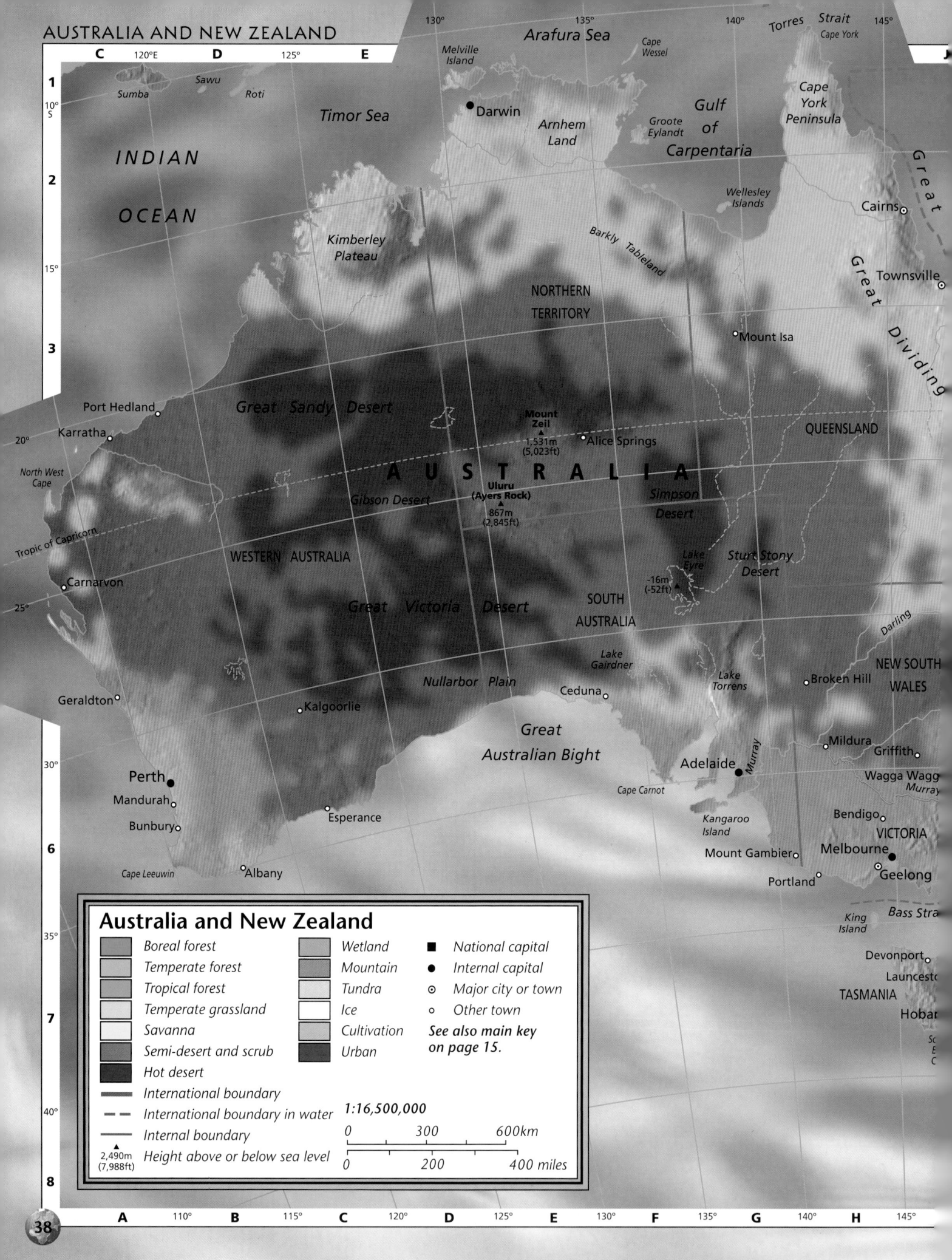
Arafura Sea
Melville Island
Cape Wessel
Torres Strait
Cape York
Sumba
Sawu
Roti
Timor Sea
Darwin
Arnhem Land
Groote Eylandt
Gulf of Carpentaria
Cape York Peninsula
INDIAN OCEAN
Wellesley Islands
Cairns
Great Dividing
Kimberley Plateau
Barkly Tableland
Townsville
NORTHERN TERRITORY
Mount Isa
Port Hedland
Great Sandy Desert
Karratha
Mount Zeil
1,531m (5,023ft)
Alice Springs
QUEENSLAND
North West Cape
AUSTRALIA
Uluru (Ayers Rock)
867m (2,845ft)
Gibson Desert
Simpson Desert
Tropic of Capricorn
WESTERN AUSTRALIA
Lake Eyre
-16m (-52ft)
Stuart Stony Desert
Carnarvon
Great Victoria Desert
SOUTH AUSTRALIA
Darling
Lake Gairdner
Lake Torrens
Broken Hill
NEW SOUTH WALES
Geraldton
Nullarbor Plain
Ceduna
Kalgoorlie
Great Australian Bight
Mildura
Griffith
Adelaide
Murray
Wagga Wagga
Murray
Perth
Mandurah
Cape Carnot
Bunbury
Esperance
Kangaroo Island
Bendigo
VICTORIA
Mount Gambier
Melbourne
Cape Leeuwin
Albany
Portland
Geelong
King Island
Bass Stra
Devonport
Launceston
TASMANIA
Hobart
Australia and New Zealand
Boreal forest
Temperate forest
Tropical forest
Temperate grassland
Savanna
Semi-desert and scrub
Hot desert
International boundary
International boundary in water
Internal boundary
2,490m (7,988ft) Height above or below sea level
Wetland
Mountain
Tundra
Ice
Cultivation
Urban
National capital
Internal capital
Major city or town
Other town
See also main key on page 15.
1:16,500,000
0 300 600km
0 200 400 miles

Copyright © Usborne Publishing Ltd.

ASIA

Asia is the largest continent and has over 40 countries, including Russia, the biggest country in the world. As well as large land masses, it has thousands of islands and inlets, giving it over 160,000km (100,000 miles) of coastline. Turkey and Russia are partly in Europe and partly in Asia, but both are shown in full on the map on the right.

The shading on this map is there to help you see clearly the different countries that make up the continent.

ARCTIC OCEAN
Franz Josef Land
Novaya Zemlya
Barents Sea
Kara Sea
Ob
Yenisey
Moscow
RUSS
Volga
Black Sea
Ankara
TURKEY
GEORGIA
Caspian Sea
ARMENIA
AZERBAIJAN
CYPRUS
LEBANON
Beirut
SYRIA
Damascus
Jerusalem
ISRAEL
Amman
JORDAN
Baghdad
IRAQ
Tehran
IRAN
Astana
KAZAKHSTAN
Aral Sea
UZBEKISTAN
TURKMENISTAN
Ashgabat
Tashkent
Bishkek
KYRGYZSTAN
Dushanbe
TAJIKISTAN
Kabul
AFGHANISTAN
Islamabad
Tropic of Cancer
KUWAIT
SAUDI ARABIA
Riyadh
BAHRAIN
QATAR
Doha
Abu Dhabi
UNITED ARAB EMIRATES
Muscat
PAKISTAN
Indus
New Delhi
NEPAL
Kathmandu
Ganges
Thimphu
BANGLADESH
Sana
YEMEN
OMAN
Arabian Sea
INDIA
Socotra (Yemen)
Bay of Bengal
INDIAN OCEAN
SRI LANKA
Sri Jayewardenepura Kotte
Colombo
Equator
MALDIVES
Male

Internet link

For a link to a website where you can read about the Great Wall of China and see a photo of it taken from space, go to **www.usborne-quicklinks.com**

This is a type of Chinese boat called a junk, sailing in the sea off Singapore.

Copyright © Usborne Publishing Ltd.

Facts

Total land area 44,537,920 sq km (17,196,090 sq miles)
Total population 3.8 billion (including all of Russia)
Biggest city Tokyo, Japan
Biggest country Russia *Total area: 17,075,200 sq km (6,592,735 sq miles) Area of Asiatic Russia: 12,780,800 sq km (4,934,667 sq miles)*
Smallest country Maldives *300 sq km (116 sq miles)*

Highest mountain Mount Everest, Nepal/China border *8,850m (29,035ft)*
Longest river Chang Jiang (Yangtze), China *6,380km (3,964 miles)*
Biggest lake Caspian Sea, western Asia *370,999 sq km (143,243 sq miles)*
Highest waterfall Jog Falls, on the Sharavati River, India *253m (830ft)*
Biggest desert Arabian Desert, in and around Saudi Arabia *2,230,000 sq km (900,000 sq miles)*
Biggest island Borneo *751,100 sq km (290,000 sq miles)*

Main mineral deposits Zinc, mica, tin, chromium, iron, nickel
Main fuel deposits Oil, coal, uranium, natural gas

These are lotus flowers, a type of water lily. In China they are associated with purity and for Buddhists they are sacred.

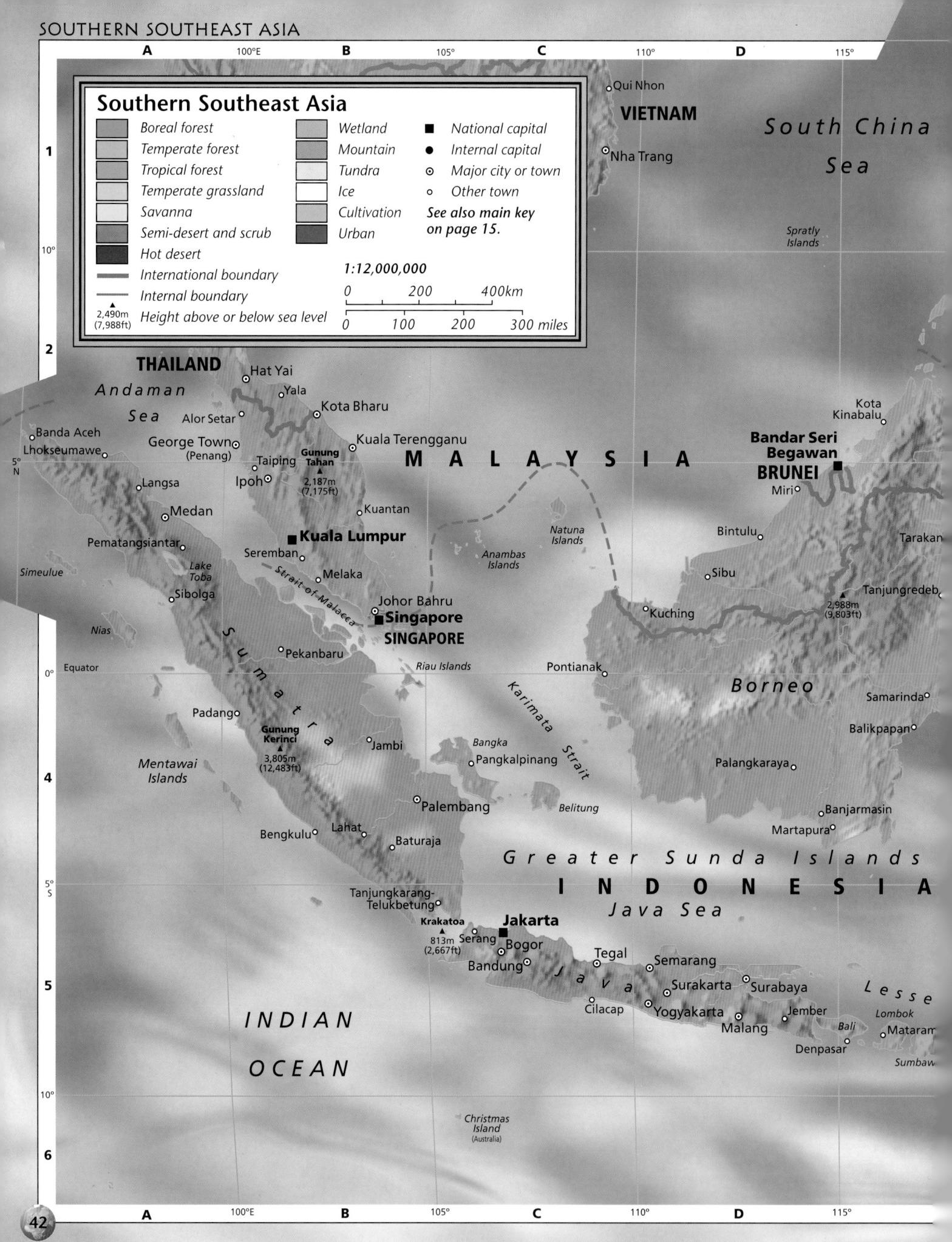
Southern Southeast Asia
Boreal forest
Temperate forest
Tropical forest
Temperate grassland
Savanna
Semi-desert and scrub
Hot desert
International boundary
Internal boundary
2,490m (7,988ft) Height above or below sea level
Wetland
Mountain
Tundra
Ice
Cultivation
Urban
National capital
Internal capital
Major city or town
Other town
See also main key on page 15.
1:12,000,000
0 200 400km
0 100 200 300 miles
A 100°E B 105° C 110° D 115°
1 10° 2 5° N 0° Equator 4 5° S 5 10° 6
Qui Nhon
VIETNAM
Nha Trang
South China Sea
Spratly Islands
THAILAND
Hat Yai
Yala
Andaman Sea
Alor Setar
Kota Bharu
Banda Aceh
Lhokseumawe
George Town (Penang)
Kuala Terengganu
Gunung Tahan 2,187m (7,175ft)
Taiping
Ipoh
Langsa
Medan
Kuantan
Pematangsiantar
Kuala Lumpur
Seremban
Lake Toba
Simeulue
Melaka
Strait of Malacca
Sibolga
Johor Bahru
Singapore
SINGAPORE
Nias
Sumatra
Pekanbaru
Riau Islands
Padang
Gunung Kerinci 3,805m (12,483ft)
Jambi
Mentawai Islands
Bangka
Pangkalpinang
Palembang
Belitung
Bengkulu
Lahat
Baturaja
Tanjungkarang-Telukbetung
Krakatoa 813m (2,667ft)
Jakarta
Serang
Bogor
Bandung
Tegal
Semarang
Surakarta
Surabaya
Cilacap
Yogyakarta
Malang
Jember
Java
Lesser
Lombok
Bali
Mataram
Denpasar
Sumbaw
INDIAN OCEAN
Christmas Island (Australia)
MALAYSIA
Natuna Islands
Anambas Islands
Kota Kinabalu
Bandar Seri Begawan
BRUNEI
Miri
Bintulu
Tarakan
Sibu
Tanjungredeb
Kuching
2,988m (9,803ft)
Pontianak
Borneo
Samarinda
Balikpapan
Karimata Strait
Palangkaraya
Banjarmasin
Martapura
Greater Sunda Islands
INDONESIA
Java Sea

Copyright © Usborne Publishing Ltd.

A
90°E
B
95°
C
100°
D
105°
E
110°
2
25° N
3
20°
4
15°
5
10°
6
5°
7
Brahmaputra
Lhasa
Himalayas
Mount Everest
8,850m
(29,035ft)
Thimphu
NEPAL
BHUTAN
Darjeeling
Biratnagar
INDIA
Dibrugarh
Jorhat
Darbhanga
Rangpur
Guwahati
Bhagalpur
Shillong
Ganges
Rajshahi
Sylhet
Asansol
BANGLADESH
Dhaka
Imphal
Jamshedpur
Aizawl
Khulna
Kolkata
(Calcutta)
Chittagong
Mouths of the Ganges
Monywa
Mount Victoria
3,053m
(10,016ft)
Mandalay
BURMA
(MYANMAR)
Sittwe
Meiktila
Taunggyi
Bay of Bengal
Pyinmana
Pye
Sandoway
Irrawaddy
Henzada
Pegu
Pathein
Rangoon
Thaton
Moulmein
Mouths of the
Irrawaddy
INDIAN
OCEAN
Tavoy
Andaman
Islands
(India)
Andaman
Sea
Mergui
Port Blair
Mergui
Archipelago
Little
Andaman
Ten Degree Channel
Nicobar Islands
(India)
Banda Aceh
Lhokseumawe
Sumatra
INDONESIA
Langsa
Chengdu
Wanxian
Gongga Shan
7,556m
(24,790ft)
Leshan
Enshi
Chongqing
Neijiang
Luzhou
Yibin
Mekong
Salween
Chang Jiang (Yangtze)
Xichang
Zunyi
Huaihua
Zhaotong
Panzhihua
Guiyang
Anshun
Myitkyina
Dali
Baoshan
Kunming
Red
Liuzhou
Kaiyuan
Gejiu
Lashio
Simao
Nanning
Ha Giang
Lao Cai
Phongsali
Thai Nguyen
Qinzhou
Son La
Hanoi
Hai Phong
Louangphrabang
Thanh Hoa
LAOS
Gulf of
Tonkin
Chiang Mai
Vinh
Vientiane
Sanya
Udon Thani
Phitsanulok
Savannakhet
Khon
Kaen
Hue
Da Nang
Nakhon Sawan
THAILAND
Ubon
Ratchathani
Pakxe
Nakhon Ratchasima
Attapu
VIETNAM
Bangkok
Stoeng Treng
Qui Nhon
Angkor
Tonle Sap
Pattaya
Batdambang
CAMBODIA
Buon Me
Thuot
Kampong
Chhnang
Kampong
Cham
Da Lat
Nha
Tran
Prachuap
Khiri Khan
Krong
Kaoh Kong
Phnom
Penh
Bien Hoa
Chumphon
Kampong Saom
Long Xuyen
Ho Chi Minh City
(Saigon)
Can Tho
Gulf of Thailand
Bac Lieu
Con Son
Nakhon Si
Thammarat
Hat Yai
Yala
Kota Bharu
Alor Setar
George Town
(Penang)
Kuala Terengganu
Gunung
Tahan
2,187m
(7,175ft)
Ipoh
Taiping
MALAYSIA
Natuna
Islands
(Indonesia)

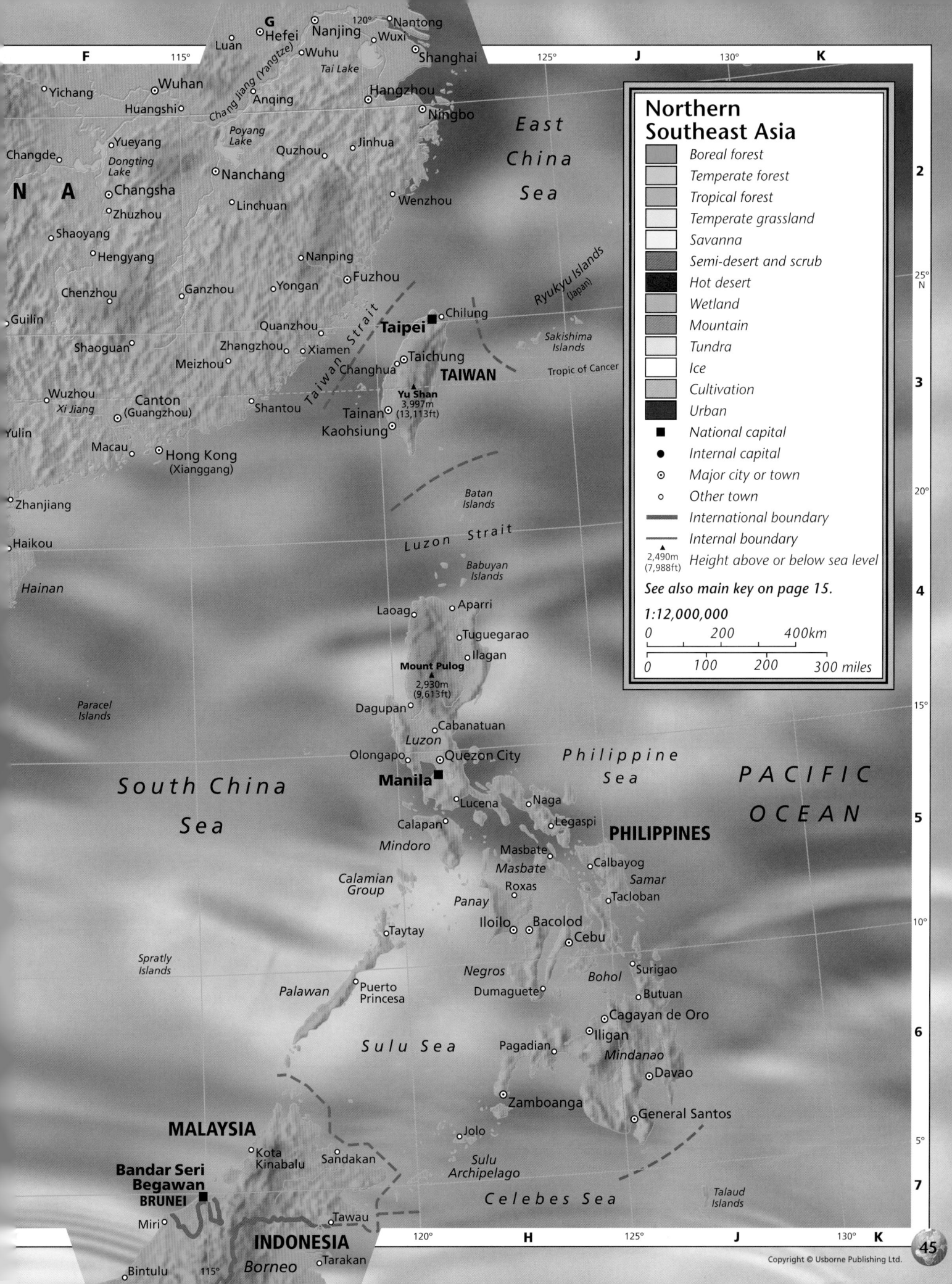

Copyright © Usborne Publishing Ltd.

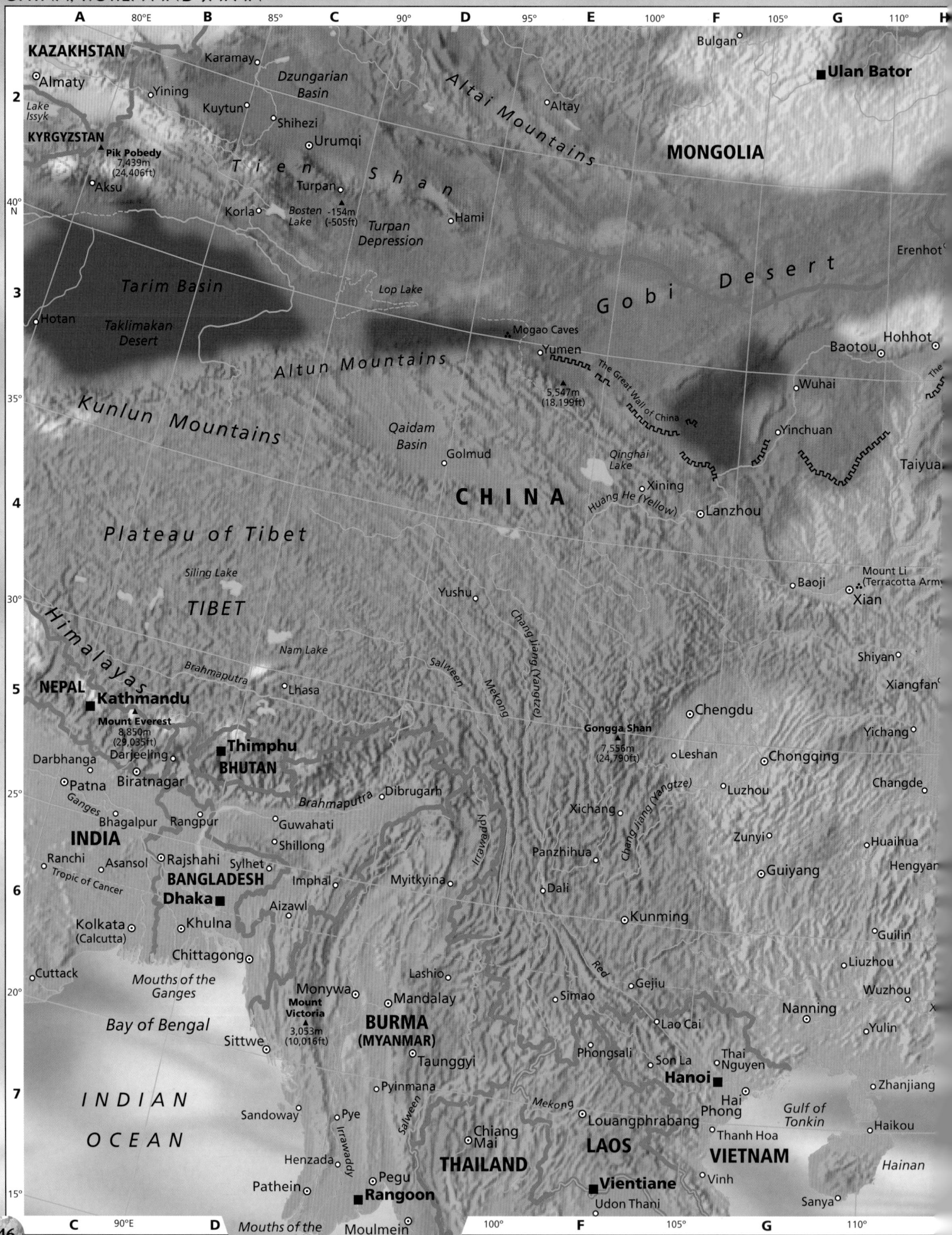
KAZAKHSTAN
Almaty
Lake Issyk
KYRGYZSTAN
Pik Pobedy
7,439m
(24,406ft)
Aksu
Karamay
Yining
Kuytun
Dzungarian Basin
Shihezi
Urumqi
Altai Mountains
Altay
Bulgan
Ulan Bator
MONGOLIA
Tien Shan
Turpan
Korla
Bosten Lake
-154m
(-505ft)
Turpan Depression
Hami
Erenhot
Gobi Desert
Tarim Basin
Lop Lake
Hotan
Taklimakan Desert
Mogao Caves
Yumen
Baotou
Hohhot
Altun Mountains
The Great Wall of China
5,547m
(18,199ft)
Wuhai
Kunlun Mountains
Qaidam Basin
Golmud
Yinchuan
Qinghai Lake
Taiyua
Xining
CHINA
Huang He (Yellow)
Lanzhou
Plateau of Tibet
Siling Lake
Yushu
Baoji
Mount Li
(Terracotta Army)
Xian
TIBET
Himalayas
Nam Lake
Chang Jiang (Yangtze)
Salween
Mekong
Brahmaputra
Lhasa
Shiyan
Xiangfan
NEPAL
Kathmandu
Mount Everest
8,850m
(29,035ft)
Chengdu
Gongga Shan
7,556m
(24,790ft)
Yichang
Thimphu
BHUTAN
Darbhanga
Darjeeling
Leshan
Chongqing
Patna
Biratnagar
Dibrugarh
Luzhou
Changde
Ganges
Bhagalpur
Rangpur
Guwahati
Xichang
INDIA
Shillong
Irrawaddy
Zunyi
Huaihua
Ranchi
Asansol
Rajshahi
Sylhet
Panzhihua
Guiyang
Hengyan
Tropic of Cancer
BANGLADESH
Imphal
Myitkyina
Dali
Dhaka
Aizawl
Kolkata
(Calcutta)
Khulna
Kunming
Guilin
Chittagong
Liuzhou
Cuttack
Mouths of the Ganges
Lashio
Red
Gejiu
Wuzhou
Monywa
Mandalay
Simao
Nanning
Mount Victoria
3,053m
(10,016ft)
Bay of Bengal
BURMA
(MYANMAR)
Lao Cai
Yulin
Sittwe
Taunggyi
Phongsali
Son La
Thai Nguyen
Hanoi
Pyinmana
Zhanjiang
INDIAN OCEAN
Sandoway
Pye
Mekong
Hai Phong
Gulf of Tonkin
Louangphrabang
Haikou
Chiang Mai
Thanh Hoa
LAOS
VIETNAM
Henzada
THAILAND
Hainan
Pegu
Vinh
Pathein
Vientiane
Rangoon
Udon Thani
Sanya
Mouths of the Irrawaddy
Moulmein
80°E
85°
90°
95°
100°
105°
110°
40° N
35°
30°
25°
20°
15°

Copyright © Usborne Publishing Ltd.

INDIA AND CENTRAL ASIA
A
B
C
H
65°E
70°
75°
80°
85°
90°
95°
45° N
40°
35°
30°
1
2
3
4
5
KAZAKHSTAN
MONGOLIA
KYRGYZSTAN
UZBEKISTAN
TAJIKISTAN
TURKMENISTAN
AFGHANISTAN
PAKISTAN
CHINA
NEPAL
BHUTAN
TIBET
JAMMU AND KASHMIR
Aral Sea
Lake Balkhash
Lake Zaysan
Lake Issyk
Bosten Lake
Lop Lake
Siling Lake
Nam Lake
Syr Darya
Amu Darya
Indus
Helmand
Ganges
Brahmaputra
Salween
Altai Mountains
Tien Shan
Karakorum Range
Hindu Kush
Kunlun Mountains
Altun Mountains
Himalayas
Dzungarian Basin
Turpan Depression
Tarim Basin
Taklimakan Desert
Qaidam Basin
Thar Desert
Plateau of Tibet
Mogao Caves
Pik Pobedy 7,439m (24,406ft)
Kongur Shan 7,719m (25,325ft)
Communism Peak 7,495m (24,590ft)
K2 8,611m (28,251ft)
Mount Everest 8,850m (29,035ft)
-154m (-505ft)
5,143m (16,873ft)
Bishkek
Tashkent
Dushanbe
Kabul
Islamabad
New Delhi
Kathmandu
Thimphu
Balqash
Altay
Karamay
Kuytun
Shihezi
Urumqi
Turpan
Hami
Yining
Almaty
Taraz
Kara-Balta
Karakol
Aksu
Korla
Qyzylorda
Shieli
Turkistan
Shymkent
Urganch
Navoiy
Buxoro
Samarqand
Turkmenabat
Mary
Jizzax
Khujand
Namangan
Angren
Fargona
Jalal-Abad
Osh
Kashi
Hotan
Golmud
Qurghonteppa
Kulob
Khorugh
Konduz
Mazar-e Sharif
Herat
Kandahar
Jalalabad
Peshawar
Gilgit
Srinagar
Jammu
Sialkot
Gujranwala
Gujrat
Lahore
Amritsar
Faisalabad
Sargodha
Ludhiana
Chandigarh
Sahiwal
Multan
Quetta
Dera Ghazi Khan
Bahawalpur
Saharanpur
Meerut
Delhi
Rahimyar Khan
Bikaner
Bareilly
Aligarh
Agra
Taj Mahal
Jaipur
Larkana
Sukkur
Panjgur
Nawabshah
Jodhpur
Ajmer
Gwalior
Lucknow
Kanpur
Jhansi
Allahabad
Gorakhpur
Pokhara
Biratnagar
Darjeeling
Darbhanga
Patna
Bhagalpur
Rangpur
Lhasa
Dibrugarh
Jorhat
Guwahati
Shillong

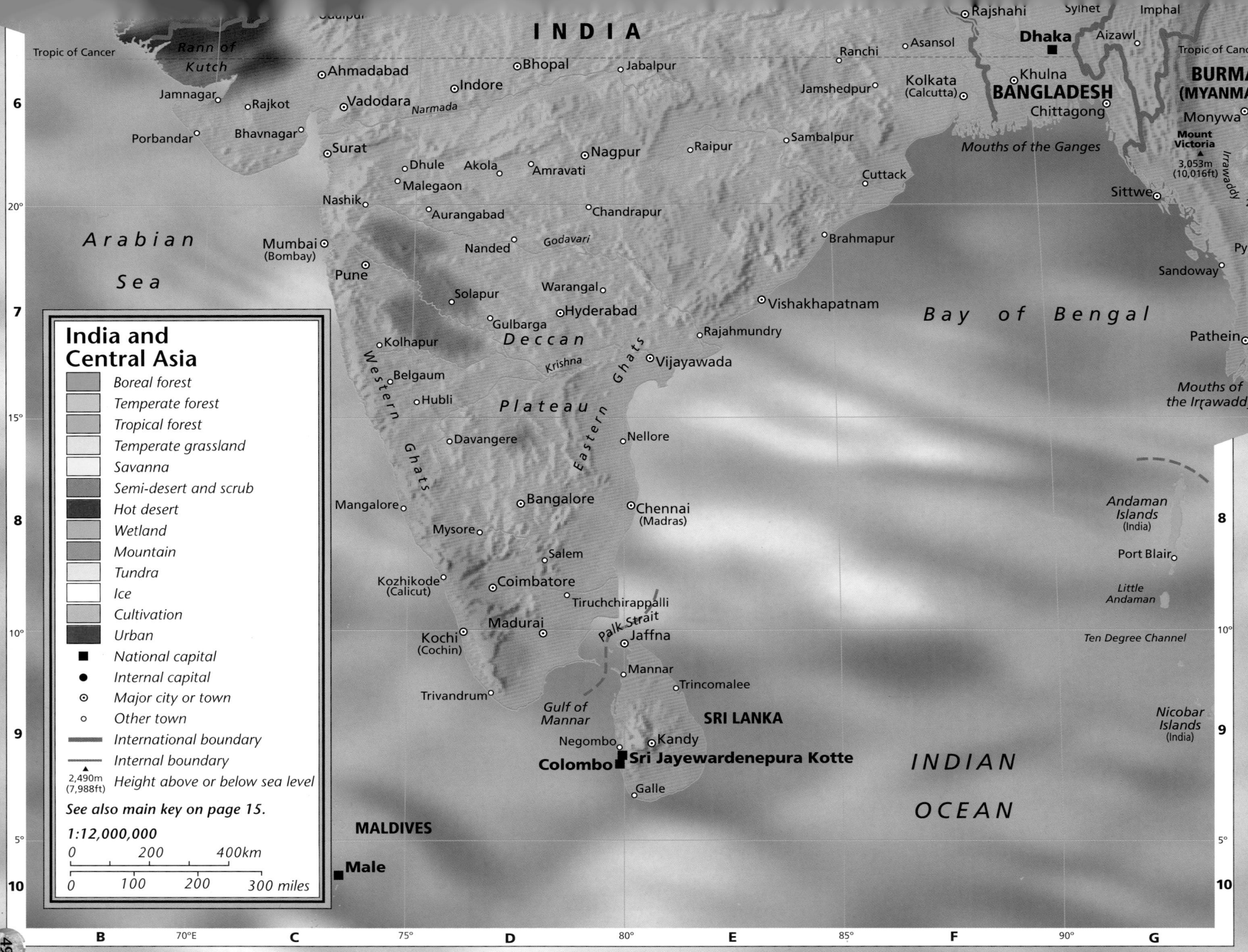

Copyright © Usborne Publishing Ltd.

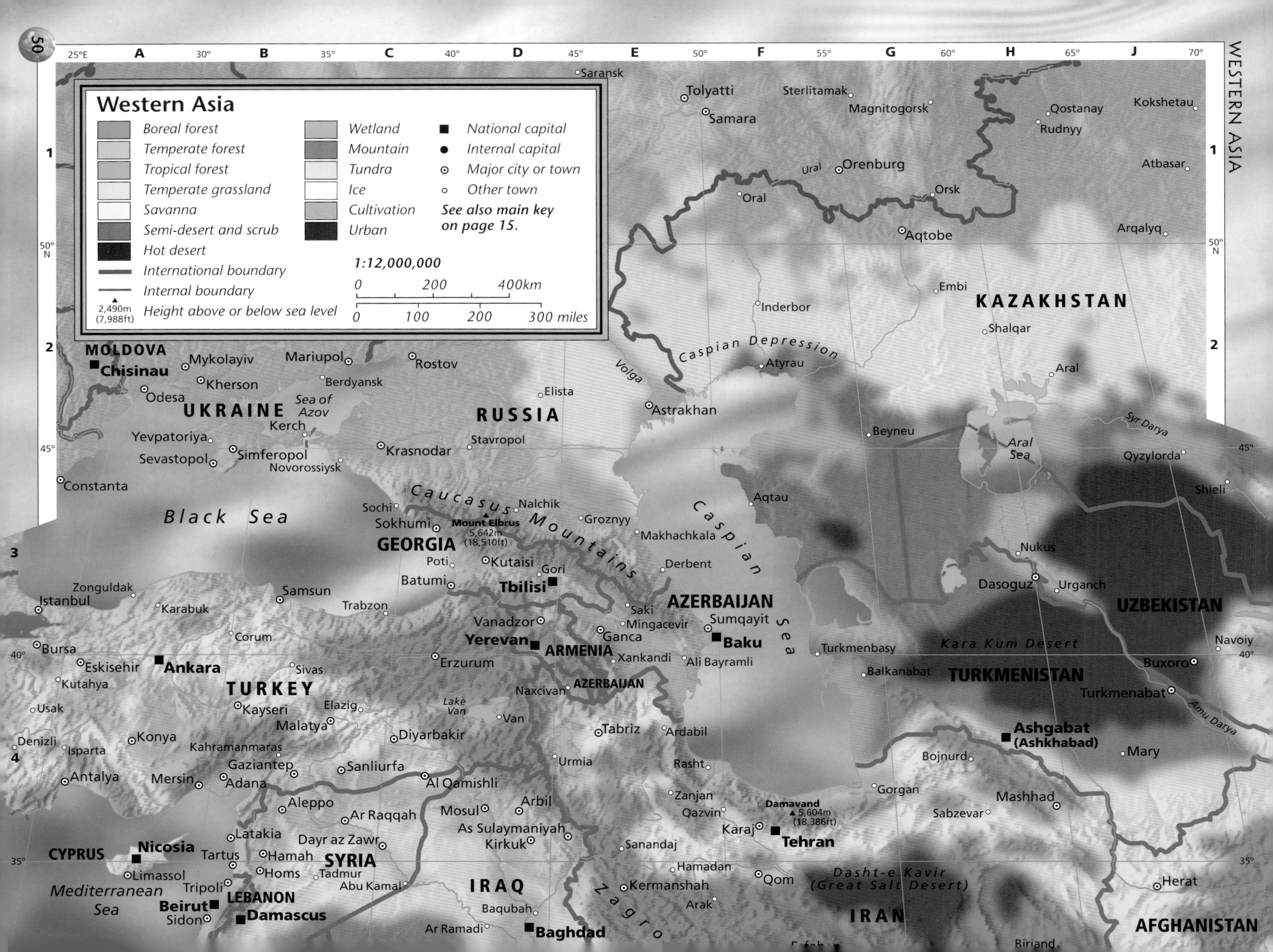
Western Asia
Boreal forest
Temperate forest
Tropical forest
Temperate grassland
Savanna
Semi-desert and scrub
Hot desert
International boundary
Internal boundary
2,490m (7,988ft) Height above or below sea level
Wetland
Mountain
Tundra
Ice
Cultivation
Urban
National capital
Internal capital
Major city or town
Other town
See also main key on page 15.
1:12,000,000
0 200 400km
0 100 200 300 miles
KAZAKHSTAN
RUSSIA
UKRAINE
MOLDOVA
Chisinau
GEORGIA
Tbilisi
ARMENIA
Yerevan
AZERBAIJAN
Baku
TURKEY
Ankara
IRAN
IRAQ
Baghdad
SYRIA
LEBANON
Damascus
Beirut
CYPRUS
Nicosia
UZBEKISTAN
TURKMENISTAN
Ashgabat (Ashkhabad)
AFGHANISTAN
Tehran
Damavand ▲5,604m (18,386ft)
Mount Elbrus ▲5,642m (18,510ft)
Black Sea
Caspian Sea
Caspian Depression
Caucasus Mountains
Aral Sea
Kara Kum Desert
Dasht-e Kavir (Great Salt Desert)
Zagros
Mediterranean Sea
Sea of Azov
Lake Van
Volga
Ural
Syr Darya
Amu Darya
Saransk
Tolyatti
Samara
Sterlitamak
Magnitogorsk
Qostanay
Rudnyy
Kokshetau
Atbasar
Orenburg
Orsk
Oral
Aqtobe
Arqalyq
Embi
Inderbor
Shalqar
Atyrau
Aral
Astrakhan
Beyneu
Qyzylorda
Shieli
Aqtau
Nukus
Dasoguz
Urganch
Navoiy
Buxoro
Turkmenbasy
Balkanabat
Turkmenabat
Mary
Bojnurd
Mashhad
Sabzevar
Gorgan
Herat
Biriand
Rasht
Zanjan
Qazvin
Karaj
Qom
Hamadan
Arak
Kermanshah
Sanandaj
Tabriz
Ardabil
Urmia
Mosul
Arbil
As Sulaymaniyah
Kirkuk
Baqubah
Ar Ramadi
Al Qamishli
Ar Raqqah
Aleppo
Dayr az Zawr
Tadmur
Abu Kamal
Homs
Hamah
Tartus
Latakia
Tripoli
Sidon
Limassol
Mersin
Adana
Sanliurfa
Gaziantep
Kahramanmaras
Diyarbakir
Malatya
Elazig
Van
Naxcivan
Kayseri
Konya
Isparta
Antalya
Denizli
Usak
Kutahya
Eskisehir
Bursa
Corum
Sivas
Erzurum
Trabzon
Samsun
Karabuk
Zonguldak
Istanbul
Constanta
Sevastopol
Simferopol
Novorossiysk
Yevpatoriya
Kerch
Odesa
Kherson
Mykolayiv
Mariupol
Berdyansk
Rostov
Elista
Stavropol
Krasnodar
Sochi
Sokhumi
Nalchik
Groznyy
Makhachkala
Derbent
Poti
Kutaisi
Gori
Batumi
Saki
Mingacevir
Sumqayit
Ganca
Xankandi
Ali Bayramli
Vanadzor
Zaqatala
1
2
3
4
50° N
45°
40°
35°
25°E
30°
35°
40°
45°
50°
55°
60°
65°
70°
A
B
C
D
E
F
G
H
J

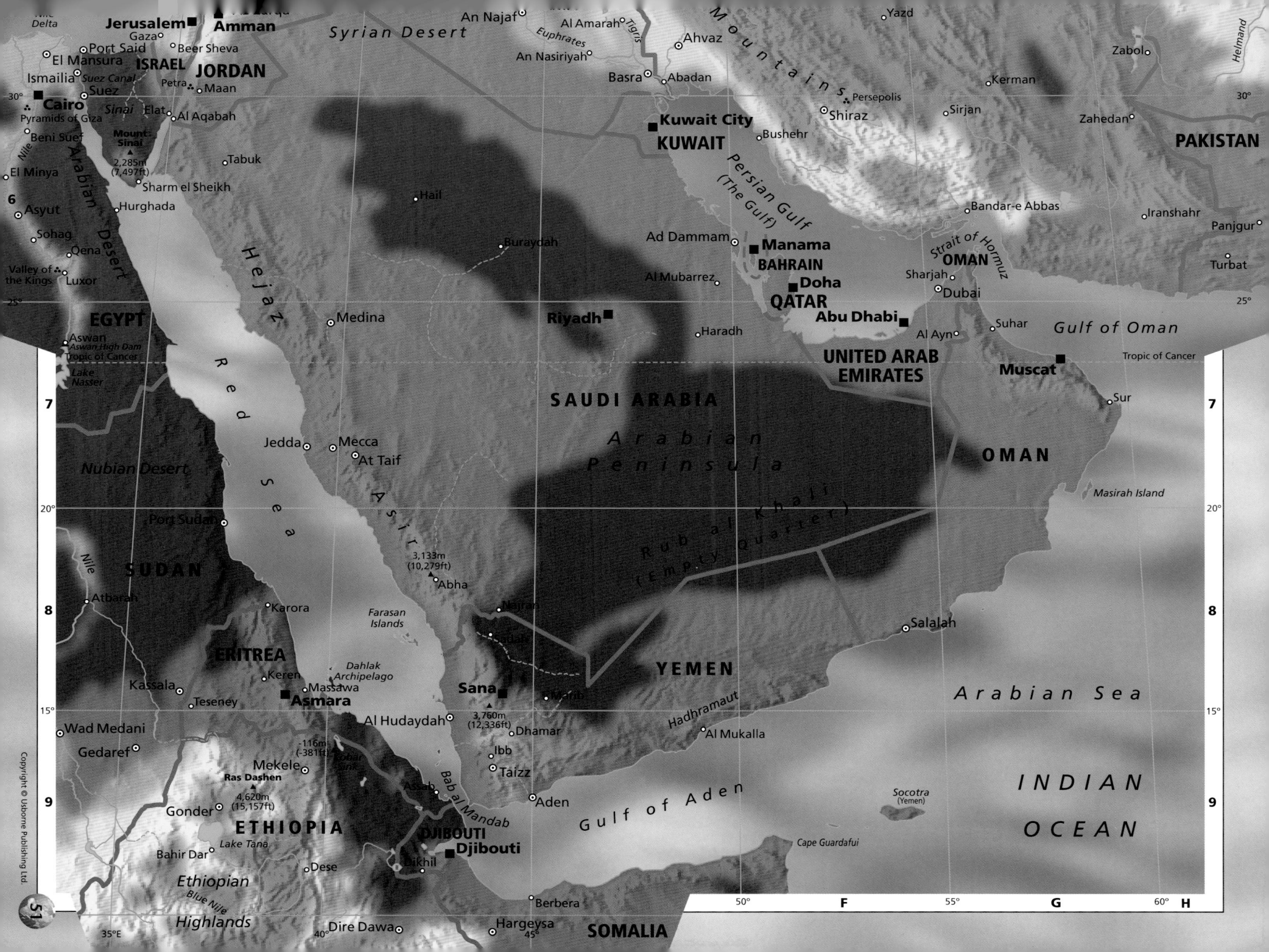

Copyright © Usborne Publishing Ltd.

UNITED KINGDOM
London
North Sea
Norwegian Sea
Arctic Circle
Svalbard (Norway)
ARCTIC
Paris
NETHERLANDS
BELGIUM
LUXEMBOURG
FRANCE
DENMARK
NORWAY
Oslo
SWEDEN
North Cape
Franz Josef Land
GERMANY
Berlin
Stockholm
FINLAND
Helsinki
Baltic Sea
Barents Sea
Novaya Zemlya
Murmansk
Kola Peninsula
Kara Sea
CZECH REPUBLIC
AUSTRIA
POLAND
Warsaw
LITHUANIA
Vilnius
ESTONIA
LATVIA
Lake Ladoga
St. Petersburg
Arkhangelsk
Lake Onega
SLOVAKIA
Budapest
HUNGARY
Minsk
BELARUS
Lviv
Cherepovets
Vorkuta
Norilsk
Moscow
Ukhta
ROMANIA
Kiev
MOLDOVA
Chisinau
UKRAINE
Ryazan
Nizhniy Novgorod
Novyy Urengoy
Ural Mountains
Ob
West Siberian Plain
Volga
Odesa
Kharkiv
Voronezh
Kazan
Perm
Dnipropetrovsk
Surgut
Yenisey
Simferopol
Samara
Yekaterinburg
Black Sea
Rostov
Volgograd
Krasnodar
Chelyabinsk
Irtysh
R U S
Ankara
Oral
Orenburg
TURKEY
Mount Elbrus
5,642m (18,510ft)
Astrakhan
Aqtobe
Omsk
Tomsk
Krasnoyarsk
Adana
Atyrau
Novosibirsk
GEORGIA
Tbilisi
KAZAKHSTAN
Astana
Pavlodar
Barnaul
ARMENIA
Yerevan
Aleppo
Aqtau
Caspian Sea
AZERBAIJAN
Baku
SYRIA
Qaraghandy
Kyzyl
Uskemen
Mosul
Tabriz
Aral Sea
Nukus
Qyzylorda
Balqash
Dasoguz
UZBEKISTAN
Lake Balkhash
Altay
Baghdad
TURKMENISTAN
IRAQ
Damavand
5,604m (18,386ft)
Tehran
Ashgabat (Ashkhabad)
Shymkent
Almaty
Tashkent
Bishkek
Urumqi
Ahvaz
Esfahan
Turkmenabat
Samarqand
KYRGYZSTAN
Tien Shan
Mashhad
Osh
Kuwait City
KUWAIT
Dushanbe
Aksu
IRAN
TAJIKISTAN
SAUDI ARABIA
Tarim Basin
Herat
Mazar-e Sharif
Taklimakan Desert
Persian (The Gulf)
Shiraz
AFGHANISTAN
Riyadh
Kabul
Hotan
Manama
K2
8,611m (28,251ft)
Bandar-e Abbas
Islamabad
QATAR
Doha
Zahedan
Kandahar
Srinagar
Abu Dhabi
Indus
Plateau of Tibet
PAKISTAN
Lahore
INDIA
60°
2
80°
A
20°
1
B
40°
C
60°
D
80°
E
3
40° N
4
C
60°E
D
80°
E

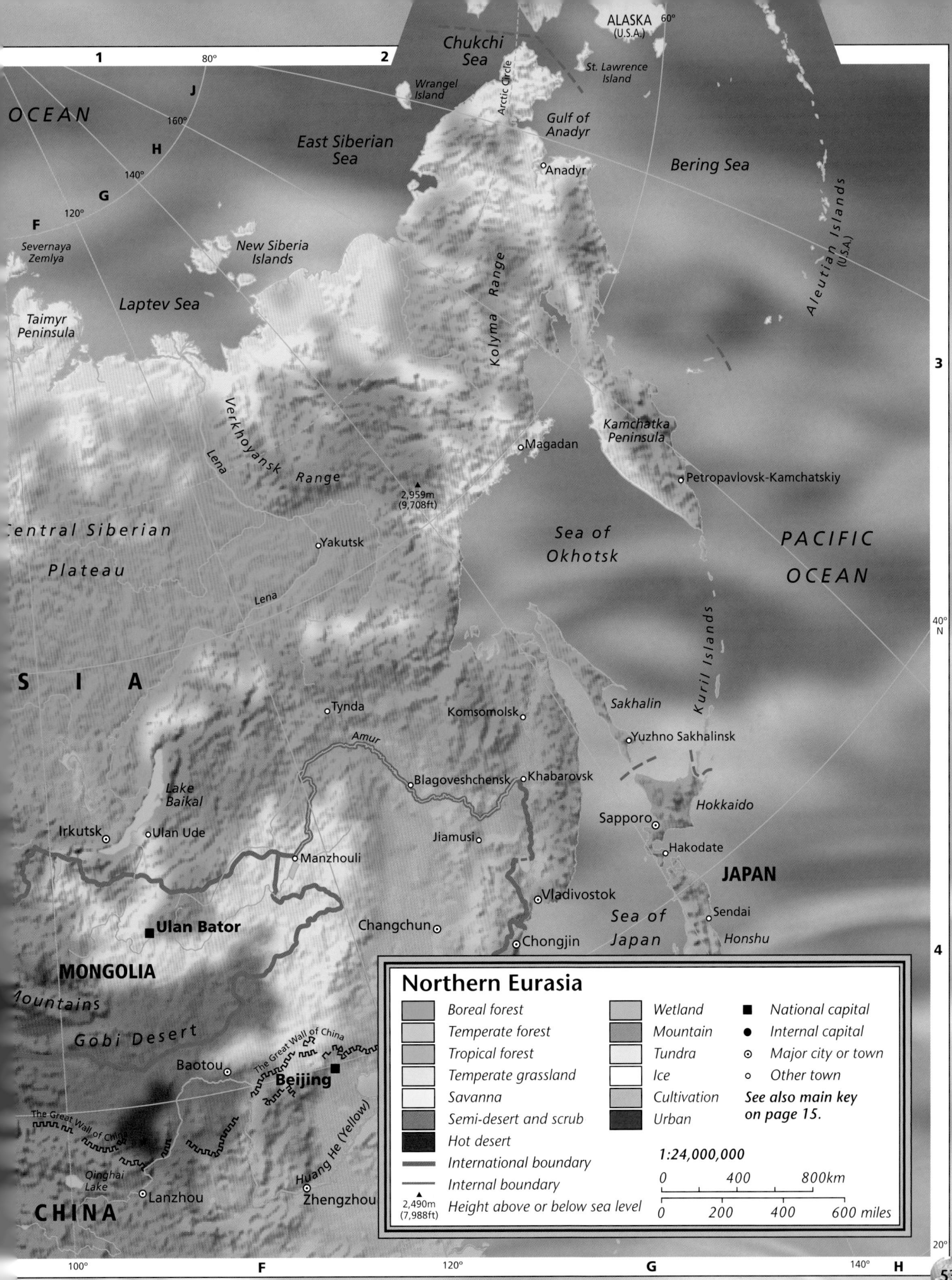

Copyright © Usborne Publishing Ltd.

EUROPE

Europe is a small continent, packed with over 40 countries and more than 700 million people. Russia is an enormous country, spanning two continents. Its western part is in Europe, while its eastern part is in Asia. The European part of Russia is larger than any other country in Europe.

The shading on this map is there to help you see clearly the different countries that make up the continent.

Internet link

For a link to a website where you can find out about the European Union and read key facts about each of its member states, go to **www.usborne-quicklinks.com**

Barents Sea
Murmansk
Arctic Circle
Arkhangelsk
FINLAND
RUSSIA
Helsinki
St. Petersburg
Tallinn
ESTONIA
Nizhniy Novgorod
Kazan
Riga
LATVIA
Moscow
LITHUANIA
Vilnius
RUSSIA
Volga
Minsk
BELARUS
Warsaw
Kiev
Volgograd
Dnieper
UKRAINE
SLOVAKIA
MOLDOVA
Chisinau
ROMANIA
Belgrade
Bucharest
Danube
Black Sea
SERBIA AND MONTENEGRO
BULGARIA
Sofia
Skopje
MACEDONIA
TURKEY
GREECE
Athens
Crete

Facts

Total land area 10,205,720 sq km (3,940,428 sq miles) (including European Russia)
Total population 727 million (including all of Russia)
Biggest city Moscow, Russia
Biggest country Russia *Total area: 17,075,200 sq km (6,592,735 sq miles) Area of European Russia: 4,294,400 sq km (1,658,068 sq miles)*
Smallest country Vatican City *0.44 sq km (0.17 sq miles)*

Highest mountain Elbrus, Russia *5,642m (18,510ft)*
Longest river Volga *3,700km (2,298 miles)*
Biggest lake Lake Ladoga, Russia *17,700 sq km (6,834 sq miles)*
Highest waterfall Utigard, on the Jostedal Glacier, Norway *800m (2,625ft)*
Biggest desert No deserts in Europe
Biggest island Great Britain *234,410 sq km (90,506 sq miles)*

Main mineral deposits Bauxite, zinc, iron, potash, fluorspar
Main fuel deposits Oil, coal, natural gas, peat, uranium

A cow in Devon, in the south of England

Copyright © Usborne Publishing Ltd

FINLAND
Helsinki
Tallinn
ESTONIA
Riga
LATVIA
LITHUANIA
Vilnius
Minsk
BELARUS
Moscow
Kiev
UKRAINE
MOLDOVA
Chisinau
ROMANIA
Baltic Sea
Gulf of Finland
Gulf of Riga
Lake Ladoga
Lake Onega
White Lake
Lake Peipus
Lake Pskov
Lake Ilmen
Rybinsk Reservoir
Gorki Reservoir
Kievske Reservoir
Kremenchukske Reservoir
Kakhovske Reservoir
Tsimlyansk Reservoir
Valdai Hills
North European Plain
Central Russian Uplands
Black Sea
Sea of Azov
Mouths of the Danube
Aland Islands
Hiiumaa
Saaremaa
Pripet Marshes
Paijanne Lake
Pihlaja Lake
Saimaa Lake
Western Dvina
Dnieper
Desna
Volga
Oka
Donets
Don
Dniester
Pripet
Turku
Hameenlinna
Lahti
Kouvola
Lappeenranta
Kotka
Espoo
Vyborg
Zelenogorsk
St. Petersburg
Kohtla-Jarve
Narva
Kingisepp
Gatchina
Pushkin
Volkhov
Tikhvin
Kirishi
Haapsalu
Kuressaare
Parnu
Tartu
Voru
Pskov
Novgorod
Cherepovets
Vologda
Konosha
Borovichi
Ventspils
Jurmala
Jelgava
Cesis
Aluksne
Jekabpils
Ludza
Siauliai
Panevezys
Daugavpils
Kaunas
Marijampole
Alytus
Navapolatsk
Polatsk
Vitsyebsk
Opochka
Velikiye Luki
Vyshniy Volochek
Rybinsk
Kostroma
Yaroslavl
Kineshma
Tver
Ivanovo
Semenov
Rzhev
Sergiyev Posad
Zelenograd
Vladimir
Nizhniy Novgorod
Podolsk
Murom
Arzamas
Hrodna
Lida
Maladzyechna
Barysaw
Zhodzina
Orsha
Smolensk
Obninsk
Kolomna
Serpukhov
Kaluga
Ryazan
Baranavichy
Mahilyow
Roslavl
Tula
Slutsk
Babruysk
Salihorsk
Zhlobin
Saransk
Pinsk
Svyetlahorsk
Homyel
Mazyr
Rechytsa
Klintsy
Bryansk
Orel
Penza
Kamenka
Michurinsk
Yelets
Lipetsk
Tambov
Lutsk
Rivne
Korosten
Chernihiv
Kursk
Shepetivka
Zhytomyr
Voronezh
Staryy Oskol
Sumy
Khmelnytskyy
Bila Tserkva
Lubny
Vinnytsya
Kamyanets-Podilskyy
Kharkiv
Cherkasy
Poltava
Kamyshin
Uman
Kremenchuk
Botosani
Balti
Kirovohrad
Oleksandriya
Rabnita
Slovyansk
Kramatorsk
Lysychansk
Iasi
Dniprodzerzhynsk
Dnipropetrovsk
Yuzhnoukrayinsk
Kryvyy Rih
Horlivka
Luhansk
Volgograd
Tiraspol
Tighina
Nikopol
Zaporizhzhya
Donetsk
Mykolayiv
Bilhorod Dnistrovskyy
Odesa
Kherson
Melitopol
Mariupol
Novocherkassk
Rostov
Volgodonsk
Galati
Braila
Tulcea
Berdyansk
343m (1,125ft)
293m (961ft)
417m (1,368ft)
20°E
25°
30°
35°
40°
45°
30°E
55° N
50°
45°
B
C
D
E
2
3
4

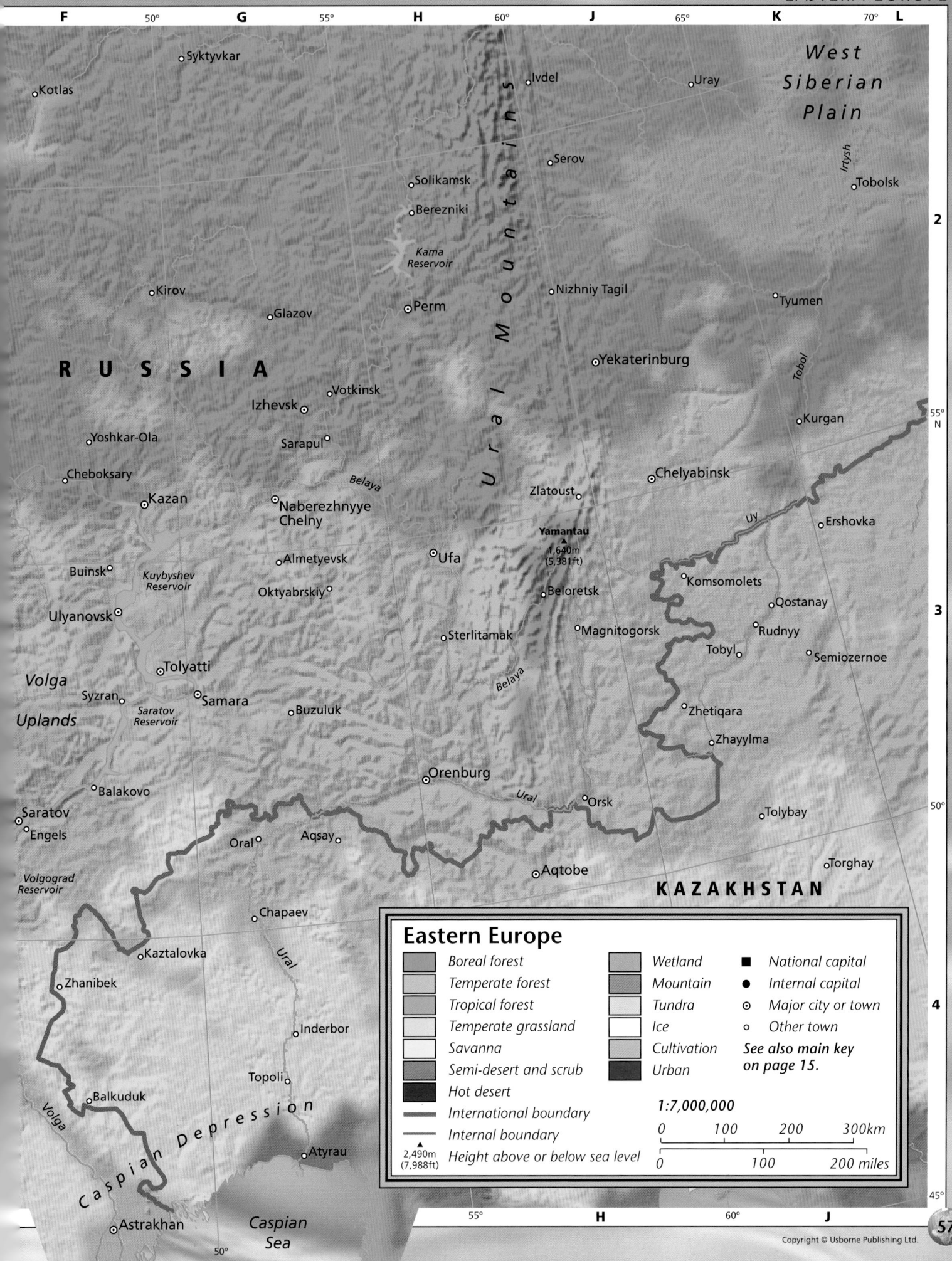

Copyright © Usborne Publishing Ltd.

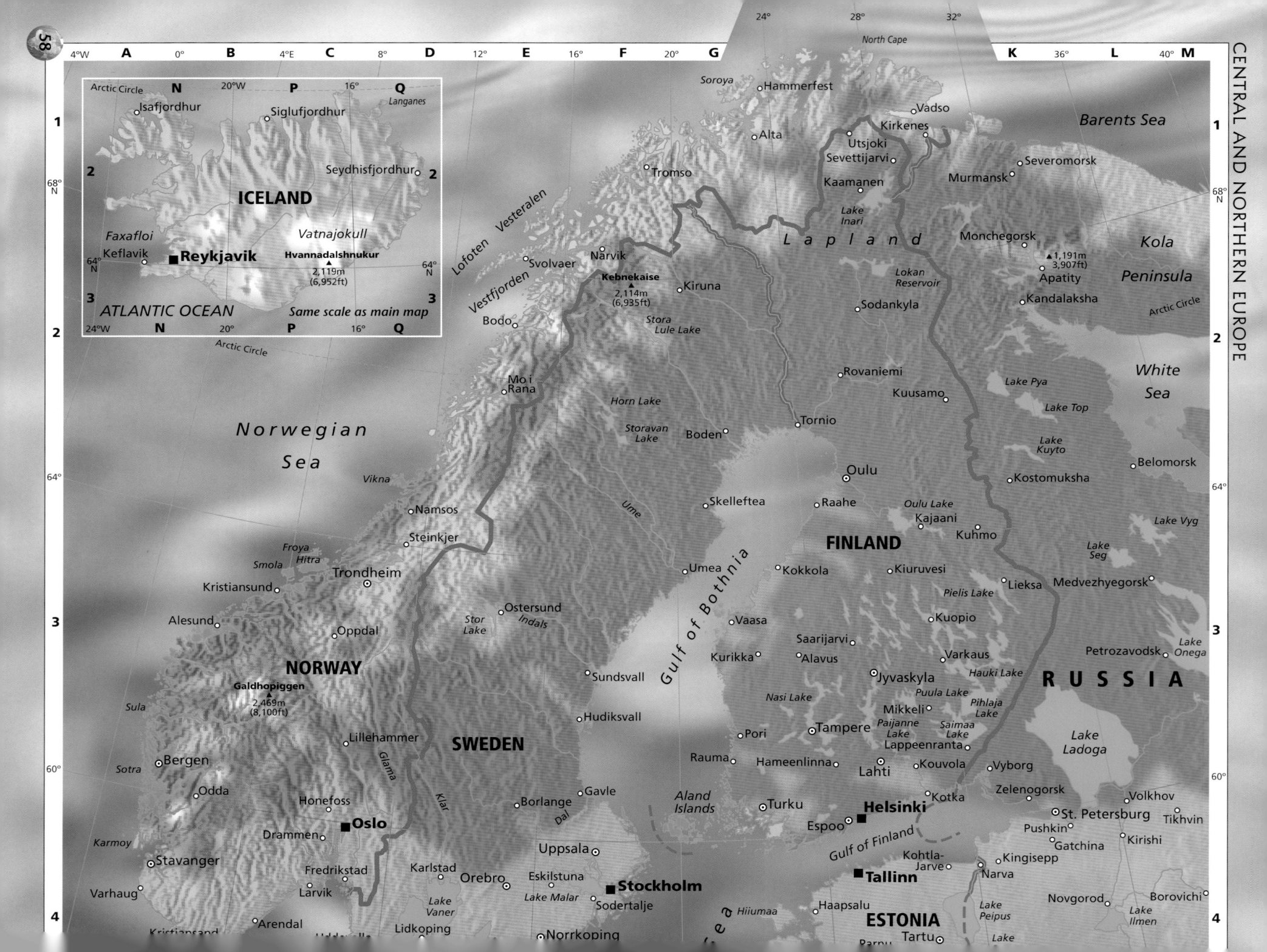
Arctic Circle
Isafjordhur
Siglufjordhur
Langanes
Seydhisfjordhur
ICELAND
Faxafloi
Vatnajokull
Keflavik
Reykjavik
Hvannadalshnukur
2,119m
(6,952ft)
ATLANTIC OCEAN
Same scale as main map
Arctic Circle
North Cape
Soroya
Hammerfest
Vadso
Kirkenes
Alta
Utsjoki
Sevettijarvi
Barents Sea
Severomorsk
Murmansk
Tromso
Kaamanen
Lake Inari
Lapland
Monchegorsk
Kola Peninsula
1,191m
3,907ft)
Apatity
Kandalaksha
Lofoten
Vesteralen
Vestfjorden
Svolvaer
Narvik
Kebnekaise
2,114m
(6,935ft)
Kiruna
Lokan Reservoir
Sodankyla
Arctic Circle
Bodo
Stora Lule Lake
Mo i Rana
Rovaniemi
Lake Pya
White Sea
Kuusamo
Lake Top
Horn Lake
Tornio
Storavan Lake
Boden
Lake Kuyto
Belomorsk
Oulu
Kostomuksha
Norwegian Sea
Vikna
Skelleftea
Raahe
Oulu Lake
Kajaani
Lake Vyg
Namsos
Ume
Kuhmo
Steinkjer
FINLAND
Lake Seg
Froya
Hitra
Smola
Trondheim
Umea
Kokkola
Kiuruvesi
Lieksa
Medvezhyegorsk
Kristiansund
Pielis Lake
Ostersund
Indals
Stor Lake
Vaasa
Kuopio
Alesund
Oppdal
Saarijarvi
Lake Onega
Petrozavodsk
Kurikka
Alavus
Varkaus
NORWAY
Sundsvall
Gulf of Bothnia
Jyvaskyla
Hauki Lake
RUSSIA
Galdhopiggen
2,469m
(8,100ft)
Sula
Nasi Lake
Puula Lake
Mikkeli
Pihlaja Lake
Hudiksvall
Paijanne Lake
Saimaa Lake
Tampere
Pori
Lillehammer
SWEDEN
Lappeenranta
Lake Ladoga
Glama
Bergen
Sotra
Rauma
Hameenlinna
Lahti
Kouvola
Vyborg
Odda
Zelenogorsk
Volkhov
Honefoss
Klar
Borlange
Gavle
Aland Islands
Turku
Kotka
Helsinki
St. Petersburg
Tikhvin
Oslo
Espoo
Pushkin
Drammen
Dal
Gatchina
Kirishi
Karmoy
Uppsala
Gulf of Finland
Kohtla-Jarve
Kingisepp
Stavanger
Fredrikstad
Karlstad
Orebro
Eskilstuna
Tallinn
Narva
Varhaug
Larvik
Lake Malar
Stockholm
Novgorod
Borovichi
Lake Vaner
Sodertalje
Hiiumaa
Haapsalu
Lake Peipus
Lake Ilmen
Arendal
ESTONIA
Lidkoping
Norrkoping
Tartu
Lake

Copyright © Usborne Publishing Ltd.

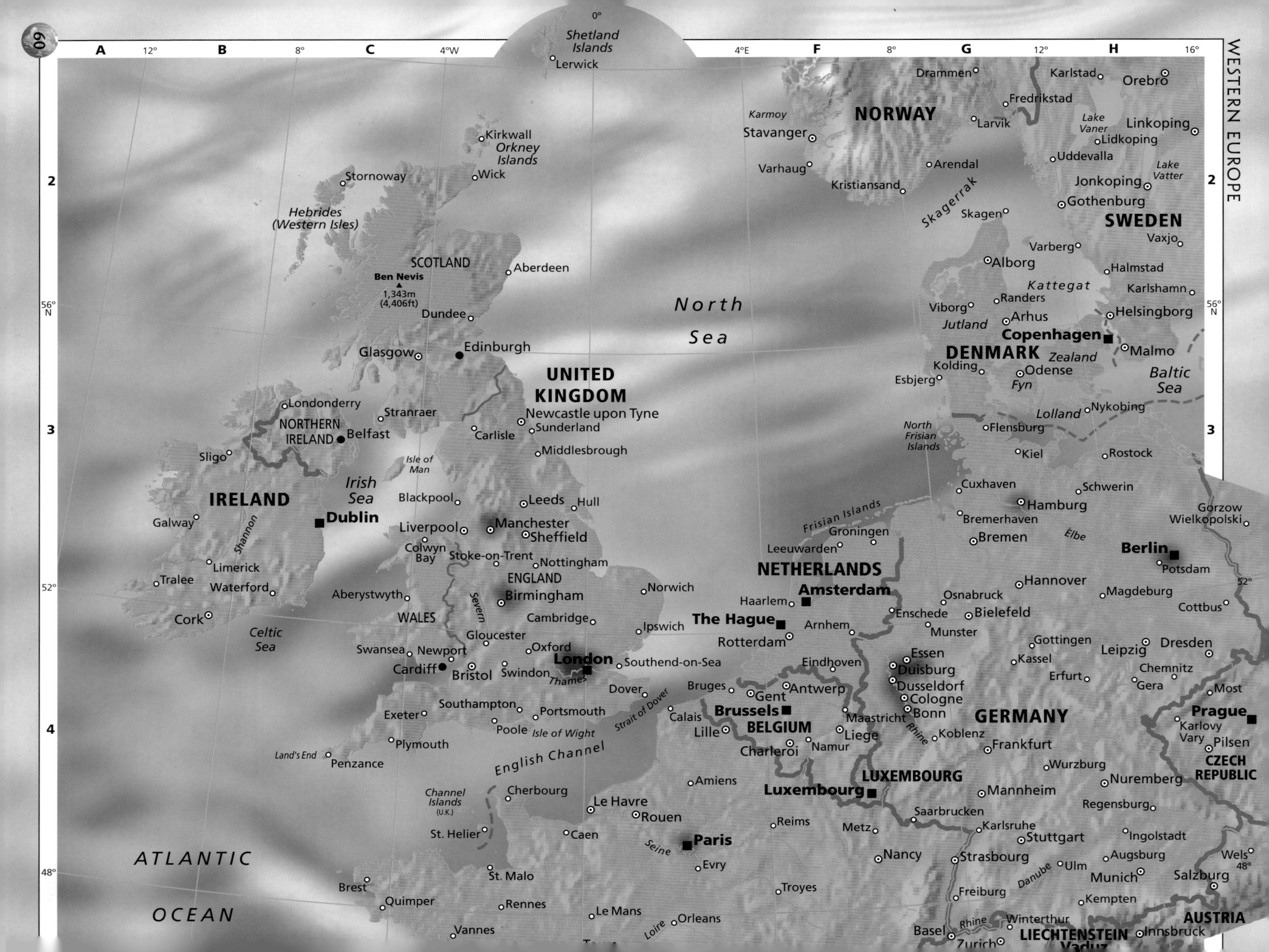
WESTERN EUROPE
A
B
C
F
G
H
12°
8°
4°W
0°
4°E
8°
12°
16°
2
3
4
56° N
52°
48°
Shetland Islands
Lerwick
Kirkwall
Orkney Islands
Wick
Stornoway
Hebrides (Western Isles)
SCOTLAND
Ben Nevis
1,343m (4,406ft)
Aberdeen
Dundee
Glasgow
Edinburgh
North Sea
UNITED KINGDOM
Newcastle upon Tyne
Sunderland
Middlesbrough
Carlisle
Stranraer
Londonderry
NORTHERN IRELAND
Belfast
Sligo
Isle of Man
Irish Sea
IRELAND
Dublin
Galway
Shannon
Limerick
Tralee
Waterford
Cork
Celtic Sea
Blackpool
Leeds
Hull
Liverpool
Manchester
Sheffield
Colwyn Bay
Stoke-on-Trent
Nottingham
ENGLAND
Birmingham
Aberystwyth
WALES
Severn
Cambridge
Norwich
Ipswich
Gloucester
Oxford
Swansea
Newport
Cardiff
Bristol
Swindon
London
Thames
Southend-on-Sea
Dover
Strait of Dover
Calais
Exeter
Southampton
Portsmouth
Poole
Isle of Wight
Plymouth
Land's End
Penzance
English Channel
Channel Islands (U.K.)
Cherbourg
St. Helier
Le Havre
Rouen
Caen
Seine
Paris
Evry
Amiens
Reims
Troyes
Orleans
Loire
Le Mans
Rennes
St. Malo
Brest
Quimper
Vannes
ATLANTIC OCEAN
Karmoy
Stavanger
Varhaug
Kristiansand
NORWAY
Drammen
Karlstad
Orebro
Fredrikstad
Larvik
Lake Vaner
Linkoping
Lidkoping
Uddevalla
Arendal
Lake Vatter
Jonkoping
Gothenburg
Skagerrak
Skagen
SWEDEN
Vaxjo
Varberg
Alborg
Halmstad
Kattegat
Karlshamn
Randers
Viborg
Arhus
Helsingborg
Jutland
Copenhagen
DENMARK
Zealand
Malmo
Kolding
Odense
Fyn
Esbjerg
Baltic Sea
Lolland
Nykobing
North Frisian Islands
Flensburg
Kiel
Rostock
Cuxhaven
Schwerin
Hamburg
Frisian Islands
Bremerhaven
Gorzow Wielkopolski
Groningen
Bremen
Elbe
Leeuwarden
Berlin
Potsdam
NETHERLANDS
Hannover
Amsterdam
Osnabruck
Magdeburg
Haarlem
Enschede
Bielefeld
Cottbus
The Hague
Arnhem
Munster
Rotterdam
Gottingen
Leipzig
Dresden
Essen
Kassel
Eindhoven
Duisburg
Chemnitz
Erfurt
Gera
Dusseldorf
Most
Antwerp
Bruges
Gent
Cologne
Brussels
Bonn
GERMANY
Prague
Maastricht
Rhine
Koblenz
Karlovy Vary
Pilsen
Lille
BELGIUM
Liege
Frankfurt
Namur
Charleroi
CZECH REPUBLIC
Wurzburg
LUXEMBOURG
Nuremberg
Luxembourg
Mannheim
Regensburg
Saarbrucken
Metz
Karlsruhe
Stuttgart
Ingolstadt
Nancy
Strasbourg
Augsburg
Wels
Danube
Ulm
Munich
Salzburg
Freiburg
Kempten
Winterthur
AUSTRIA
Basel
Rhine
LIECHTENSTEIN
Innsbruck
Zurich

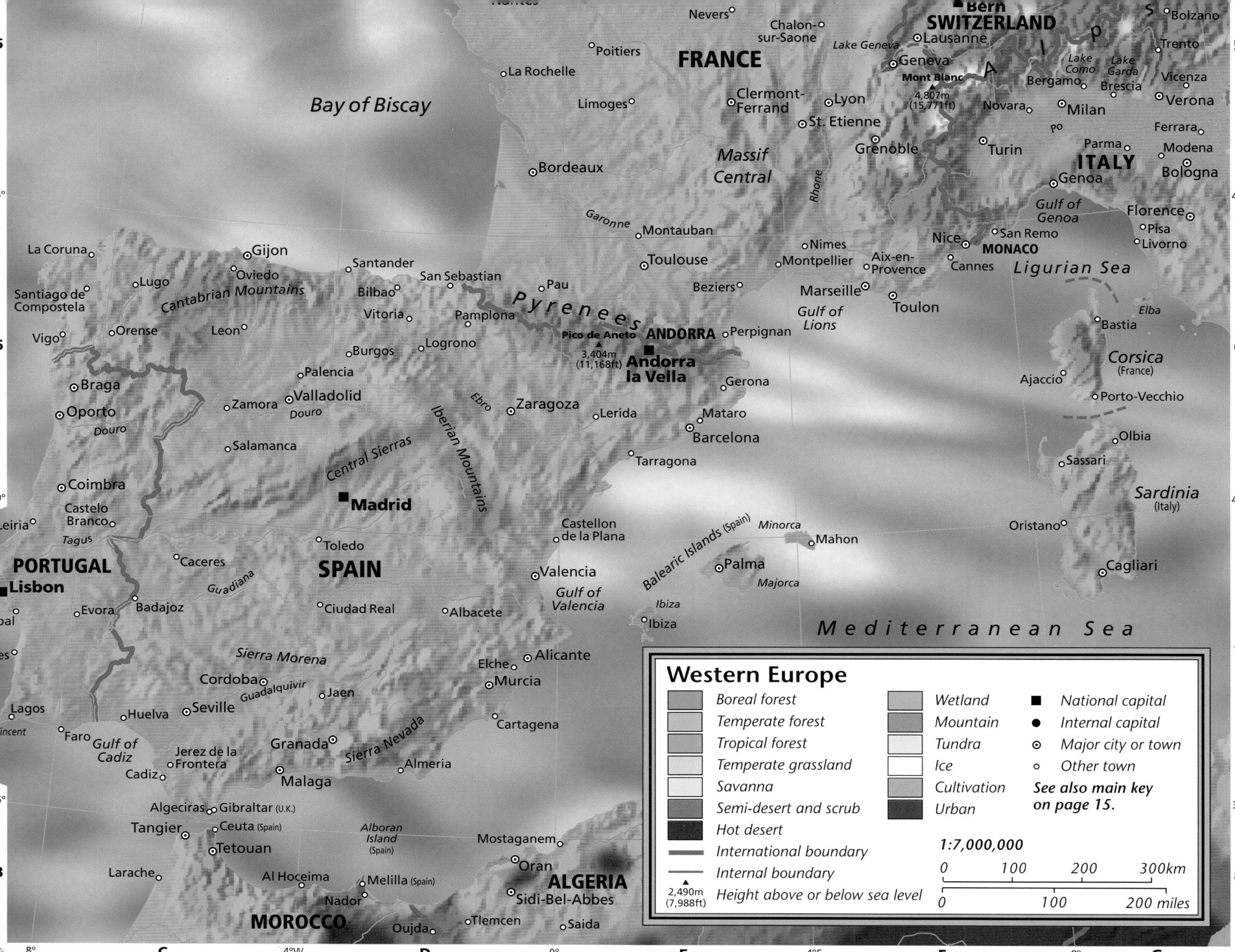

Copyright © Usborne Publishing Ltd.

Southern Europe
Boreal forest
Temperate forest
Tropical forest
Temperate grassland
Savanna
Semi-desert and scrub
Hot desert
Wetland
Mountain
Tundra
Ice
Cultivation
Urban
National capital
Internal capital
Major city or town
Other town
International boundary
Internal boundary
2,490m (7,988ft) Height above or below sea level
See also main key on page 15.
1:7,000,000
0 100 200 300km
0 100 200 miles
BELGIUM
LUXEMBOURG
Luxembourg
GERMANY
CZECH REPUBLIC
Prague
FRANCE
SWITZERLAND
Bern
LIECHTENSTEIN
Vaduz
AUSTRIA
Vienna
Bratislava
SLOVENIA
Ljubljana
CROATIA
Zagreb
BOSNIA AND HERZEGOVINA
ITALY
SAN MARINO
VATICAN CITY
Rome
MONACO
Andorra la Vella
MALTA
Valletta
TUNISIA
Tunis
Paris
Massif Central
Mont Blanc 4,807m (15,771ft)
Grossglockner 3,798m (12,461ft)
Corsica (France)
Sardinia (Italy)
Sicily
Mount Etna 3,323m (10,902ft)
Lipari Islands
Pantelleria (Italy)
Pelagian Islands (Italy)
Elba
Ligurian Sea
Gulf of Genoa
Gulf of Lions
Tyrrhenian Sea
Adriatic Sea
Mediterranean Sea
Apennines
Dinaric Alps
Lake Geneva
Lake Como
Lake Garda
Lake Balaton
Seine
Loire
Rhine
Danube
Elbe
Oder
Rhone
Garonne
Po
Cherbourg
Le Havre
Rouen
Caen
Amiens
Charleroi
Namur
Koblenz
Frankfurt
Erfurt
Gera
Chemnitz
Dresden
Wroclaw
Walbrzych
Opole
Liberec
Most
Hradec Kralove
Karlovy Vary
Pilsen
Wurzburg
Mannheim
Saarbrucken
Metz
Nuremberg
Olomouc
Brno
Zlin
Ceske Budejovice
Reims
Evry
Le Mans
Angers
Orleans
Tours
Troyes
Nancy
Karlsruhe
Stuttgart
Regensburg
Ingolstadt
Strasbourg
Ulm
Augsburg
Freiburg
Munich
Linz
Wels
St. Polten
Trnava
Poitiers
Nevers
Dijon
Besancon
Basel
Zurich
Winterthur
Kempten
Salzburg
Biel
Lucerne
Chalon-sur-Saone
Innsbruck
Knittelfeld
Graz
Szombathely
Gyor
Limoges
Lausanne
Geneva
Clermont-Ferrand
Lyon
Villach
Klagenfurt
Zalaegerszeg
Bolzano
Maribor
St. Etienne
Kranj
Trento
Bergamo
Brescia
Vicenza
Novara
Milan
Grenoble
Trieste
Novo Mesto
Montauban
Turin
Verona
Venice
Rijeka
Karlovac
Slavonski Brod
Toulouse
Parma
Ferrara
Pula
Banja Luka
Genoa
Modena
Bologna
Montpellier
Nimes
Ravenna
Zenica
Beziers
Aix-en-Provence
Nice
San Remo
Rimini
Zadar
Marseille
Cannes
Pisa
Livorno
Florence
Ancona
Split
Mostar
Toulon
Perugia
Bastia
Terni
Pescara
Ajaccio
Porto-Vecchio
Foggia
Olbia
Bari
Sassari
Naples
Pompeii
Salerno
Taranto
Oristano
Cagliari
Cosenza
Catanzaro
Trapani
Palermo
Messina
Agrigento
Catania
Bizerte
Annaba
Menzel Bourguiba
Carthage
Syracuse
Guelma
Souk Ahras
Nabeul
Ragusa
Sousse
Tebessa
Kairouan
Monastir
Kasserine
El Jem
Biskra
0°
4°E
8°
12°
16°
48° N
44°
40°
36°
A
B
C
D
E
F
1
2
3
4
5

Copyright © Usborne Publishing Ltd.

AFRICA

Africa is the second-biggest continent in the world, and has 53 countries. These range from the vast, dry Sudan, to small, tropical islands such as the Seychelles. More than a quarter of Africa's countries are landlocked, with no access to the sea except through other countries.

Here is a group of Masai people from East Africa, silhouetted against a sunset over the flat grasslands of Africa.

Algiers
Tunis
Rabat
Madeira (Portugal)
MOROCCO
TUNISIA
Tripoli
Canary Islands (Spain)
Laayoune
ALGERIA
LIBYA
Tropic of Cancer
WESTERN SAHARA (Morocco)
MAURITANIA
Nouakchott
MALI
Niger
NIGER
CAPE VERDE
Praia
Dakar
SENEGAL
THE GAMBIA
Banjul
Bissau
GUINEA-BISSAU
Bamako
Ouagadougou
Niamey
CHAD
Ndjamena
GUINEA
BURKINA FASO
Conakry
Freetown
SIERRA LEONE
Monrovia
LIBERIA
IVORY COAST
Yamoussoukro
GHANA
Accra
TOGO
Lome
BENIN
Porto-Novo
NIGERIA
Abuja
CENTRAL AFRICAN REPUBLIC
Bangui
CAMEROON
Yaounde
Malabo
EQUATORIAL GUINEA
Congo
Equator
Libreville
GABON
CONGO
SAO TOME AND PRINCIPE
Brazzaville
Kinshasa
ATLANTIC OCEAN
Luanda
ANGOLA
NAMIBIA
Tropic of Capricorn
Windhoek
Orange
Cape Town

Copyright © Usborne Publishing Ltd.

The shading on this map is there to help you see clearly the different countries that make up the continent.

Cairo
EGYPT
Tropic of Cancer
Nile
Khartoum
ERITREA
Asmara
SUDAN
DJIBOUTI
Djibouti
Addis Ababa
SOMALIA
ETHIOPIA
Mogadishu
UGANDA
Kampala
KENYA
Equator
Nairobi
Kigali
RWANDA
BURUNDI
Bujumbura
Victoria
SEYCHELLES
Dodoma
TANZANIA
Dar es Salaam
INDIAN
OCEAN
MALAWI
Moroni
COMOROS
Lilongwe
ZAMBIA
Lusaka
Zambezi
Harare
ZIMBABWE
MOZAMBIQUE
Antananarivo
MAURITIUS
Port Louis
MADAGASCAR
Reunion
(France)
Tropic of Capricorn
Pretoria
Maputo
Mbabane
SWAZILAND
Lobamba
Maseru
LESOTHO

Internet link

For a link to a website where you can find facts, photos and a quiz about Madagascar's amazing wildlife, go to **www.usborne-quicklinks.com**

Facts

Total land area 30,311,690 sq km (11,703,343 sq miles)
Total population 794 million
Biggest city Lagos, Nigeria
Biggest country Sudan *2,505,810 sq km (967,493 sq miles)*
Smallest country Seychelles *455 sq km (176 sq miles)*

Highest mountain Kilimanjaro, Tanzania *5,895m (19,340ft)*
Longest river Nile, running from to Burundi to Egypt *6,671km (4,145 miles)*
Biggest lake Lake Victoria, between Tanzania, Kenya and Uganda *69,215 sq km (26,724 sq miles)*
Highest waterfall Tugela Falls, on the Tugela River, South Africa *610m (2,000ft)*
Biggest desert Sahara, North Africa *9,100,000 sq km (3,500,000 sq miles)*
Biggest island Madagascar *587,040 sq km (226,656 sq miles)*

Main mineral deposits Gold, copper, diamonds, iron ore, manganese, bauxite
Main fuel deposits Coal, uranium, natural gas

This greater flamingo is from the Transvaal National Park, South Africa.

A
B
C
D
E
F
0°
5°E
10°
15°
20°
30° N
25°
20°
15°
10°
2
3
4
5
6
7
Annaba
Bizerte
Menzel
Carthage
Bourguiba
Tunis
Sicily
(Italy)
Catania
Syracuse
Pantelleria
(Italy)
GREECE
Athens
Saida
Djelfa
Batna
Tebessa
Kairouan
Sousse
Monastir
El Jem
Pelagian Islands
(Italy)
MALTA
Valletta
Biskra
Atlas Mountains
Sfax
Gafsa
Kerkenah Islands
Tozeur
Gulf of Gabes
Jerba
El Oued
Touggourt
Chott el Jerid
Gabes
Mediterranean
Ghardaia
Tataouine
Tripoli
TUNISIA
Ouargla
Al Khums
Leptis Magna
Misratah
Cyrene
Al Bayda
Darnah
Gharyan
Benghazi
Tubruq
Surt
Gulf of Sidra
Ajdabiya
Tademait Plateau
Ghadamis
Great Eastern Erg
ALGERIA
Illizi
Sabha
LIBYA
Murzuq
Ahaggar Mountains
Ghat
Libyan
Tropic of Cancer
Mount Tahat
2,918m
(9,573ft)
Tamanrasset
Al Jawf
Djado Plateau
Tibesti Mountains
Emi Koussi
3,415m
(11,204ft)
MALI
SAHARA
Agadez
NIGER
Faya-Largeau
Bodele Depression
Ennedi Plateau
Tahoua
CHAD
Dosso
Sokoto
Maradi
Zinder
Mao
SAHEL
Birnin-Kebbi
Katsina
Abeche
Lake Chad
Gusau
Kano
Kandi
Ndjamena
Mount Ma
3,088
(10,13
Zaria
Potiskum
Maiduguri
Mongo
Nya
Kainji Reservoir
Kaduna
NIGERIA
Maroua
Am Timan
Minna
Jos
Kumo
Niger
CAMEROON
Bongor
Saki
Bida
Abuja
Birao

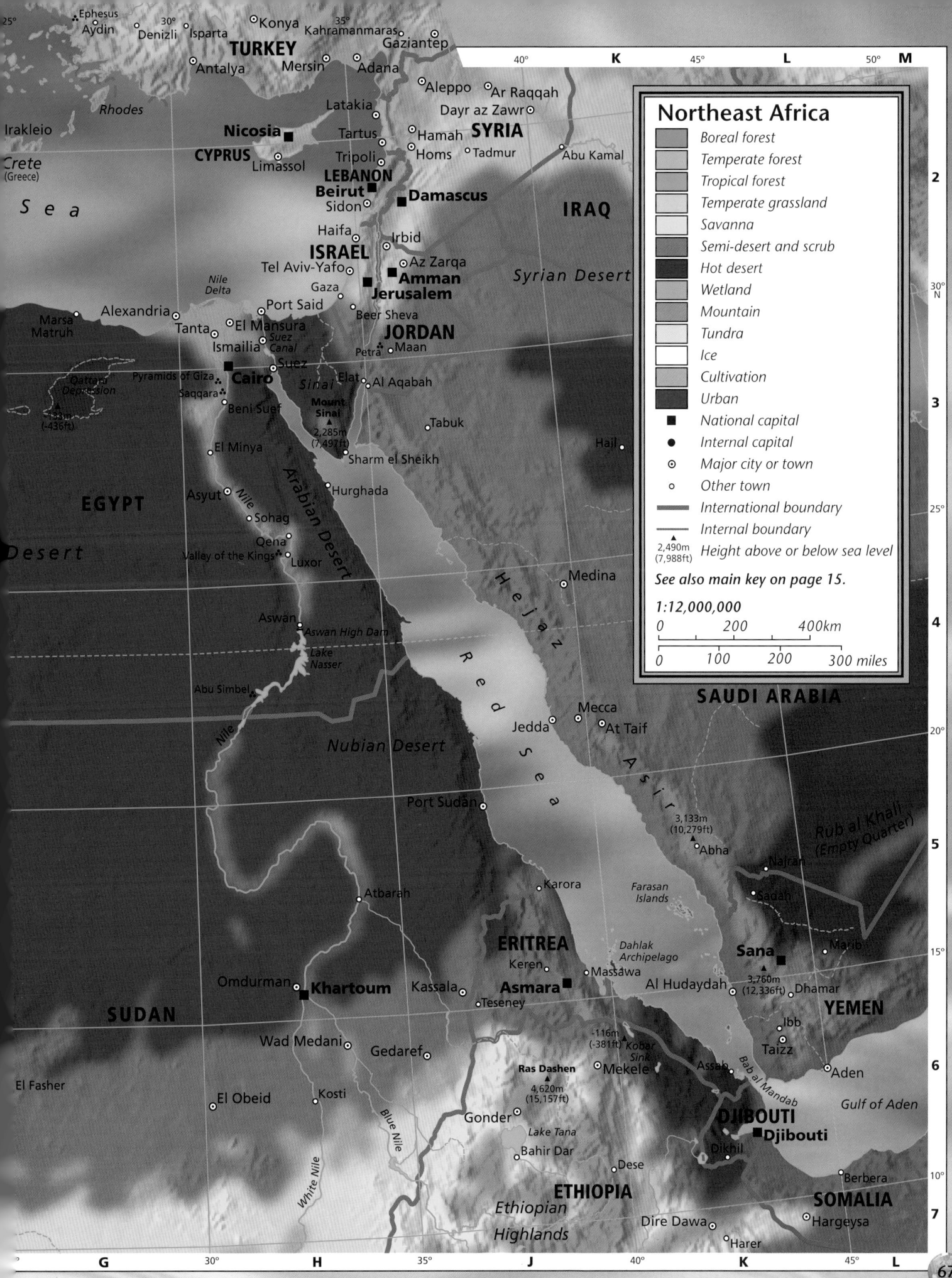

Copyright © Usborne Publishing Ltd.

A
B
C
D
E
F
G
H
20°
15°
10°
5°W
0°
5°E
10°
1
2
3
4
35°
30°
25°
20°
J
K
30°W
40° N
ATLANTIC OCEAN
Flores
Terceira
Azores
(Portugal)
Pico
Angra do Heroismo
Sao Miguel
Ponta Delgada
Same scale as main map
25°
Lisbon
PORTUGAL
Sines
Lagos
SPAIN
Cordoba
Seville
Granada
Malaga
Almeria
Cadiz
Gibraltar (U.K.)
Tangier
Ceuta (Spain)
Tetouan
Larache
Al Hoceima
Alicante
Murcia
Ibiza
Majorca
Balearic Islands
(Spain)
Sardinia
(Italy)
Cagliari
Mediterranean Sea
Algiers
Bejaia
Skikda
Menzel Bourguiba
Bizerte
Carthage
Tunis
Annaba
Blida
Djemila
Constantine
Bordj Bou Arreridj
Setif
Sousse
Kairouan
Monastir
Oran
Mostaganem
Melilla
(Spain)
Sidi-Bel-Abbes
Batna
Tebessa
El Jem
Saida
Sfax
Oujda
Tlemcen
Djelfa
Kerkenah Islands
Rabat
Kenitra
Taza
Fes
Meknes
Casablanca
Gafsa
Jerba
El Jadida
Khouribga
Tozeur
Chott el Jerid
Tataouine
Madeira
(Portugal)
Funchal
Safi
Beni Mellal
Atlas Mountains
Ghardaia
TUNISIA
MOROCCO
Ouargla
Essaouira
Marrakech
Toubkal
4,165m
(13,665ft)
Er Rachidia
Erfoud
Bechar
Ouarzazate
Agadir
Great Western Erg
Ghadamis
LIBYA
Canary Islands
(Spain)
Lanzarote
Fuerteventura
La Palma
Tenerife
La Gomera
El Hierro
Gran Canaria
Tan-Tan
Tademait Plateau
Great Eastern Erg
Adrar
Tindouf
Laayoune
ALGERIA
Es Semara
Boujdour
Illizi
Chech Erg
WESTERN SAHARA
(Morocco)
Ahaggar Mountains
Ad Dakhla
Mount Tahat
2,918m
(9,573ft)
Tropic of Cancer
Tropic of Cancer
Zouerat
Tamanrasset
Nouadhibou
Cape Blanc
Atar
S A H A R A
Akjoujt
MAURITANIA
Tidjikja
Nouakchott
MALI
Kidal

Copyright © Usborne Publishing Ltd.

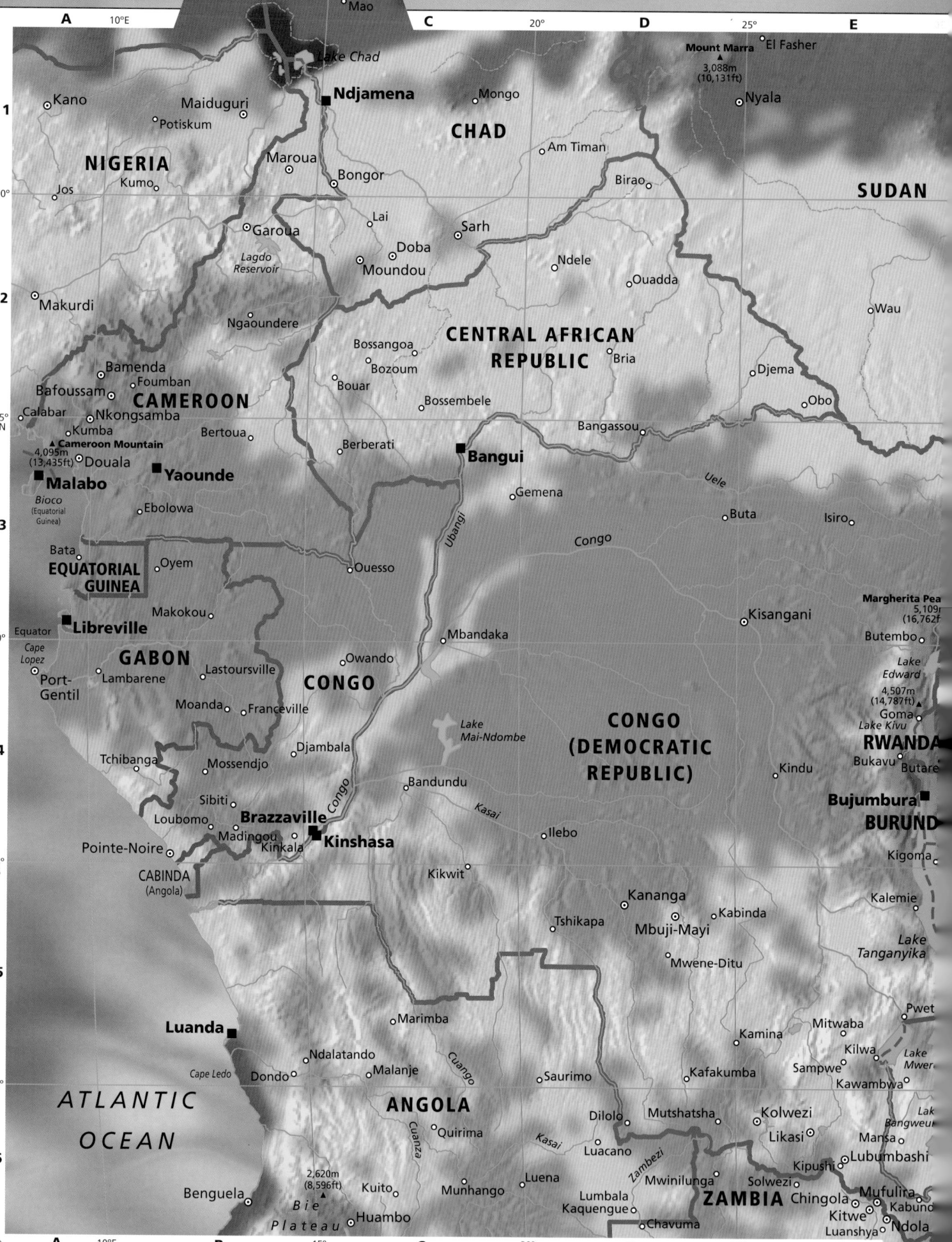
Mao
Lake Chad
Ndjamena
Mongo
Mount Marra
3,088m
(10,131ft)
El Fasher
Nyala
Kano
Maiduguri
Potiskum
CHAD
NIGERIA
Maroua
Am Timan
Kumo
Jos
Bongor
Birao
SUDAN
Lai
Sarh
Garoua
Doba
Lagdo
Reservoir
Moundou
Ndele
Ouadda
Makurdi
Wau
Ngaoundere
CENTRAL AFRICAN
REPUBLIC
Bossangoa
Bria
Bozoum
Bamenda
Fourban
Bouar
Djema
Bafoussam
CAMEROON
Bossembele
Obo
Calabar
Nkongsamba
Kumba
Bangassou
Cameroon Mountain
4,095m
(13,435ft)
Bertoua
Berberati
Douala
Bangui
Malabo
Yaounde
Uele
Bioco
(Equatorial
Guinea)
Gemena
Ebolowa
Buta
Isiro
Ubangi
Congo
Bata
EQUATORIAL
GUINEA
Oyem
Ouesso
Makokou
Kisangani
Libreville
Equator
Mbandaka
Butembo
Cape
Lopez
GABON
Owando
Lake
Edward
Port-
Gentil
Lambarene
Lastoursville
CONGO
4,507m
(14,787ft)
Moanda
Franceville
Goma
Lake Kivu
Lake
Mai-Ndombe
CONGO
(DEMOCRATIC
REPUBLIC)
RWANDA
Djambala
Tchibanga
Mossendjo
Bukavu
Butare
Kindu
Bandundu
Sibiti
Bujumbura
Kasai
Loubomo
Brazzaville
Madingou
Kinkala
Kinshasa
Ilebo
Pointe-Noire
Kigoma
CABINDA
(Angola)
Kikwit
Kananga
Kalemie
Kabinda
Tshikapa
Mbuji-Mayi
Lake
Tanganyika
Mwene-Ditu
Luanda
Marimba
Pwet
Mitwaba
Kamina
Ndalatando
Kilwa
Lake
Mwer
Cuango
Cape Ledo
Dondo
Malanje
Saurimo
Kafakumba
Sampwe
Kawambwa
ATLANTIC
OCEAN
ANGOLA
Dilolo
Mutshatsha
Kolwezi
Lak
Bangweu
Quirima
Cuanza
Kasai
Luacano
Likasi
Mansa
Zambezi
Lubumbashi
Kipushi
2,620m
(8,596ft)
Luena
Mwinilunga
Solwezi
Benguela
Kuito
Munhango
Lumbala
Kaquengue
ZAMBIA
Chingola
Mufulira
Kabund
Bie
Plateau
Huambo
Kitwe
Chavuma
Luanshya
Ndola
Mkush
A
B
C
D
E
10°E
15°
20°
25°
10°
5° N
0°
5° S
10°
1
2
3
4
5
6

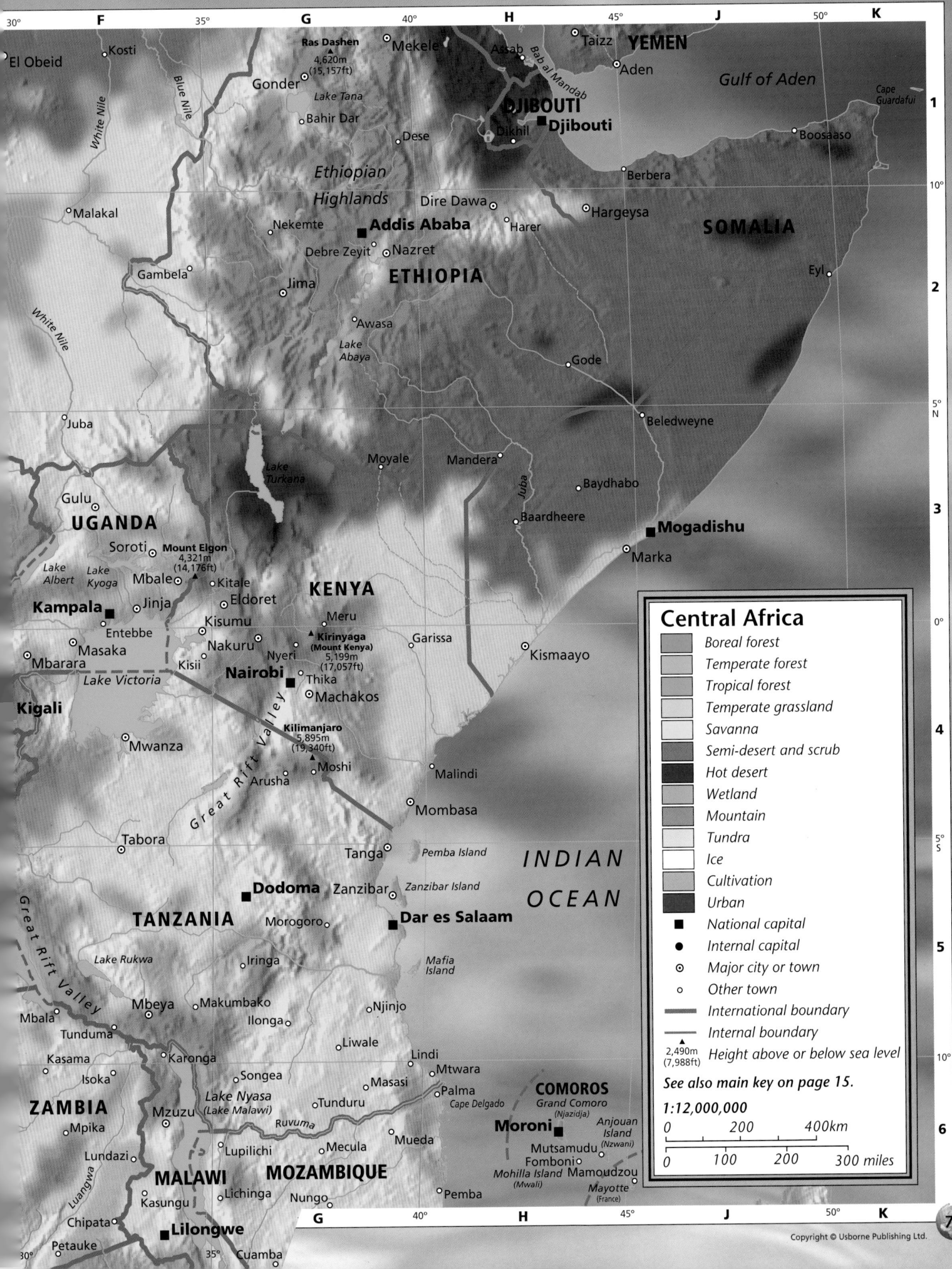

Copyright © Usborne Publishing Ltd.

ANGOLA
CONGO (DEMOCRATIC REPUBLIC)
ZAMBIA
ZIMBABWE
NAMIBIA
BOTSWANA
SOUTH AFRICA
LESOTHO
SWAZILAND
ATLANTIC OCEAN
Luanda
Ndalatando
Dondo
Cape Ledo
Malanje
Marimba
Cuango
Saurimo
Kafakumba
Kamina
Mitwaba
Pweto
Mbala
Great
Kilwa
Sampwe
Lake Mweru
Kawambwa
Kasama
Dilolo
Mutshatsha
Kolwezi
Likasi
Lake Bangweulu
Mansa
Lubumbashi
Mpika
Kipushi
Mufulira
Kabunda
Ndola
Kitwe
Chingola
Luanshya
Mkushi
Luangwa
Petauke
Kabwe
Rufunsa
Lusaka
Kafue
Zambezi
Cabora Bassa Reservoir
Zumbo
Mount Darwin
Mutoko
Bindura
Harare
Kadoma
Kamativi
Chinhoyi
Kariba
Lake Kariba
Binga
Zimba
Livingstone
Victoria Falls
Hwange
Sesheke
Luiana
Zambezi
Mwinilunga
Solwezi
Luacano
Luena
Lumbala Kaquengue
Chavuma
Zambezi
Lukulu
Mongu
Kataba
Ngoma
Mavinga
Caiundo
Menongue
Lumbala Nguimbo
Cangombe
Mumbue
Kuito
Munhango
Quirima
Cuanza
Kasai
Huambo
Bie Plateau
2,620m (8,596ft)
Benguela
Lucira
Cape St. Martha
Matala
Lubango
Namibe
Albino Point
Cunene
Xangongo
Foz do Cunene
Cuangar
Rundu
Andara
Caprivi Strip
Okavango Swamp
Okavango
Ondangwa
Opuwo
Etosha Pan
Okaukuejo
Tsumeb
Otavi
Kamanjab
Otjiwarongo
Sukses
Kaukau Veld
Nokaneng
Maun
Tsau
Lake Ngami
Makgadikgadi Pans (Makarikari)
Rakops
Francistown
Orapa
Selebi-Phikwe
Plumtree
Bulawayo
Gweru
Masvingo
Zvishavane
Chiredzi
Karibib
Okahandja
Mamuno
Gobabis
Swakopmund
Windhoek
Walvis Bay
Rehoboth
Leonardville
Tropic of Capricorn
Kalkrand
Mariental
Gochas
Tshwane
Serowe
Mahalapye
Messina
Pafuri
Limpopo
Kang
Molepolole
Mochudi
Gaborone
Tshane
Kalahari Desert
Werda
Kanye
Warmbad
Graskop
Pietersburg
Nelspruit
Pretoria
Krugersdorp
Benoni
Mbabane
Lobamba
Terra Firma
Mmabatho
Johannesburg
Springs
Tshabong
Molopo
Tses
Keetmanshoop
Luderitz
Seeheim
Orkneyo
Standerton
Hotazel
Kroonstad
Grunau
Welkom
Bethlehem
Harrismith
Upington
Kimberley
Tugela Falls
Ladysmith
Richards Bay
Maseru
Orange
Alexander Bay
Kenhardt
Douglas
Bloemfontein
Pietermaritzburg
Mafeteng
Durban
Prieska
Drakensberg
2,770m (9,088ft)
De Aar
Bitterfontein
Carnarvon
Umtata
Beaufort West
Graaff-Reinet
Cradock
Great Karoo
Bisho
East London
Cape Columbine
Groot
Grahamstown
Uitenhage
Port Elizabeth
Paarl
Worcester
Oudtshoorn
Cape Town
Stellenbosch
Cape St. Francis
Cape of Good Hope
Cape Agulhas
15°E
20°
25°
30°
10°E
10° S
15°
20°
25°
30°
A
B
C
D
E
F
1
2
3
4
5
6

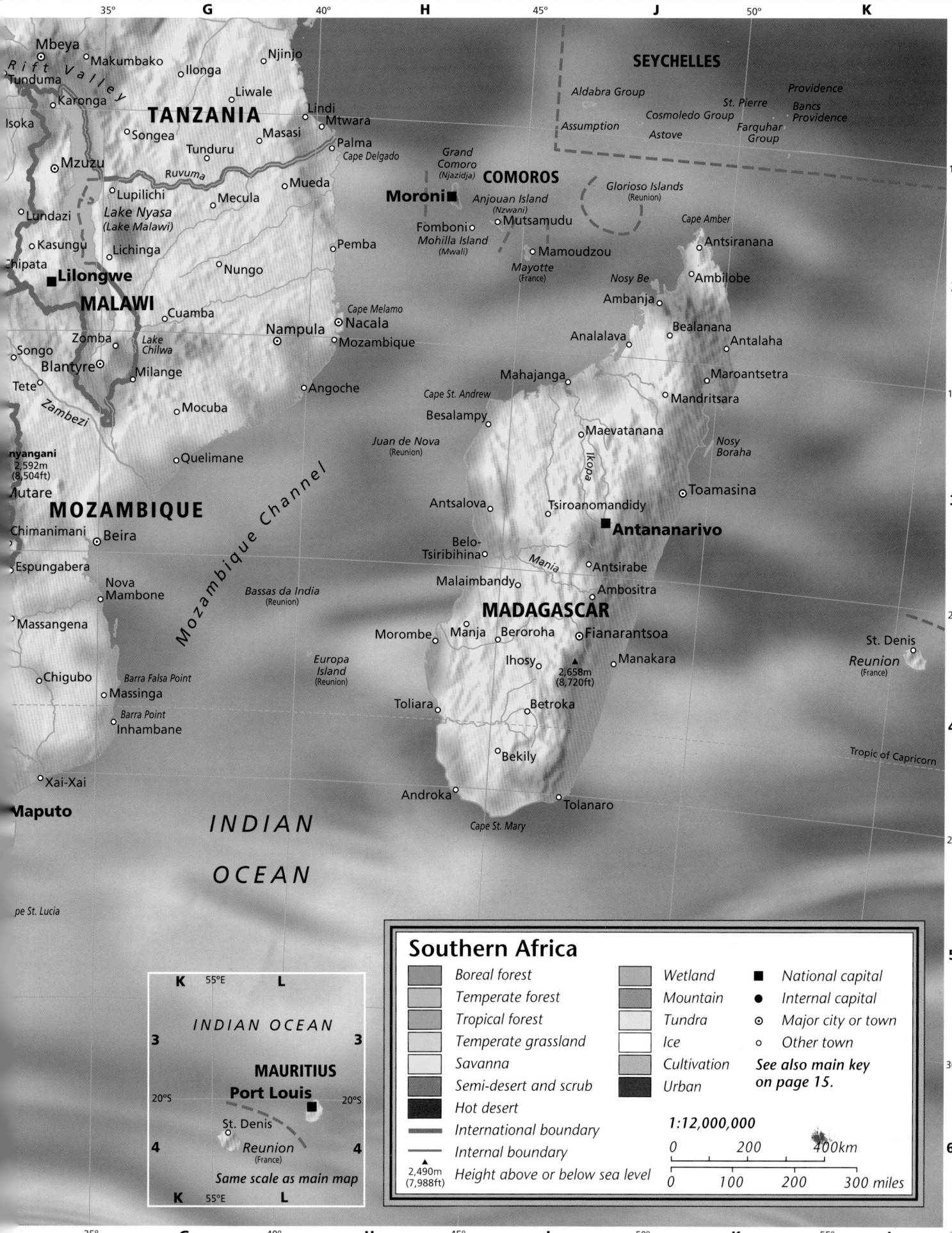

Copyright © Usborne Publishing Ltd.

THE ARCTIC

The Arctic is not a continent. It is a region north of the Arctic Circle line of latitude, around the North Pole. The Arctic consists of the Arctic Ocean, islands such as Greenland and the most northerly parts of mainland Europe, North America and Asia. The Arctic region is covered in ice and snow almost all year round.

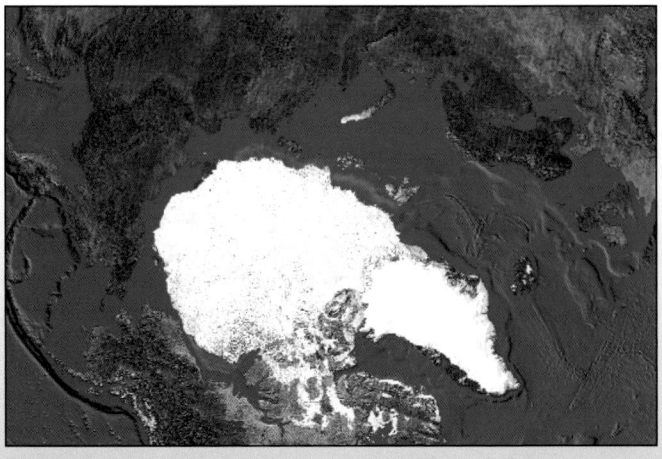

The large white area in this satellite image is ice covering the Arctic Ocean and Greenland. At the top left of the image is the edge of Russia and at the top right is part of Europe.

These Inuit people are wearing thick, animal-skin coats, boots and gloves to keep warm.

Internet link

For a link to a website where you can discover more about the Arctic, including its wildlife, climate and native peoples, go to **www.usborne-quicklinks.com**

Facts

Size of Arctic Ocean
14,056,000 sq km (5,426,000 sq miles)

Highest point Gunnbjorns Mountain, Greenland *3,700m (12,139ft)*

Lowest point Fram Basin, Arctic Ocean *-4,665m (-15,305ft)*

Lowest recorded temperature
-67.8°C (-90°F)

Main mineral deposits
Diamonds, gold

Main fuel deposits
Oil, natural gas

Seals living in Arctic regions have a thick layer of fat under their skin to keep them warm in the freezing weather.

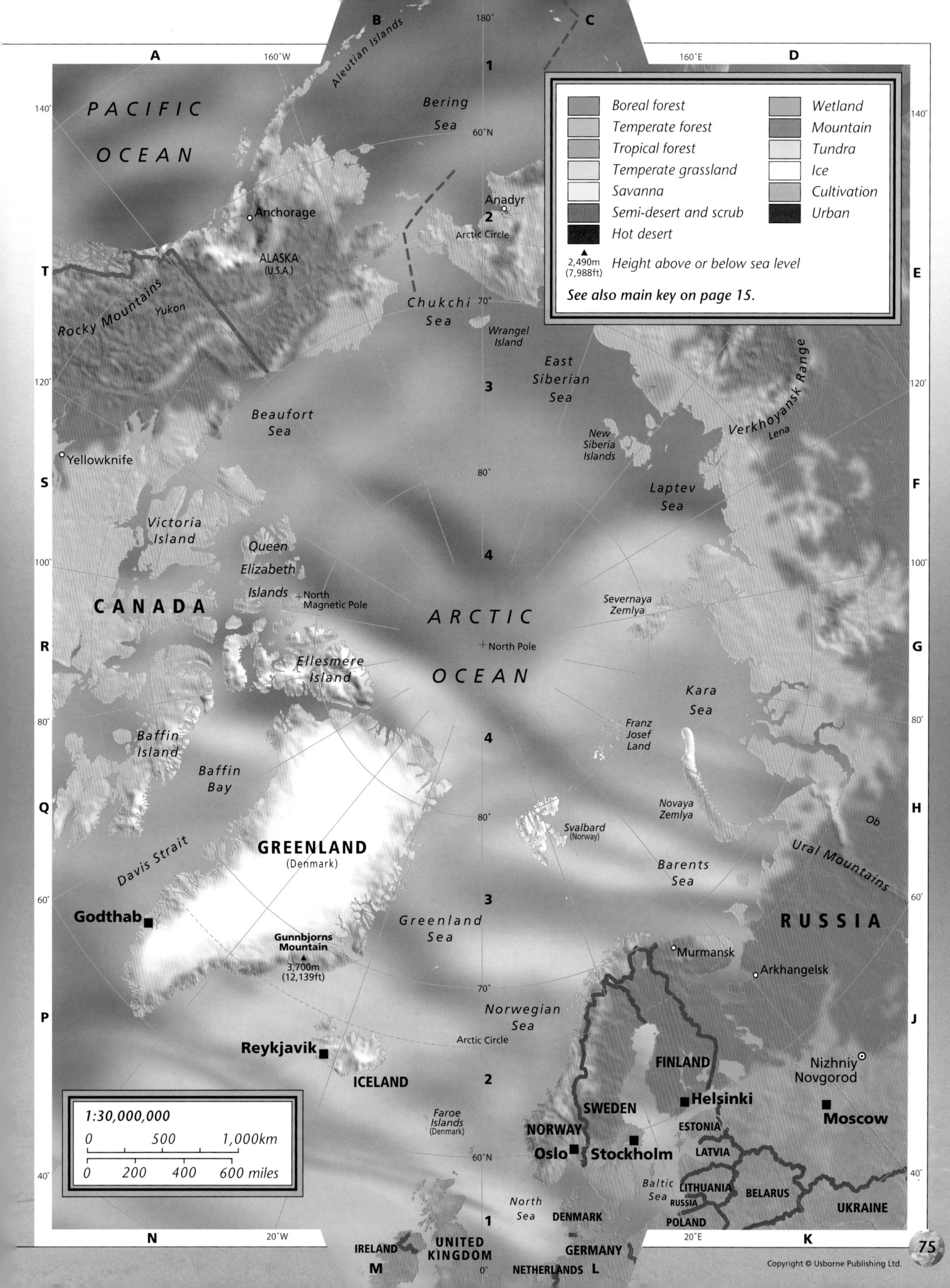

Copyright © Usborne Publishing Ltd.

ANTARCTICA

Antarctica is a huge, frozen continent within the Antarctic Circle. It is almost completely covered by an enormous ice sheet, which is more than 3km (2 miles) deep in some places. Nobody lives permanently in Antarctica, though many scientists visit to study the area. No plants grow in the ice, and the only land animals are tiny mites. But many animals, including penguins, seals, whales and fish, live in the seas around Antarctica.

This ship takes tourists on Antarctic expeditions. Visitors can see animals such as these gentoo penguins, which come onto land to breed.

Internet link

For a link to a website where you can find out more about Antarctica and the creatures that live in the seas around it, go to **www.usborne-quicklinks.com**

Facts

Total land area 14,000,000 sq km (5,405,442 sq miles), of which 13,720,000 sq km (5,297,333 sq miles) are covered in ice

Highest point Vinson Massif *5,140m (16,863ft)*

Lowest point Bentley Subglacial Trench *-2,555m (-8,382ft)*

Lowest recorded temperature -89.2°C (-128.6°F)

Main mineral deposits Iron ore, chromium, copper, gold, nickel, platinum

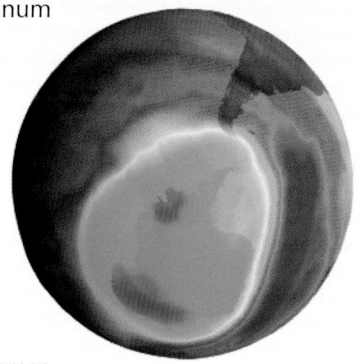

The green area in this satellite photograph is a hole in the ozone layer over Antarctica. The hole is caused by atmospheric pollution.

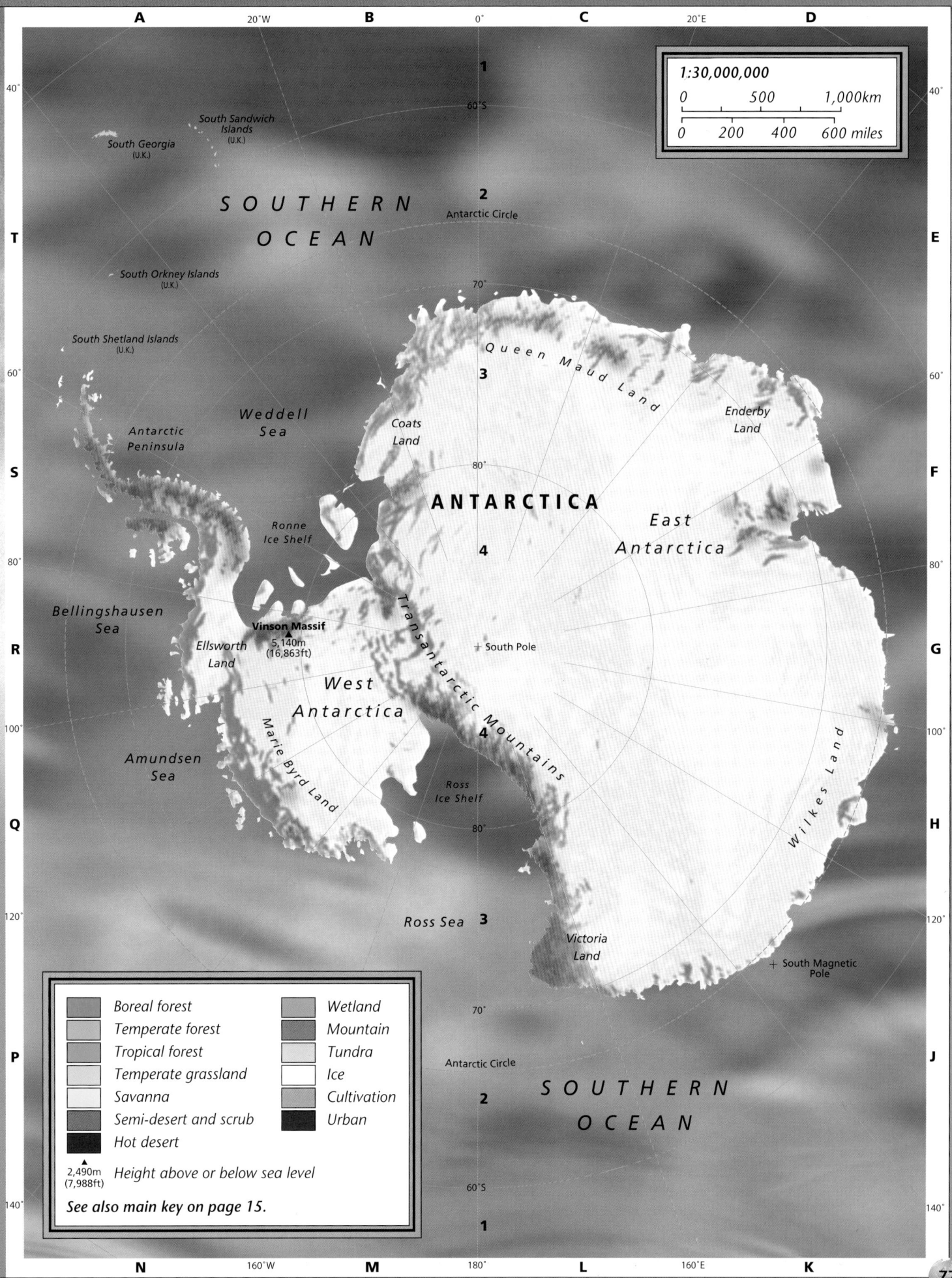

Copyright © Usborne Publishing Ltd.

WORLD RECORDS

Here are some of the Earth's longest rivers, highest mountains and other amazing world records. But the world is always changing; mountains wear down, rivers change shape, and new buildings are constructed. Ways of measuring things can also change. That's why you may find slightly different figures in different books.

Highest mountains	
Everest, Nepal/China	8,850m (29,035ft)
K2, Pakistan/China	8,611m (28,251ft)
Kanchenjunga, India/Nepal	8,597m (28,208ft)
Lhotse I, Nepal/China	8,511m (27,923ft)
Makalu I, Nepal/China	8,481m (27,824ft)
Lhotse II, Nepal/China	8,400m (27,560ft)
Dhaulagiri, Nepal	8,172m (26,810ft)
Manaslu I, Nepal	8,156m (26,760ft)
Cho Oyu, Nepal/China	8,153m (26,750ft)
Nanga Parbat, Pakistan	8,126m (26,660ft)

Longest rivers	
Nile, Africa	6,671km (4,145 miles)
Amazon, South America	6,440km (4,000 miles)
Chang Jiang (Yangtze), China	6,380km (3,964 miles)
Mississippi/Missouri, U.S.A.	6,019km (3,741 miles)
Yenisey/Angara, Russia	5,540km (3,442 miles)
Huang He (Yellow), China	5,464km (3,395 miles)
Ob/Irtysh/Black Irtysh, Asia	5,411km (3,362 miles)
Amur/Shilka/Onon, Asia	4,416km (2,744 miles)
Lena, Russia	4,400km (2,734 miles)
Congo, Africa	4,374km (2,718 miles)

Biggest natural lakes	
Caspian Sea	370,999 sq km (143,243 sq miles)
Lake Superior	82,414 sq km (31,820 sq miles)
Lake Victoria	69,215 sq km (26,724 sq miles)
Lake Huron	59,596 sq km (23,010 sq miles)
Lake Michigan	58,016 sq km (22,400 sq miles)
Lake Tanganyika	32,764 sq km (12,650 sq miles)
Lake Baikal	31,500 sq km (12,162 sq miles)
Great Bear Lake	31,328 sq km (12,096 sq miles)
Lake Nyasa	29,928 sq km (11,555 sq miles)
Aral Sea	28,600 sq km (11,042 sq miles)

Deepest ocean
The Mariana Trench, part of the Pacific Ocean, is the deepest part of the sea at 10,911m (35,797ft) deep.

Deepest lake
Lake Baikal in Russia is the deepest lake in the world. At its deepest point it is 1,637m (5,370ft) deep.

Biggest islands	
Greenland	2,175,600 sq km (840,000 sq miles)
New Guinea	800,000 sq km (309,000 sq miles)
Borneo	751,100 sq km (290,000 sq miles)
Madagascar	587,040 sq km (226,656 sq miles)
Baffin Island	507,451 sq km (195,928 sq miles)
Sumatra	437,607 sq km (184,706 sq miles)
Great Britain	234,410 sq km (90,506 sq miles)
Honshu	227,920 sq km (88,000 sq miles)
Victoria Island	217,290 sq km (83,896 sq miles)
Ellesmere Island	196,236 sq km (75,767 sq miles)

Tallest inhabited buildings	
Petronas Towers, Malaysia	452m (1,483ft)
Sears Tower, U.S.A.	443m (1,454ft)
Jin Mao Building, China	420m (1,378ft)
CITIC Plaza, China	391m (1,283ft)
Shun Hing Square, China	384m (1,260ft)
Plaza Rakyat, Malaysia	382m (1,254ft)
Empire State Building, U.S.A.	381m (1,250ft)
Central Plaza, China	373m (1,227ft)
Bank of China, China	368m (1,209ft)
Emirates Tower, U.A.E.	350m (1,148ft)

Biggest cities/urban areas	
Tokyo, Japan	26.4 million
Mexico City, Mexico	18.1 million
Bombay, India	18.1 million
Sao Paulo, Brazil	17.8 million
New York, U.S.A.	16.6 million
Lagos, Nigeria	13.4 million
Los Angeles, U.S.A.	13.1 million
Calcutta, India	12.9 million
Shanghai, China	12.9 million
Buenos Aires, Argentina	12.6 million

Famous waterfalls	Height
Angel Falls, Venezuela	979m (3,212ft)
Sutherland Falls, New Zealand	580m (1,904ft)
Mardalfossen, Norway	517m (1,696ft)
Jog Falls, India	253m (830ft)
Victoria Falls, Zimbabwe/Zambia	108m (355ft)
Iguacu Falls, Brazil/Argentina	82m (269ft)
Niagara Falls, Canada/U.S.A.	57m (187ft)

Natural disasters

Natural disasters can be measured in different ways. For example, some earthquakes score highly on the Richter scale, while others cause more destruction. The earthquakes, volcanic eruptions, floods, hurricanes and tornadoes listed here are among the most famous and destructive disasters in history.

Earthquakes	Richter scale	Disastrous effects
San Francisco, U.S.A., 1906	7.9	3,000 died in resulting fire
Messina, Italy, 1908	7.5	More than 70,000 people died
Tokyo-Kanto, Japan, 1923	8.3	Great Tokyo Fire; 142,807 died
Quetta, Pakistan, 1935	7.5	30–60,000 died; city destroyed
Concepcion, Chile, 1960	8.7	2,000 died; strongest quake ever
Alaska, U.S.A., 1964	8.6	125 died; strongest U.S. quake ever
Tangshan, China, 1976	7.9	More than 655,000 people died
Manjil-Rudbar, Iran, 1990	7.7	50,000 died; cities destroyed
Kobe, Japan, 1995	6.8	6,400 died; over $147bn damage
Gujarat, India, 2001	8.0	20,085 died; 2nd strongest Indian quake

Volcanic eruptions	Disastrous effects
Mount Vesuvius, Italy, AD79	Pompeii flattened; up to 20,000 died
Tambora, Indonesia, 1815	92,000 people starved to death
Krakatau, Indonesia, 1883	36,500 drowned in resulting tsunami
Mount Pelee, Martinique, 1902	Nearly 30,000 people buried in ash flows
Kelut, Indonesia, 1919	Over 5,000 people drowned in mud
Agung, Indonesia, 1963	1,200 people suffocated in hot ash
Mount St. Helens, U.S.A., 1980	Only 61 died but a large area was destroyed
Ruiz, Colombia, 1985	25,000 people died in giant mud flows
Mt. Pinatubo, Philippines, 1991	800 killed by collapsing roofs and disease
Island of Montserrat, 1995	Volcano left most of the island uninhabitable

Floods	Disastrous effects
Holland, 1228	100,000 drowned by a sea flood
Kaifeng, China, 1642	300,000 died after rebels destroyed a dyke
Johnstown, U.S.A., 1889	2,200 killed in a flood caused by rain
Italy, 1963	Vaoint Dam overflowed; 2–3,000 killed
East Pakistan, 1970	Giant wave caused by cyclone killed 250,000
Bangladesh, 1988	1,300 died, 30m homeless in monsoon flood
Southern U.S.A., 1993	$12bn of damage after Mississippi flooded
China, 1998	Chang Jiang overflow left 14m homeless
Papua New Guinea, 1998	Tsunamis killed 2,000 people
Venezuela, 1999	Floods and mudslides killed 5,000–20,000

Storms	Disastrous effects
Caribbean "Great Hurricane", 1780	Biggest ever hurricane killed over 20,000
Hong Kong typhoon, China, 1906	10,000 people died in this giant hurricane
Killer tornado, U.S.A., 1925	Up to 700 people died in Ellington, Missouri
Tropical Storm Agnes, U.S.A., 1972	$3.5bn damage, 129 dead
Hurricane Fifi, Honduras, 1974	8,000 people died and 100,000 left homeless
Hurricane Georges, U.S.A., 1998	Caribbean and U.S.A. hit; $5bn of damage
Hurricane Mitch, C. America, 1998	Over 9,000 killed across Central America

Amazing Earth facts

The Earth is 12,103km (7,520 miles) across. Its circumference (the distance around the Equator) is 38,022km (23,627 miles) and it is 149,503,000 km (92,897,000 miles) away from the Sun.

To make one complete orbit around the Sun, the Earth has to travel 938,900,000km (583,400,000 miles). To do this in just a year, it has to travel very fast. Because of the atmosphere surrounding the Earth, you can't feel it moving. But in fact you are zooming through space faster than any rocket.

• **Orbit speed** The Earth travels around the Sun at a speed of about 106,000kph (65,868mph).

• **Spinning speed** The Earth also spins around an axis, but the speed you are spinning at depends on where you live. Places on the Equator move at 1,600kph (995mph). New York moves at around 1,100kph (684mph). Near the poles, the spinning is not very fast at all. (You can see how this works by looking at a spinning globe.)

• **Solar System speed** The whole Solar System, including the Sun, the Earth and its moon, and the other planets and their moons, is moving at 72,400kph (45,000 mph) through the galaxy.

• **Galaxy speed** Our galaxy, the Milky Way, whizzes through the universe at a speed of 2,172,150kph (1,350,000mph).

TIME ZONES

The Earth is divided into different time zones. Within each zone, people usually set their clocks to the same time. If you fly between two zones, you change your watch to the time in the new zone.

Dividing up time

There are 25 time zones. They are separated by one-hour intervals and there is a time zone every 15 degrees of longitude. There are 12 one-hour zones both ahead of and behind Greenwich Mean Time (GMT), the time at the Prime Meridian Line.

For convenience, whole countries usually keep the same local time instead of sticking to the zones exactly. For example, China could be divided into several time zones, but instead the whole country has the same time. A few places, such as India, use non-standard half hour deviations.

Summer time

Some places adjust their clocks in summer. For example, in the U.K. all clocks go forward one hour. It is a way of getting more out of the days by having an extra hour of light.

Changing dates

The International Date Line runs mostly through the Pacific Ocean and bends to avoid the land. Places to the west of it are 24 hours ahead of places to the east. This means that if you travel east across it you lose a day and if you travel west across it you gain a day.

This map shows the time zones. The times at the top of the map tell you the time in the different zones when it is noon at the Prime Meridian Line. There are two midnight zones, one for each day on either side of the International Date Line. The numbers in circles tell you how many hours ahead of or behind Greenwich Mean Time an area is.

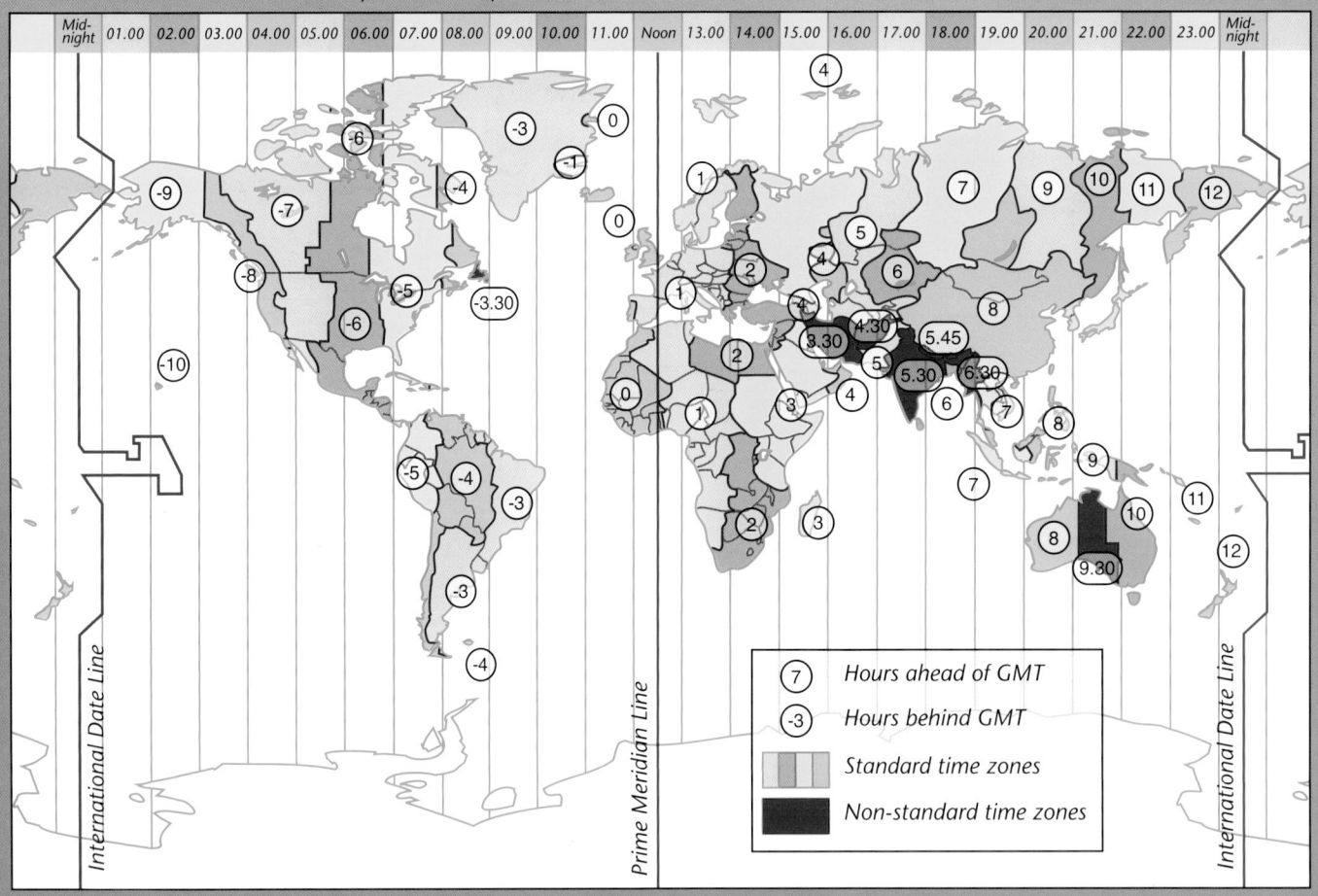

TYPES OF GOVERNMENTS

Most states have one main leader along with a parliament or assembly of politicians. The main types of governments are listed and explained below. A state can have a combination of more than one of these types of governments. For example, the United States of America is a federal republic.

Anarchy
Anarchy means a situation where there is no government. This can happen after a civil war, when a government has been destroyed and rival groups are battling to take its place.

Capitalist state
In a Capitalist or free-market state, people can own their own businesses and property, and buy services such as healthcare privately. However, most Capitalist governments also provide national health, education and welfare services.

Commonwealth
This word is sometimes used to mean a democratic republic, in which all the state's citizens are seen as having an equal interest in the functioning of the state.

Communist state
Under Communism, the state owns things like factories, farms and businesses, and provides healthcare, welfare and education for its people.

Democracy
In a democracy, the government is elected by the people, using a voting system.

Dictatorship
This is a state run by a single, unelected leader, who may use force to keep control. In a military dictatorship, the army is in power.

Federal government
In a federal system, such as that of the U.S.A., a central government shares power with a number of smaller regional governments.

Monarchy
A monarchy is a state with a king or queen. In some traditional monarchies, the monarch has complete power. A constitutional monarchy, however, also has a separate, usually democratic, government and the monarch's powers are limited.

Regional or local government
A government that controls a smaller area within a state. Some regional governments have very limited powers, and are largely directed by the central government. Others, such as the regional governments in the U.S.A., have much more power and can make their own laws.

Republic
A republic is a state with no monarch. The head of state is usually an elected president.

Revolutionary government
After a revolution, when a government is overthrown by force, the new regime is sometimes called a revolutionary government.

Totalitarian state
This is a state with only one political party, in which individuals are forced to obey the government and may also be prevented from leaving the country.

Transitional government
A government that is changing from one system to another is known as a transitional government. For example, a dictatorship may become a democracy after the dictator dies, but the transition between the systems can take several years.

GAZETTEER OF STATES

Afghanistan

Albania

Algeria

Andorra

Angola

Antigua and Barbuda

• Argentina

This gazetteer lists the world's 193 independent states, along with key facts about each one. In the lists of languages, the language that is most widely spoken is given first, even if it is not the official language. In the lists of religions, the one followed by the most people is also placed first. Every state has a national flag, which is usually used to represent the country abroad. A few states also have a state flag which they prefer to use instead. The state flags appear here with a dot • beside them.

AFGHANISTAN (Asia)
Area: 647,500 sq km (249,935 sq miles)
Population: 27,755,775
Capital city: Kabul
Main languages: Dari, Pashto
Main religion: Muslim
Government: transitional
Currency: 1 afghani = 100 puls

ALBANIA (Europe)
Area: 28,750 sq km (11,100 sq miles)
Population: 3,544,841
Capital city: Tirana
Main language: Albanian
Main religions: Muslim, Albanian Orthodox
Government: emerging democracy
Currency: 1 lek = 100 qintars

ALGERIA (Africa)
Area: 2,381,740 sq km (919,589 sq miles)
Population: 32,277,942
Capital city: Algiers
Main languages: Arabic, French, Berber dialects
Main religion: Sunni Muslim
Government: republic
Currency: 1 Algerian dinar = 100 centimes

ANDORRA (Europe)
Area: 468 sq km (181 sq miles)
Population: 68,403
Capital city: Andorra la Vella
Main languages: Catalan, Spanish
Main religion: Roman Catholic
Government: parliamentary democracy
Currency: 1 euro = 100 cents

ANGOLA (Africa)
Area: 1,246,700 sq km (481,351 sq miles)
Population: 10,593,171
Capital city: Luanda
Main languages: Kilongo, Kimbundu, other Bantu languages, Portuguese
Main religions: indigenous, Roman Catholic, Protestant
Government: transitional
Currency: 1 kwanza = 100 lwei

ANTIGUA AND BARBUDA (North America)
Area: 442 sq km (171 sq miles)
Population: 67,448
Capital city: Saint John's
Main languages: Caribbean Creole, English
Main religion: Protestant
Government: constitutional monarchy
Currency: 1 East Caribbean dollar = 100 cents

ARGENTINA (South America)
Area: 2,766,890 sq km (1,068,305 sq miles)
Population: 37,812,817
Capital city: Buenos Aires
Main language: Spanish
Main religion: Roman Catholic
Government: republic
Currency: 1 peso = 100 centavos

ARMENIA (Asia)
Area: 29,800 sq km (11,506 sq miles)
Population: 3,336,100
Capital city: Yerevan
Main language: Armenian
Main religion: Armenian Orthodox
Government: republic
Currency: 1 dram = 100 luma

AUSTRALIA (Australasia/Oceania)
Area: 7,686,850 sq km (2,967,124 sq miles)
Population: 19,546,792
Capital city: Canberra
Main language: English
Main religion: Christian
Government: federal democratic monarchy
Currency: 1 Australian dollar = 100 cents

AUSTRIA (Europe)
Area: 83,858 sq km (32,378 sq miles)
Population: 8,169,929
Capital city: Vienna
Main language: German
Main religion: Roman Catholic
Government: federal republic
Currency: 1 euro = 100 cents

Armenia

Australia

Austria

Azerbaijan

Bahamas, The

Bahrain

Bangladesh

Barbados

Belarus

Belgium

Belize

Benin

Bhutan

• Bolivia

AZERBAIJAN (Asia)
Area: 86,600 sq km (33,436 sq miles)
Population: 7,798,497
Capital city: Baku
Main language: Azeri
Main religion: Muslim
Government: republic
Currency: 1 manat = 100 gopiks

BAHAMAS, THE (North America)
Area: 13,940 sq km (5,382 sq miles)
Population: 300,529
Capital city: Nassau
Main languages: Bahamian Creole, English
Main religion: Christian
Government: parliamentary democracy
Currency: 1 Bahamian dollar = 100 cents

BAHRAIN (Asia)
Area: 665 sq km (257 sq miles)
Population: 656,397
Capital city: Manama
Main languages: Arabic, English
Main religion: Muslim
Government: traditional monarchy
Currency: 1 Bahraini dinar = 1,000 fils

BANGLADESH (Asia)
Area: 144,000 sq km (55,598 sq miles)
Population: 133,376,684
Capital city: Dhaka
Main languages: Bengali, English
Main religions: Muslim, Hindu
Government: republic
Currency: 1 taka = 100 poisha

BARBADOS (North America)
Area: 430 sq km (166 sq miles)
Population: 276,607
Capital city: Bridgetown
Main languages: Bajan, English
Main religion: Christian
Government: parliamentary democracy
Currency: 1 Barbadian dollar = 100 cents

BELARUS (Europe)
Area: 207,600 sq km (80,154 sq miles)
Population: 10,335,382
Capital city: Minsk
Main language: Belarusian
Main religion: Eastern Orthodox
Government: republic
Currency: 1 Belarusian ruble = 100 kopecks

BELGIUM (Europe)
Area: 30,510 sq km (11,780 sq miles)
Population: 10,274,595
Capital city: Brussels
Main languages: Dutch, French
Main religions: Roman Catholic, Protestant
Government: constitutional monarchy
Currency: 1 euro = 100 cents

BELIZE (North America)
Area: 22,960 sq km (8,865 sq miles)
Population: 262,999
Capital city: Belmopan
Main languages: Spanish, Belize Creole, English, Garifuna, Maya
Main religions: Roman Catholic, Protestant
Government: parliamentary democracy
Currency: 1 Belizean dollar = 100 cents

BENIN (Africa)
Area: 112,620 sq km (43,483 sq miles)
Population: 6,787,625
Capital city: Porto-Novo
Main languages: Fon, French, Yoruba
Main religions: indigenous, Christian, Muslim
Government: republic
Currency: 1 CFA* franc = 100 centimes

BHUTAN (Asia)
Area: 47,000 sq km (18,146 sq miles)
Population: 2,094,176
Capital city: Thimphu
Main languages: Dzongkha, Nepali
Main religions: Buddhist, Hindu
Government: monarchy
Currency: 1 ngultrum = 100 chetrum

BOLIVIA (South America)
Area: 1,098,580 sq km (424,162 sq miles)
Population: 8,445,134
Capital cities: La Paz, Sucre
Main languages: Spanish, Quechua, Aymara
Main religion: Roman Catholic
Government: republic
Currency: 1 boliviano = 100 centavos

BOSNIA AND HERZEGOVINA (Europe)
Area: 51,129 sq km (19,741 sq miles)
Population: 3,964,388
Capital city: Sarajevo
Main languages: Bosnian, Serbian, Croatian
Main religions: Muslim, Orthodox, Roman Catholic
Government: emerging federal democracy
Currency: 1 marka = 100 pfenninga

BOTSWANA (Africa)
Area: 600,372 sq km (231,743 sq miles)
Population: 1,591,232
Capital city: Gaborone
Main languages: Setswana, Kalanga, English
Main religions: indigenous, Christian
Government: parliamentary republic
Currency: 1 pula = 100 thebe

BRAZIL (South America)
Area: 8,547,400 sq km (3,300,151 sq miles)
Population: 176,029,560
Capital city: Brasilia
Main language: Portuguese
Main religion: Roman Catholic
Government: federal republic
Currency: 1 real = 100 centavos

BRUNEI (Asia)
Area: 5,770 sq km (2,228 sq miles)
Population: 350,898
Capital city: Bandar Seri Begawan
Main languages: Malay, English, Chinese
Main religions: Muslim, Buddhist
Government: constitutional sultanate (a type of monarchy)
Currency: 1 Bruneian dollar = 100 cents

Bosnia and Herzegovina

Botswana

Brazil

Brunei

Bulgaria

Burkina Faso

Burma (Myanmar)

*CFA = Communaute Financiere Africaine

Burundi

Cambodia

Cameroon

Canada

Cape Verde

Central African Republic

Chad

BULGARIA (Europe)
Area: 110,910 sq km (42,822 sq miles)
Population: 7,621,337
Capital city: Sofia
Main language: Bulgarian
Main religions: Bulgarian Orthodox, Muslim
Government: parliamentary democracy
Currency: 1 lev = 100 stotinki

BURKINA FASO (Africa)
Area: 274,200 sq km (105,869 sq miles)
Population: 12,603,185
Capital city: Ouagadougou
Main languages: Moore, Jula, French
Main religions: Muslim, indigenous
Government: republic
Currency: 1 CFA* franc = 100 centimes

BURMA (MYANMAR) (Asia)
Area: 678,500 sq km (261,969 sq miles)
Population: 42,238,224
Capital city: Rangoon
Main language: Burmese
Main religion: Buddhist
Government: military dictatorship
Currency: 1 kyat = 100 pyas

BURUNDI (Africa)
Area: 27,830 sq km (10,745 sq miles)
Population: 6,373,002
Capital city: Bujumbura
Main languages: Kirundi, French, Swahili
Main religions: Christian, indigenous
Government: republic
Currency: 1 Burundi franc = 100 centimes

CAMBODIA (Asia)
Area: 181,040 sq km (69,900 sq miles)
Population: 12,775,324
Capital city: Phnom Penh
Main language: Khmer
Main religion: Buddhist
Government: constitutional monarchy
Currency: 1 new riel = 100 sen

CAMEROON (Africa)
Area: 475,440 sq km (183,567 sq miles)
Population: 16,184,748
Capital city: Yaounde
Main languages: Cameroon Pidgin English, Ewondo, Fula, French, English
Main religions: indigenous, Christian, Muslim
Government: republic
Currency: 1 CFA* franc = 100 centimes

CANADA (North America)
Area: 9,970,610 sq km (3,849,653 sq miles)
Population: 31,902,268
Capital city: Ottawa
Main languages: English, French
Main religions: Roman Catholic, Protestant
Government: federal democracy
Currency: 1 Canadian dollar = 100 cents

CAPE VERDE (Africa)
Area: 4,033 sq km (1,557 sq miles)
Population: 408,760
Capital city: Praia
Main languages: Crioulo*, Portuguese
Main religions: Roman Catholic, Protestant
Government: republic
Currency: 1 Cape Verdean escudo = 100 centavos

CENTRAL AFRICAN REPUBLIC (Africa)
Area: 622,984 sq km (240,536 sq miles)
Population: 3,642,739
Capital city: Bangui
Main languages: Sangho, French
Main religions: indigenous, Christian, Muslim
Government: republic
Currency: 1 CFA* franc = 100 centimes

CHAD (Africa)
Area: 1,284,000 sq km (495,752 sq miles)
Population: 8,997,237
Capital city: Ndjamena
Main languages: Arabic, Sara, French
Main religions: Muslim, Christian, indigenous
Government: republic
Currency: 1 CFA* franc = 100 centimes

CHILE (South America)
Area: 756,626 sq km (292,133 sq miles)
Population: 15,498,930
Capital city: Santiago
Main language: Spanish
Main religions: Roman Catholic, Protestant
Government: republic
Currency: 1 Chilean peso = 100 centavos

CHINA (Asia)
Area: 9,596,960 sq km (3,705,386 sq miles)
Population: 1,284,303,705
Capital city: Beijing
Main languages: Mandarin Chinese, Yue, Wu
Main religions: Taoist, Buddhist
Government: Communist state
Currency: 1 yuan = 10 jiao

COLOMBIA (South America)
Area: 1,138,910 sq km (439,733 sq miles)
Population: 41,008,227
Capital city: Bogota
Main language: Spanish
Main religion: Roman Catholic
Government: republic
Currency: 1 Colombian peso = 100 centavos

COMOROS (Africa)
Area: 2,170 sq km (838 sq miles)
Population: 614,382
Capital city: Moroni
Main languages: Comorian*, French, Arabic
Main religion: Sunni Muslim
Government: republic
Currency: 1 Comoran franc = 100 centimes

CONGO (Africa)
Area: 342,000 sq km (132,046 sq miles)
Population: 2,958,448
Capital city: Brazzaville
Main languages: Munukutuba, Lingala, French
Main religions: Christian, animist
Government: republic
Currency: 1 CFA* franc = 100 centimes

Chile

China

Colombia

Comoros

Congo

Congo (Democratic Republic)

Costa Rica

**CFA = Communaute Financiere Africaine; Comorian = a blend of Swahili and Arabic; Crioulo = a blend of Portuguese and West African*

Croatia

Cuba

Cyprus

Czech Republic

Denmark

Djibouti

Dominica

CONGO (DEMOCRATIC REPUBLIC) (Africa)
Area: 2,345,410 sq km (905,563 sq miles)
Population: 55,225,478
Capital city: Kinshasa
Main languages: Lingala, Swahili, Kikongo, Tshiluba, French
Main religions: Roman Catholic, Protestant, Kimbanguist, Muslim
Government: transitional
Currency: 1 Congolese franc = 100 centimes

COSTA RICA (North America)
Area: 51,100 sq km (19,730 sq miles)
Population: 3,834,934
Capital city: San Jose
Main language: Spanish
Main religions: Roman Catholic, Evangelical
Government: democratic republic
Currency: 1 Costa Rican colon = 100 centimos

CROATIA (Europe)
Area: 56,538 sq km (21,829 sq miles)
Population: 4,390,751
Capital city: Zagreb
Main language: Croatian
Main religions: Roman Catholic, Orthodox
Government: parliamentary democracy
Currency: 1 kuna = 100 lipas

CUBA (North America)
Area: 110,860 sq km (42,803 sq miles)
Population: 11,224,321
Capital city: Havana
Main language: Spanish
Main religion: Roman Catholic
Government: Communist state
Currency: 1 Cuban peso = 100 centavos

CYPRUS (Europe)
Area: 9,250 sq km (3,571 sq miles)
Population: 767,314
Capital city: Nicosia
Main languages: Greek, Turkish
Main religions: Greek Orthodox, Muslim
Government: republic with a self-proclaimed independent Turkish area
Currency: Greek Cypriot area: 1 Cypriot pound = 100 cents; Turkish Cypriot area: 1 Turkish lira = 100 kurus

CZECH REPUBLIC (Europe)
Area: 78,866 sq km (30,450 sq miles)
Population: 10,256,760
Capital city: Prague
Main language: Czech
Main religion: Roman Catholic
Government: parliamentary democracy
Currency: 1 koruna = 100 haleru

DENMARK (Europe)
Area: 43,094 sq km (16,639 sq miles)
Population: 5,368,854
Capital city: Copenhagen
Main language: Danish
Main religion: Evangelical Lutheran
Government: constitutional monarchy
Currency: 1 Danish krone = 100 oere

DJIBOUTI (Africa)
Area: 23,200 sq km (8,957 sq miles)
Population: 472,810
Capital city: Djibouti
Main languages: Afar, Somali, Arabic, French
Main religion: Muslim
Government: republic
Currency: 1 Djiboutian franc = 100 centimes

DOMINICA (North America)
Area: 751 sq km (290 sq miles)
Population: 70,158
Capital city: Roseau
Main languages: English, French patois
Main religions: Roman Catholic, Protestant
Government: democratic republic
Currency: 1 East Caribbean dollar = 100 cents

DOMINICAN REPUBLIC (North America)
Area: 48,730 sq km (18,815 sq miles)
Population: 8,721,594
Capital city: Santo Domingo
Main language: Spanish
Main religion: Roman Catholic
Government: democratic republic
Currency: 1 Dominican peso = 100 centavos

EAST TIMOR (Asia)
Area: 15,007 sq km (5,794 sq miles)
Population: 952,618
Capital city: Dili
Main languages: Tetum, Portuguese, Indonesian
Main religions: Roman Catholic, animist
Government: republic
Currency: 1 U.S. dollar = 100 cents

ECUADOR (South America)
Area: 283,560 sq km (109,483 sq miles)
Population: 13,447,494
Capital city: Quito
Main languages: Spanish, Quechua
Main religion: Roman Catholic
Government: republic
Currency: 1 sucre = 100 centavos

EGYPT (Africa)
Area: 1,001,450 sq km (386,660 sq miles)
Population: 70,712,345
Capital city: Cairo
Main language: Arabic
Main religion: Sunni Muslim
Government: republic
Currency: 1 Egyptian pound = 100 piasters

EL SALVADOR (North America)
Area: 21,040 sq km (8,124 sq miles)
Population: 6,353,681
Capital city: San Salvador
Main language: Spanish
Main religion: Roman Catholic
Government: republic
Currency: 1 Salvadoran colon = 100 centavos

EQUATORIAL GUINEA (Africa)
Area: 28,050 sq km (10,830 sq miles)
Population: 498,144
Capital city: Malabo

• Dominican Republic

East Timor

• Ecuador

Egypt

• El Salvador

Equatorial Guinea

Eritrea

Estonia

Ethiopia

Federated States of Micronesia

Fiji

Finland

France

Gabon

Main languages: Fang, Bubi, other Bantu languages, Spanish, French, Pidgin English
Main religion: Christian
Government: republic
Currency: 1 CFA* franc = 100 centimes

ERITREA (Africa)
Area: 121,320 sq km (46,842 sq miles)
Population: 4,465,651
Capital city: Asmara
Main languages: Tigrinya, Afar, Arabic
Main religions: Muslim, Coptic Christian, Roman Catholic, Protestant
Government: transitional
Currency: 1 nafka = 100 cents

ESTONIA (Europe)
Area: 45,226 sq km (17,462 sq miles)
Population: 1,415,681
Capital city: Tallinn
Main languages: Estonian, Russian
Main religions: Evangelical Lutheran, Russian and Estonian Orthodox, other Christian
Government: parliamentary democracy
Currency: 1 Estonian kroon = 100 senti

ETHIOPIA (Africa)
Area: 1,127,127 sq km (435,184 sq miles)
Population: 67,673,031
Capital city: Addis Ababa
Main languages: Amharic, Tigrinya, Arabic
Main religions: Muslim, Ethiopian Orthodox, animist
Government: federal republic
Currency: 1 birr = 100 cents

FEDERATED STATES OF MICRONESIA (Australasia/Oceania)
Area: 702 sq km (271 sq miles)
Population: 135,869
Capital city: Palikir
Main languages: Chuuk, Ponapean, English
Main religions: Roman Catholic, Protestant
Government: democracy
Currency: 1 U.S. dollar = 100 cents

FIJI (Australasia/Oceania)
Area: 18,270 sq km (7,054 sq miles)
Population: 856,346
Capital city: Suva
Main languages: Fijian, Hindustani, English
Main religions: Christian, Hindu
Government: republic
Currency: 1 Fijian dollar = 100 cents

FINLAND (Europe)
Area: 337,030 sq km (130,127 sq miles)
Population: 5,183,545
Capital city: Helsinki
Main language: Finnish
Main religion: Evangelical Lutheran
Government: republic
Currency: 1 euro = 100 cents

FRANCE (Europe)
Area: 547,030 sq km (211,208 sq miles)
Population: 59,765,983
Capital city: Paris
Main language: French
Main religion: Roman Catholic
Government: republic
Currency: 1 euro = 100 cents

GABON (Africa)
Area: 267,670 sq km (103,347 sq miles)
Population: 1,233,353
Capital city: Libreville
Main languages: Fang, Myene, French
Main religions: Christian, animist
Government: republic
Currency: 1 CFA* franc = 100 centimes

GAMBIA, THE (Africa)
Area: 11,300 sq km (4,363 sq miles)
Population: 1,455,842
Capital city: Banjul
Main languages: Mandinka, Fula, Wolof, English
Main religion: Muslim
Government: democratic republic
Currency: 1 dalasi = 100 butut

GEORGIA (Asia)
Area: 69,700 sq km (26,911 sq miles)
Population: 4,960,951
Capital city: Tbilisi
Main languages: Georgian, Russian
Main religions: Georgian Orthodox, Muslim, Russian Orthodox
Government: republic
Currency: 1 lari = 100 tetri

GERMANY (Europe)
Area: 357,021 sq km (137,846 sq miles)
Population: 83,251,851
Capital city: Berlin
Main language: German
Main religions: Protestant, Roman Catholic
Government: federal republic
Currency: 1 euro = 100 cents

GHANA (Africa)
Area: 239,460 sq km (92,456 sq miles)
Population: 20,244,154
Capital city: Accra
Main languages: Twi, Fante, Ga, Hausa, Dagbani, Ewe, Nzemi, English
Main religions: indigenous, Muslim, Christian
Government: democratic republic
Currency: 1 new cedi = 100 pesewas

GREECE (Europe)
Area: 131,940 sq km (50,942 sq miles)
Population: 10,645,343
Capital city: Athens
Main language: Greek
Main religion: Greek Orthodox
Government: parliamentary republic
Currency: 1 euro = 100 cents

GRENADA (North America)
Area: 340 sq km (131 sq miles)
Population: 89,211
Capital city: Saint George's
Main languages: English, French patois
Main religions: Roman Catholic, Protestant
Government: constitutional monarchy
Currency: 1 East Caribbean dollar = 100 cents

Gambia, The

Georgia

Germany

Ghana

Greece

Grenada

Guatemala

*CFA = Communaute Financiere Africaine

Guinea

Guinea-Bissau

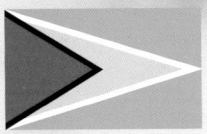

Guyana

• Haiti

Honduras

Hungary

Iceland

GUATEMALA (North America)
Area: 108,890 sq km (42,042 sq miles)
Population: 13,314,079
Capital city: Guatemala City
Main languages: Spanish, Amerindian languages including Quiche, Kekchi, Cakchiquel, Mam
Main religions: Roman Catholic, Protestant, indigenous Mayan beliefs
Government: democratic republic
Currency: 1 quetzal = 100 centavos

GUINEA (Africa)
Area: 245,860 sq km (94,927 sq miles)
Population: 7,775,065
Capital city: Conakry
Main languages: Fuuta Jalon, Mallinke, Susu, French
Main religion: Muslim
Government: republic
Currency: 1 Guinean franc = 100 centimes

GUINEA-BISSAU (Africa)
Area: 36,120 sq km (13,946 sq miles)
Population: 1,345,479
Capital city: Bissau
Main languages: Crioulo*, Balante, Pulaar, Mandjak, Mandinka, Portuguese
Main religions: indigenous, Muslim
Government: republic
Currency: 1 CFA* franc = 100 centimes

GUYANA (South America)
Area: 214,970 sq km (83,000 sq miles)
Population: 698,209
Capital city: Georgetown
Main languages: Guyanese Creole, English, Amerindian languages, Caribbean Hindi
Main religions: Christian, Hindu
Government: republic
Currency: 1 Guyanese dollar = 100 cents

HAITI (North America)
Area: 27,750 sq km (10,714 sq miles)
Population: 7,063,722
Capital city: Port-au-Prince
Main languages: Haitian Creole, French
Main religions: Roman Catholic, Protestant, Voodoo
Government: republic
Currency: 1 gourde = 100 centimes

HONDURAS (North America)
Area: 112,090 sq km (43,278 sq miles)
Population: 6,560,608
Capital city: Tegucigalpa
Main language: Spanish
Main religion: Roman Catholic
Government: republic
Currency: 1 lempira = 100 centavos

HUNGARY (Europe)
Area: 93,030 sq km (35,919 sq miles)
Population: 10,075,034
Capital city: Budapest
Main language: Hungarian
Main religions: Roman Catholic, Calvinist
Government: parliamentary democracy
Currency: 1 forint = 100 filler

ICELAND (Europe)
Area: 103,000 sq km (39,768 sq miles)
Population: 279,384
Capital city: Reykjavik
Main language: Icelandic
Main religion: Evangelical Lutheran
Government: republic
Currency: 1 Icelandic krona = 100 aurar

INDIA (Asia)
Area: 3,287,590 sq km (1,269,339 sq miles)
Population: 1,045,845,226
Capital city: New Delhi
Main languages: Hindi, English, Bengali, Urdu, over 1,600 other languages and dialects
Main religions: Hindu, Muslim
Government: federal republic
Currency: 1 Indian rupee = 100 paise

INDONESIA (Asia)
Area: 1,919,440 sq km (741,096 sq miles)
Population: 231,328,092
Capital city: Jakarta
Main languages: Bahasa Indonesia, English, Dutch, Javanese
Main religion: Muslim
Government: republic
Currency: 1 Indonesian rupiah = 100 sen

IRAN (Asia)
Area: 1,648,000 sq km (636,293 sq miles)
Population: 66,622,704
Capital city: Tehran
Main languages: Farsi and other Persian dialects, Azeri
Main religions: Shi'a Muslim, Sunni Muslim
Government: Islamic republic
Currency: 10 Iranian rials = 1 toman

IRAQ (Asia)
Area: 437,072 sq km (168,754 sq miles)
Population: 24,001,816
Capital city: Baghdad
Main languages: Arabic, Kurdish
Main religion: Muslim
Government: republic under a military regime
Currency: 1 Iraqi dinar = 1,000 fils

IRELAND (Europe)
Area: 70,280 sq km (27,135 sq miles)
Population: 3,883,159
Capital city: Dublin
Main languages: English, Irish (Gaelic)
Main religion: Roman Catholic
Government: republic
Currency: 1 euro = 100 cents

ISRAEL (Asia)
Area: 20,770 sq km (8,019 sq miles)
Population: 6,029,529
Capital city: Jerusalem
Main languages: Hebrew, Arabic
Main religions: Jewish, Muslim
Government: parliamentary democracy
Currency: 1 Israeli shekel = 100 agorot

India

Indonesia

Iran

Iraq

Ireland

Israel

Italy

*CFA = Communaute Financiere Africaine;
Crioulo = a blend of Portuguese and West African

Ivory Coast

Jamaica

Japan

Jordan

Kazakhstan

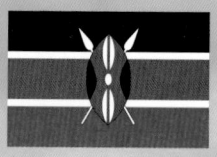

Kenya

Kiribati

ITALY (Europe)
Area: 301,230 sq km (116,305 sq miles)
Population: 57,715,625
Capital city: Rome
Main language: Italian
Main religion: Roman Catholic
Government: republic
Currency: 1 euro = 100 cents

IVORY COAST (Africa)
Area: 322,460 sq km (124,502 sq miles)
Population: 16,804,784
Capital city: Yamoussoukro
Main languages: Baoule, Dioula, French
Main religions: Christian, Muslim, animist
Government: republic
Currency: 1 CFA* = 100 centimes

JAMAICA (North America)
Area: 10,990 sq km (4,243 sq miles)
Population: 2,680,029
Capital city: Kingston
Main languages: Southwestern Caribbean Creole, English
Main religion: Protestant
Government: parliamentary democracy
Currency: 1 Jamaican dollar = 100 cents

JAPAN (Asia)
Area: 377,835 sq km (145,882 sq miles)
Population: 126,974,628
Capital city: Tokyo
Main language: Japanese
Main religions: Shinto, Buddhist
Government: constitutional monarchy
Currency: 1 yen = 100 sen

JORDAN (Asia)
Area: 92,300 sq km (35,637 sq miles)
Population: 5,307,470
Capital city: Amman
Main languages: Arabic, English
Main religion: Sunni Muslim
Government: constitutional monarchy
Currency: 1 Jordanian dinar = 1,000 fils

KAZAKHSTAN (Asia)
Area: 2,717,300 sq km (1,049,150 sq miles)
Population: 16,741,519
Capital city: Astana
Main languages: Kazakh, Russian
Main religions: Muslim, Russian Orthodox
Government: republic
Currency: 1 Kazakhstani tenge = 100 tiyn

KENYA (Africa)
Area: 582,650 sq km (224,961 sq miles)
Population: 31,138,735
Capital city: Nairobi
Main languages: Swahili, English, Bantu languages
Main religions: Christian, indigenous
Government: republic
Currency: 1 Kenyan shilling = 100 cents

KIRIBATI (Australasia/Oceania)
Area: 811 sq km (313 sq miles)
Population: 96,335
Capital city: Bairiki (on Tarawa island)
Main languages: Gilbertese, English
Main religions: Roman Catholic, Protestant
Government: republic
Currency: 1 Australian dollar = 100 cents

KUWAIT (Asia)
Area: 17,820 sq km (6,880 sq miles)
Population: 2,111,561
Capital city: Kuwait City
Main languages: Arabic, English
Main religion: Muslim
Government: monarchy
Currency: 1 Kuwaiti dinar = 1,000 fils

KYRGYZSTAN (Asia)
Area: 198,500 sq km (76,641 sq miles)
Population: 4,822,166
Capital city: Bishkek
Main languages: Kyrgyz, Russian
Main religions: Muslim, Russian Orthodox
Government: republic
Currency: 1 Kyrgyzstani som = 100 tyiyn

LAOS (Asia)
Area: 236,800 sq km (91,428 sq miles)
Population: 5,777,180
Capital city: Vientiane
Main languages: Lao, French, English
Main religions: Buddhist, animist
Government: Communist state
Currency: 1 new kip = 100 at

LATVIA (Europe)
Area: 64,589 sq km (24,938 sq miles)
Population: 2,366,515
Capital city: Riga
Main languages: Latvian, Russian
Main religions: Lutheran, Roman Catholic, Russian Orthodox
Government: parliamentary democracy
Currency: 1 Latvian lat = 100 santims

LEBANON (Asia)
Area: 10,400 sq km (4,015 sq miles)
Population: 3,677,780
Capital city: Beirut
Main languages: Arabic, French, English
Main religions: Muslim, Christian
Government: republic
Currency: 1 Lebanese pound = 100 piasters

LESOTHO (Africa)
Area: 30,350 sq km (11,718 sq miles)
Population: 2,207,954
Capital cities: Maseru, Lobamba
Main languages: Sesotho, English, Zulu, Xhosa
Main religions: Christian, indigenous
Government: constitutional monarchy
Currency: 1 loti = 100 lisente

LIBERIA (Africa)
Area: 111,370 sq km (43,000 sq miles)
Population: 3,288,198
Capital city: Monrovia
Main languages: Kpelle, English, Bassa
Main religions: indigenous, Christian, Muslim
Government: republic
Currency: 1 Liberian dollar = 100 cents

Kuwait

Kyrgyzstan

Laos

Latvia

Lebanon

Lesotho

Liberia

*CFA = Communaute Financiere Africaine

Libya

Liechtenstein

Lithuania

Luxembourg

Macedonia

Madagascar

Malawi

LIBYA (Africa)
Area: 1,759,540 sq km (679,358 sq miles)
Population: 5,368,585
Capital city: Tripoli
Main languages: Arabic, Italian, English
Main religion: Sunni Muslim
Government: military rule
Currency: 1 Libyan dinar = 1,000 dirhams

LIECHTENSTEIN (Europe)
Area: 160 sq km (62 sq miles)
Population: 32,842
Capital city: Vaduz
Main languages: German, Alemannic
Main religion: Roman Catholic
Government: constitutional monarchy
Currency: 1 Swiss franc = 100 centimes

LITHUANIA (Europe)
Area: 65,200 sq km (25,174 sq miles)
Population: 3,601,138
Capital city: Vilnius
Main languages: Lithuanian, Polish, Russian
Main religions: Roman Catholic, Lutheran, Russian Orthodox
Government: democracy
Currency: 1 Lithuanian litas = 100 centas

LUXEMBOURG (Europe)
Area: 2,586 sq km (998 sq miles)
Population: 448,569
Capital city: Luxembourg
Main languages: Luxemburgish, German, French
Main religion: Roman Catholic
Government: constitutional monarchy
Currency: 1 euro = 100 cents

MACEDONIA (Europe)
Area: 25,333 sq km (9,781 sq miles)
Population: 2,054,800
Capital city: Skopje
Main languages: Macedonian, Albanian
Main religions: Macedonian Orthodox, Muslim
Government: emerging democracy
Currency: 1 Macedonian denar = 100 deni

MADAGASCAR (Africa)
Area: 587,040 sq km (226,656 sq miles)
Population: 16,473,477
Capital city: Antananarivo
Main languages: Malagasy, French
Main religions: indigenous beliefs, Christian
Government: republic
Currency: 1 Malagasy franc = 100 centimes

MALAWI (Africa)
Area: 118,480 sq km (45,745 sq miles)
Population: 10,701,824
Capital city: Lilongwe
Main languages: Chichewa, English
Main religions: Protestant, Roman Catholic, Muslim
Government: parliamentary democracy
Currency: 1 Malawian kwacha = 100 tambala

MALAYSIA (Asia)
Area: 329,750 sq km (127,316 sq miles)
Population: 22,662,365
Capital city: Kuala Lumpur
Main languages: Bahasa Melayu, English, Chinese dialects, Tamil
Main religions: Muslim, Buddhist, Daoist
Government: constitutional monarchy
Currency: 1 ringgit = 100 sen

MALDIVES (Asia)
Area: 300 sq km (116 sq miles)
Population: 320,165
Capital city: Male
Main languages: Maldivian, English
Main religion: Sunni Muslim
Government: republic
Currency: 1 rufiyaa = 100 laari

MALI (Africa)
Area: 1,240,000 sq km (478,764 sq miles)
Population: 11,340,480
Capital city: Bamako
Main languages: Bambara, Fulani, Songhai, French
Main religion: Muslim
Government: republic
Currency: 1 CFA* franc = 100 centimes

MALTA (Europe)
Area: 316 sq km (122 sq miles)
Population: 397,499
Capital city: Valletta
Main languages: Maltese, English
Main religion: Roman Catholic
Government: republic
Currency: 1 Maltese lira = 100 cents

MARSHALL ISLANDS (Australasia/Oceania)
Area: 181 sq km (70 sq miles)
Population: 73,630
Capital city: Majuro
Main languages: Marshallese, English
Main religion: Protestant
Government: republic
Currency: 1 U.S. dollar = 100 cents

MAURITANIA (Africa)
Area: 1,030,700 sq km (397,953 sq miles)
Population: 2,828,858
Capital city: Nouakchott
Main languages: Arabic, Wolof, French
Main religion: Muslim
Government: republic
Currency: 1 ouguiya = 5 khoums

MAURITIUS (Africa)
Area: 2,040 sq km (788 sq miles)
Population: 1,200,206
Capital city: Port Louis
Main languages: Mauritius Creole French, French, Hindi, Bhojpuri, Urdu, Tamil, English
Main religions: Hindu, Christian, Muslim
Government: parliamentary democracy
Currency: 1 Mauritian rupee = 100 cents

MEXICO (North America)
Area: 1,972,550 sq km (761,602 sq miles)
Population: 103,400,165
Capital city: Mexico City
Main languages: Spanish, Mayan, Nahuatl

Malaysia

Maldives

Mali

Malta

Marshall Islands

Mauritania

Mauritius

*CFA = Communaute Financiere Africaine

Mexico

Moldova

Monaco

Mongolia

Morocco

Mozambique

Namibia

Main religion: Roman Catholic
Government: federal republic
Currency: 1 Mexican peso = 100 centavos

MOLDOVA (Europe)
Area: 33,843 sq km (13,067 sq miles)
Population: 4,434,547
Capital city: Chisinau
Main languages: Moldovan, Russian, Gagauz
Main religion: Eastern Orthodox
Government: republic
Currency: 1 Moldovan leu = 100 bani

MONACO (Europe)
Area: 1.95 sq km (0.75 sq miles)
Population: 31,987
Capital city: Monaco
Main languages: French, Monegasque, Italian
Main religion: Roman Catholic
Government: constitutional monarchy
Currency: 1 euro = 100 cents

MONGOLIA (Asia)
Area: 1,565,000 sq km (604,247 sq miles)
Population: 2,694,432
Capital city: Ulan Bator
Main language: Khalkha Mongol
Main religion: Tibetan Buddist Lamaist
Government: republic
Currency: 1 tugrik = 100 mongos

MOROCCO (Africa)
Area: 446,550 sq km (172,413 sq miles)
Population: 31,167,783
Capital city: Rabat
Main languages: Arabic, Berber, French
Main religion: Muslim
Government: constitutional monarchy
Currency: 1 Moroccan dirham = 100 centimes

MOZAMBIQUE (Africa)
Area: 801,590 sq km (309,494 sq miles)
Population: 19,607,519
Capital city: Maputo
Main languages: Makua, Tsonga, Portuguese
Main religions: indigenous, Christian, Muslim
Government: republic
Currency: 1 metical = 100 centavos

NAMIBIA (Africa)
Area: 825,418 sq km (318,694 sq miles)
Population: 1,820,916
Capital city: Windhoek
Main languages: Afrikaans, German, English
Main religions: Christian, indigenous
Government: republic
Currency: 1 Namibian dollar = 100 cents

NAURU (Australasia/Oceania)
Area: 21 sq km (8 sq miles)
Population: 12,329
Capital city: Yaren
Main languages: Nauruan, English
Main religion: Christian
Government: republic
Currency: 1 Australian dollar = 100 cents

NEPAL (Asia)
Area: 140,800 sq km (54,363 sq miles)
Population: 25,873,917
Capital city: Kathmandu
Main languages: Nepali, Maithili
Main religions: Hindu, Buddhist
Government: constitutional monarchy
Currency: 1 Nepalese rupee = 100 paisa

NETHERLANDS (Europe)
Area: 41,532 sq km (16,036 sq miles)
Population: 16,067,754
Capital cities: Amsterdam, The Hague
Main language: Dutch
Main religion: Christian
Government: constitutional monarchy
Currency: 1 euro = 100 cents

NEW ZEALAND (Australasia/Oceania)
Area: 268,680 sq km (103,737 sq miles)
Population: 3,908,037
Capital city: Wellington
Main languages: English, Maori
Main religion: Christian
Government: parliamentary democracy
Currency: 1 New Zealand dollar = 100 cents

NICARAGUA (North America)
Area: 129,494 sq km (49,998 sq miles)
Population: 5,023,818
Capital city: Managua
Main language: Spanish
Main religion: Roman Catholic
Government: republic
Currency: 1 gold cordoba = 100 centavos

NIGER (Africa)
Area: 1,267,000 sq km (489,189 sq miles)
Population: 10,639,744
Capital city: Niamey
Main languages: Hausa, Djerma, French
Main religion: Muslim
Government: republic
Currency: 1 CFA* franc = 100 centimes

NIGERIA (Africa)
Area: 923,768 sq km (356,667 sq miles)
Population: 129,934,911
Capital city: Abuja
Main languages: Hausa, Yoruba, Igbo, English
Main religions: Muslim, Christian, indigenous
Government: republic
Currency: 1 naira = 100 kobo

NORTH KOREA (Asia)
Area: 120,540 sq km (46,540 sq miles)
Population: 22,224,195
Capital city: Pyongyang
Main language: Korean
Main religions: Buddhist, Confucianist
Government: authoritarian socialist
Currency: 1 North Korean won = 100 chon

NORWAY (Europe)
Area: 324,220 sq km (125,181 sq miles)
Population: 4,525,116
Capital city: Oslo
Main language: Norwegian

Nauru

Nepal

Netherlands

New Zealand

Nicaragua

Niger

Nigeria

*CFA = Communaute Financiere Africaine

North Korea

Norway

Oman

Pakistan

Palau

Panama

Papua New Guinea

Main religion: Evangelical Lutheran
Government: constitutional monarchy
Currency: 1 Norwegian krone = 100 oere

OMAN (Asia)
Area: 212,460 sq km (82,031 sq miles)
Population: 2,713,462
Capital city: Muscat
Main languages: Arabic, English, Baluchi
Main religion: Muslim
Government: monarchy
Currency: 1 Omani rial = 1,000 baiza

PAKISTAN (Asia)
Area: 803,940 sq km (310,401 sq miles)
Population: 147,663,429
Capital city: Islamabad
Main languages: Punjabi, Sindhi, Urdu, English
Main religion: Muslim
Government: federal republic
Currency: 1 Pakistani rupee = 100 paisa

PALAU (Australasia/Oceania)
Area: 459 sq km (177 sq miles)
Population: 19,409
Capital city: Koror
Main languages: Palauan, English
Main religions: Christian, Modekngei
Government: democratic republic
Currency: 1 U.S. dollar = 100 cents

PANAMA (North America)
Area: 78,200 sq km (30,193 sq miles)
Population: 2,882,329
Capital city: Panama City
Main languages: Spanish, English
Main religions: Roman Catholic, Protestant
Government: democracy
Currency: 1 balboa = 100 centesimos

PAPUA NEW GUINEA (Australasia/Oceania)
Area: 462,840 sq km (178,703 sq miles)
Population: 5,172,033
Capital city: Port Moresby
Main languages: Tok Pisin, Hiri Motu, English
Main religions: Christian, indigenous
Government: parliamentary democracy
Currency: 1 kina = 100 toea

PARAGUAY (South America)
Area: 406,750 sq km (157,046 sq miles)
Population: 5,884,491
Capital city: Asuncion
Main languages: Guarani, Spanish
Main religion: Roman Catholic
Government: republic
Currency: 1 guarani = 100 centimos

PERU (South America)
Area: 1,285,220 sq km (496,223 sq miles)
Population: 27,949,639
Capital city: Lima
Main languages: Spanish, Quechua, Aymara
Main religion: Roman Catholic
Government: republic
Currency: 1 nuevo sol = 100 centimos

PHILIPPINES (Asia)
Area: 300,000 sq km (115,830 sq miles)
Population: 84,525,639
Capital city: Manila
Main languages: Tagalog, English, Ilocano
Main religion: Roman Catholic
Government: republic
Currency: 1 Philippine peso = 100 centavos

POLAND (Europe)
Area: 312,685 sq km (120,727 sq miles)
Population: 38,625,478
Capital city: Warsaw
Main language: Polish
Main religion: Roman Catholic
Government: democratic republic
Currency: 1 zloty = 100 groszy

PORTUGAL (Europe)
Area: 92,391 sq km (35,672 sq miles)
Population: 10,084,245
Capital city: Lisbon
Main language: Portuguese
Main religion: Roman Catholic
Government: parliamentary democracy
Currency: 1 euro = 100 cents

QATAR (Asia)
Area: 11,437 sq km (4,416 sq miles)
Population: 793,341
Capital city: Doha
Main languages: Arabic, English
Main religion: Muslim
Government: monarchy
Currency: 1 Qatari riyal = 100 dirhams

ROMANIA (Europe)
Area: 237,500 sq km (91,699 sq miles)
Population: 22,317,730
Capital city: Bucharest
Main languages: Romanian, Hungarian, German
Main religion: Romanian Orthodox
Government: republic
Currency: 1 leu = 100 bani

RUSSIA (Europe and Asia)
Area: 17,075,200 sq km (6,592,735 sq miles)
Population: 144,978,573
Capital city: Moscow
Main language: Russian
Main religions: Russian Orthodox, Muslim
Government: federal government
Currency: 1 ruble = 100 kopeks

RWANDA (Africa)
Area: 26,338 sq km (10,169 sq miles)
Population: 7,398,074
Capital city: Kigali
Main languages: Kinyarwanda, French, English, Swahili
Main religions: Roman Catholic, Protestant, Adventist
Government: republic
Currency: 1 Rwandan franc = 100 centimes

SAINT KITTS AND NEVIS (North America)
Area: 261 sq km (101 sq miles)
Population: 38,736

Paraguay

• Peru

Philippines

Poland

Portugal

Qatar

Romania

Russia

Rwanda

Saint Kitts and Nevis

Saint Lucia

Saint Vincent and the Grenadines

Samoa

• San Marino

Capital city: Basseterre
Main language: English
Main religions: Protestant, Roman Catholic
Government: constitutional monarchy
Currency: 1 East Caribbean dollar = 100 cents

SAINT LUCIA (North America)
Area: 620 sq km (239 sq miles)
Population: 160,145
Capital city: Castries
Main languages: French patois, English
Main religion: Roman Catholic
Government: parliamentary democracy
Currency: 1 East Caribbean dollar = 100 cents

SAINT VINCENT AND THE GRENADINES (North America)
Area: 389 sq km (150 sq miles)
Population: 116,394
Capital city: Kingstown
Main languages: English, French patois
Main religions: Protestant, Roman Catholic
Government: parliamentary democracy
Currency: 1 East Caribbean dollar = 100 cents

SAMOA (Australasia/Oceania)
Area: 2,860 sq km (1,104 sq miles)
Population: 178,631
Capital city: Apia
Main languages: Samoan, English
Main religion: Christian
Government: constitutional monarchy
Currency: 1 tala = 100 sene

SAN MARINO (Europe)
Area: 61 sq km (24 sq miles)
Population: 27,730
Capital city: San Marino
Main language: Italian
Main religion: Roman Catholic
Government: republic
Currency: 1 euro = 100 cents

SAO TOME AND PRINCIPE (Africa)
Area: 1,001 sq km (386 sq miles)
Population: 170,372
Capital city: Sao Tome
Main languages: Crioulo* dialects, Portuguese
Main religion: Christian
Government: republic
Currency: 1 dobra = 100 centimos

SAUDI ARABIA (Asia)
Area: 1,960,582 sq km (756,987 sq miles)
Population: 23,513,330
Capital city: Riyadh
Main language: Arabic
Main religion: Muslim
Government: monarchy
Currency: 1 Saudi riyal = 100 halalah

SENEGAL (Africa)
Area: 196,190 sq km (75,749 sq miles)
Population: 10,589,571
Capital city: Dakar
Main languages: Wolof, French, Pulaar
Main religion: Muslim
Government: democratic republic
Currency: 1 CFA* franc = 100 centimes

SERBIA AND MONTENEGRO (Europe)
Area: 102,350 sq km (39,517 sq miles)
Population: 10,656,929
Capital city: Belgrade
Main language: Serbian
Main religions: Orthodox, Muslim
Government: republic
Currency: 1 Yugoslavian new dinar = 100 paras

SEYCHELLES (Africa)
Area: 455 sq km (176 sq miles)
Population: 80,098
Capital city: Victoria
Main languages: Seselwa, English, French
Main religion: Roman Catholic
Government: republic
Currency: 1 Seychelles rupee = 100 cents

SIERRA LEONE (Africa)
Area: 71,740 sq km (27,699 sq miles)
Population: 5,614,743
Capital city: Freetown
Main languages: Mende, Temne, Krio, English
Main religions: Muslim, indigenous, Christian
Government: constitutional democracy
Currency: 1 leone = 100 cents

SINGAPORE (Asia)
Area: 692 sq km (267 sq miles)
Population: 4,452,732
Capital city: Singapore
Main languages: Chinese, Malay, English, Tamil
Main religions: Buddhist, Muslim
Government: parliamentary republic
Currency: 1 Singapore dollar = 100 cents

SLOVAKIA (Europe)
Area: 48,845 sq km (18,859 sq miles)
Population: 5,422,366
Capital city: Bratislava
Main languages: Slovak, Hungarian
Main religion: Roman Catholic
Government: parliamentary democracy
Currency: 1 koruna = 100 halierov

SLOVENIA (Europe)
Area: 20,273 sq km (7,827 sq miles)
Population: 1,932,917
Capital city: Ljubljana
Main language: Slovenian
Main religion: Roman Catholic
Government: democratic republic
Currency: 1 tolar = 100 stotins

SOLOMON ISLANDS (Australasia/Oceania)
Area: 28,450 sq km (10,985 sq miles)
Population: 494,786
Capital city: Honiara
Main languages: Solomon pidgin, Kwara'ae, To'abaita, English
Main religion: Christian
Government: parliamentary democracy
Currency: 1 Solomon Islands dollar = 100 cents

SOMALIA (Africa)
Area: 637,657 sq km (246,199 sq miles)
Population: 7,753,310
Capital city: Mogadishu
Main languages: Somali, Arabic, Oromo

Sao Tome and Principe

Saudi Arabia

Senegal

Serbia and Montenegro

Seychelles

Sierra Leone

Singapore

**CFA = Communaute Financiere Africaine; Crioulo = a blend of Portuguese and West African*

Slovakia

• Slovenia

Solomon Islands

Somalia

South Africa

South Korea

• Spain

Main religion: Sunni Muslim
Government: currently has no government
Currency: 1 Somali shilling = 100 cents

SOUTH AFRICA (Africa)
Area: 1,219,912 sq km (471,008 sq miles)
Population: 43,647,658
Capital cities: Pretoria, Cape Town, Bloemfontein
Main languages: Zulu, Xhosa, Afrikaans, Pedi, English, Tswana, Sotho, Tsonga, Swati, Venda, Ndebele
Main religions: Christian, indigenous
Government: republic
Currency: 1 rand = 100 cents

SOUTH KOREA (Asia)
Area: 98,480 sq km (38,023 sq miles)
Population: 48,324,000
Capital city: Seoul
Main language: Korean
Main religions: Christian, Buddhist
Government: republic
Currency: 1 South Korean won = 100 chun

SPAIN (Europe)
Area: 504,782 sq km (194,898 sq miles)
Population: 40,077,100
Capital city: Madrid
Main languages: Castilian Spanish, Catalan
Main religion: Roman Catholic
Government: constitutional monarchy
Currency: 1 euro = 100 cents

SRI LANKA (Asia)
Area: 65,610 sq km (25,332 sq miles)
Population: 19,576,783
Capital cities: Colombo, Sri Jayewardenepura Kotte
Main languages: Sinhala, Tamil, English
Main religions: Buddhist, Hindu
Government: republic
Currency: 1 Sri Lankan rupee = 100 cents

SUDAN (Africa)
Area: 2,505,810 sq km (967,493 sq miles)
Population: 37,090,298
Capital city: Khartoum
Main languages: Arabic, English
Main religions: Sunni Muslim, indigenous
Government: Islamic republic
Currency: 1 Sudanese dinar = 100 piastres

SURINAM (South America)
Area: 163,270 sq km (63,039 sq miles)
Population: 436,494
Capital city: Paramaribo
Main languages: Sranang Tongo, Dutch, English
Main religions: Christian, Hindu, Muslim
Government: constitutional democracy
Currency: 1 Surinamese guilder = 100 cents

SWAZILAND (Africa)
Area: 17,363 sq km (6,704 sq miles)
Population: 1,123,605
Capital cities: Mbabane, Lobamba
Main languages: Swati, English
Main religions: Christian, indigenous, Muslim
Government: monarchy
Currency: 1 lilangeni = 100 cents

SWEDEN (Europe)
Area: 449,964 sq km (173,731 sq miles)
Population: 8,876,744
Capital city: Stockholm
Main language: Swedish
Main religion: Lutheran
Government: constitutional monarchy
Currency: 1 Swedish krona = 100 oere

SWITZERLAND (Europe)
Area: 41,290 sq km (15,942 sq miles)
Population: 7,301,994
Capital city: Bern
Main languages: German, French, Italian
Main religions: Roman Catholic, Protestant
Government: federal republic
Currency: 1 Swiss franc = 100 centimes

SYRIA (Asia)
Area: 185,180 sq km (71,498 sq miles)
Population: 17,155,814
Capital city: Damascus
Main languages: Arabic, Kurdish
Main religions: Muslim, Christian
Government: republic under military regime
Currency: 1 Syrian pound = 100 piastres

TAIWAN (Asia)
Area: 35,980 sq km (13,892 sq miles)
Population: 22,548,009
Capital city: Taipei
Main languages: Taiwanese, Mandarin Chinese, Hakka Chinese
Main religions: Buddhist, Confucian, Daoist
Government: democracy
Currency: 1 New Taiwan dollar = 100 cents

TAJIKISTAN (Asia)
Area: 143,100 sq km (55,251 sq miles)
Population: 6,719,567
Capital city: Dushanbe
Main languages: Tajik, Russian
Main religion: Sunni Muslim
Government: republic
Currency: 1 somoni = 100 dirams

TANZANIA (Africa)
Area: 945,087 sq km (364,898 sq miles)
Population: 37,187,939
Capital cities: Dar es Salaam, Dodoma
Main languages: Swahili, English, Sukuma
Main religions: Christian, Muslim, indigenous
Government: republic
Currency: 1 Tanzanian shilling = 100 cents

THAILAND (Asia)
Area: 514,000 sq km (198,455 sq miles)
Population: 62,354,402
Capital city: Bangkok
Main languages: Thai, English, Chaochow
Main religion: Buddhist
Government: constitutional monarchy
Currency: 1 baht = 100 satang

Sri Lanka

Sudan

Surinam

Swaziland

Sweden

Switzerland

Syria

Taiwan

Tajikistan

Tanzania

Thailand

Togo

Tonga

TOGO (Africa)
Area: 56,785 sq km (21,925 sq miles)
Population: 5,285,501
Capital city: Lome
Main languages: Mina, Ewe, Kabye, French
Main religions: indigenous, Christian, Muslim
Government: republic
Currency: 1 CFA* franc = 100 centimes

TONGA (Australasia/Oceania)
Area: 748 sq km (289 sq miles)
Population: 106,137
Capital city: Nukualofa
Main languages: Tongan, English
Main religion: Christian
Government: constitutional monarchy
Currency: 1 pa'anga = 100 seniti

TRINIDAD AND TOBAGO (North America)
Area: 5,128 sq km (1,980 sq miles)
Population: 1,163,724
Capital city: Port-of-Spain
Main languages: English, French, Spanish, Hindi
Main religions: Christian, Hindu
Government: parliamentary democracy
Currency: 1 Trinidad and Tobago dollar = 100 cents

TUNISIA (Africa)
Area: 163,610 sq km (63,170 sq miles)
Population: 9,815,644
Capital city: Tunis
Main languages: Arabic, French
Main religion: Muslim
Government: republic
Currency: 1 Tunisian dinar = 1,000 millimes

TURKEY (Europe and Asia)
Area: 780,580 sq km (301,382 sq miles)
Population: 67,308,928
Capital city: Ankara
Main language: Turkish
Main religion: Muslim
Government: democratic republic
Currency: 1 Turkish lira = 100 kurus

TURKMENISTAN (Asia)
Area: 488,100 sq km (188,455 sq miles)
Population: 4,688,963
Capital city: Ashgabat (Ashkhabad)
Main languages: Turkmen, Russian
Main religion: Muslim
Government: republic
Currency: 1 Turkmen manat = 100 tenesi

TUVALU (Australasia/Oceania)
Area: 26 sq km (10 sq miles)
Population: 11,146
Capital city: Funafuti
Main languages: Tuvaluan, English
Main religion: Congregationalist
Government: constitutional monarchy
Currency: 1 Tuvaluan dollar or 1 Australian dollar = 100 cents

UGANDA (Africa)
Area: 236,040 sq km (91,135 sq miles)
Population: 24,699,073
Capital city: Kampala
Main languages: Luganda, English, Swahili
Main religion: Christian, Muslim, indigenous
Government: republic
Currency: 1 Ugandan shilling = 100 cents

UKRAINE (Europe)
Area: 603,700 sq km (233,089 sq miles)
Population: 48,396,470
Capital city: Kiev
Main languages: Ukrainian, Russian
Main religion: Ukrainian Orthodox
Government: republic
Currency: 1 hryvnia = 100 kopiykas

UNITED ARAB EMIRATES (Asia)
Area: 82,880 sq km (32,000 sq miles)
Population: 2,445,989
Capital city: Abu Dhabi
Main languages: Arabic, English
Main religion: Muslim
Government: federation
Currency: 1 Emirati dirham = 100 fils

UNITED KINGDOM (Europe)
Area: 244,820 sq km (94,525 sq miles)
Population: 59,778,002
Capital city: London
Main language: English
Main religions: Anglican, Roman Catholic
Government: constitutional monarchy
Currency: 1 British pound = 100 pence

UNITED STATES OF AMERICA (North America)
Area: 9,629,091 sq km (3,717,792 sq miles)
Population: 280,562,489
Capital city: Washington D.C.
Main language: English
Main religions: Protestant, Roman Catholic
Government: federal republic
Currency: 1 U.S. dollar = 100 cents

URUGUAY (South America)
Area: 176,220 sq km (68,039 sq miles)
Population: 3,386,575
Capital city: Montevideo
Main language: Spanish
Main religion: Roman Catholic
Government: republic
Currency: 1 Uruguayan peso = 100 centesimos

UZBEKISTAN (Asia)
Area: 447,400 sq km (172,741 sq miles)
Population: 25,563,441
Capital city: Tashkent
Main languages: Uzbek, Russian
Main religions: Muslim, Eastern Orthodox
Government: republic
Currency: 1 Uzbekistani sum = 100 tyyn

VANUATU (Australasia/Oceania)
Area: 12,189 sq km (4,706 sq miles)
Population: 196,178
Capital city: Port-Vila
Main languages: Bislama, French, English
Main religion: Christian
Government: republic
Currency: 1 vatu = 100 centimes

Trinidad and Tobago

Tunisia

Turkey

Turkmenistan

Tuvalu

Uganda

*CFA = Communaute Financiere Africaine

Ukraine

United Arab Emirates

United Kingdom

United States of America

Uruguay

Uzbekistan

VATICAN CITY (Europe)
Area: 0.44 sq km (0.17 sq miles)
Population: 900
Capital city: Vatican City
Main languages: Italian, Latin
Main religion: Roman Catholic
Government: led by the Pope
Currency: 1 euro = 100 cents

VENEZUELA (South America)
Area: 912,050 sq km (352,143 sq miles)
Population: 24,287,670
Capital city: Caracas
Main language: Spanish
Main religion: Roman Catholic
Government: federal republic
Currency: 1 bolivar = 100 centimos

VIETNAM (Asia)
Area: 329,560 sq km (127,243 sq miles)
Population: 81,098,416
Capital city: Hanoi
Main languages: Vietnamese, French, English, Khmer, Chinese
Main religion: Buddhist
Government: Communist state
Currency: 1 new dong = 100 xu

YEMEN (Asia)
Area: 527,970 sq km (203,849 sq miles)
Population: 18,701,257
Capital city: Sana
Main language: Arabic
Main religion: Muslim
Government: republic
Currency: 1 Yemeni rial = 100 fils

ZAMBIA (Africa)
Area: 752,614 sq km (290,584 sq miles)
Population: 9,959,037
Capital city: Lusaka
Main languages: Bemba, Tonga, Nyanja, English
Main religions: Christian, Muslim, Hindu
Government: republic
Currency: 1 Zambian kwacha = 100 ngwee

ZIMBABWE (Africa)
Area: 390,580 sq km (150,803 sq miles)
Population: 11,376,676
Capital city: Harare
Main languages: Shona, Ndebele, English
Main religions: Christian, indigenous
Government: republic
Currency: 1 Zimbabwean dollar = 100 cents

The United Nations

The United Nations (U.N.) is an organization which aims to bring countries together to work for peace and development. Of the world's 193 states, 191 belong to the U.N. Those that don't belong are Taiwan and the Vatican City.

Internet link

For a link to a website where you can match countries and their flags in a great game, go to **www.usborne-quicklinks.com**

Kofi Annan, the Secretary-General of the U.N., with U.N. ambassador Pele

Vanuatu

Vatican City

Venezuela

Vietnam

Yemen

Zambia

Zimbabwe

USEFUL WEBSITES

On these pages, there are descriptions of websites that have information, photographs and games on the theme of maps and geography. For links to these sites, go to the Usborne Quicklinks website at **www.usborne-quicklinks.com** and enter the keywords "essential atlas". There you will find links to take you to all the sites.

Map resources

Website 1
Find street maps of any town or city in the world.

Website 2
See maps that show which parts of the Earth are in daylight or darkness at this very moment, plus up-to-date weather conditions across the globe.

Website 3
Download clip art of world, continent, country and state maps, as well as flags and globes.

Website 4
Find maps of any country in the world, plus information about their geography, people, government, economy and more.

World wildlife

Website 1
Discover some of the weird and wonderful creatures that live in the world's oceans and seas.

Website 2
Learn about the world's endangered animals and find out what can be done to stop them from becoming extinct.

Website 3
Find out about amazing animals and watch videos of them in the wild.

Website 4
Learn about the unusual animals that live in the Galapagos Islands, including iguanas and giant tortoises.

Website 5
Read about animals that live in the Arctic, such as walruses, snowy owls, polar bears and arctic foxes.

This is part of Kluane National Park, in Yukon Territory, Canada. A huge mass of ice known as a glacier flows slowly downhill, cutting valleys through the mountains.

Amazing Earth

Website 1
Read fascinating facts about some of the world's most interesting locations, including the Amazon Rainforest, Greenland and Madagascar. This site also has short films to watch and quiz questions to answer.

Website 2
Find out about natural disasters such as earthquakes and tsunamis and see animated diagrams of how each forms.

Website 3
Take an interactive tour of Everest, the highest mountain in the world.

Website 4
Read up-to-date information about all the current volcanic eruptions around the world.

Website 5
Explore the vast Sahara Desert and learn about its landscape and peoples.

Website 6
Discover all kinds of underground caves and find out how they were formed.

A birdwing butterfly feeds from a tropical flower. Birdwings are the world's largest butterflies and live in the rainforests of Asia and Australasia.

Quizzes and games

Website 1
See if you can identify and name countries and capital cities.

Website 2
Try all kinds of geography quizzes and have a go at some online crosswords.

Website 3
Take a safari quiz and find out if you have what it takes to survive in the wild.

Website 4
Test your knowledge of the world's deserts.

MAP INDEX

This is an index of the places and features named on the maps. Each entry consists of the following parts: the name (given in bold type), the country or region within which it is located (given in italics), the page on which the name can be found (given in bold type), and the grid reference (also given in bold type). For some names, there is also a description explaining what kind of place it is – for example a country, internal administrative area (state or province), national capital or internal capital. To find a place on a map, first find the map indicated by the page reference. Then use the grid reference to find the square containing the name or town symbol. See page 9 for help with using the grid.

a

Abaco, *The Bahamas,* **25 L5**
Abadan, *Iran,* **51 E5**
Abakan, *Russia,* **52 E3**
Abaya, Lake, *Ethiopia,* **71 G2**
Abeche, *Chad,* **66 F6**
Abeokuta, *Nigeria,* **69 F7**
Aberdeen, *United Kingdom,* **60 D2**
Aberystwyth, *United Kingdom,* **60 C3**
Abha, *Saudi Arabia,* **51 D8**
Abidjan, *Ivory Coast,* **69 E7**
Abilene, *U.S.A.,* **24 G4**
Abomey, *Benin,* **69 F7**
Abu Dhabi, *United Arab Emirates, national capital,* **51 F7**
Abuja, *Nigeria, national capital,* **69 G7**
Abu Kamal, *Syria,* **50 D5**
Abu Simbel, *Egypt,* **67 H4**
Acapulco, *Mexico,* **26 E4**
Accra, *Ghana, national capital,* **69 E7**
Acklins Island, *The Bahamas,* **25 L6**
Aconcagua, *Argentina,* **32 E6**
Adana, *Turkey,* **50 C4**
Adapazari, *Turkey,* **63 J3**
Ad Dakhla, *Western Sahara,* **68 B4**
Ad Dammam, *Saudi Arabia,* **51 F6**
Addis Ababa, *Ethiopia, national capital,* **71 G2**
Adelaide, *Australia, internal capital,* **38 G6**
Aden, *Yemen,* **51 E9**
Aden, Gulf of, *Africa/Asia,* **51 E9**
Admiralty Islands, *Papua New Guinea,* **43 L4**
Adrar, *Algeria,* **68 E3**
Adriatic Sea, *Europe,* **62 E3**
Adzope, *Ivory Coast,* **69 E7**
Aegean Sea, *Europe,* **63 H4**
Afghanistan, *Asia, country,* **48 A4**
Africa, **19**
Agadez, *Niger,* **66 C5**
Agadir, *Morocco,* **68 D2**
Agra, *India,* **48 D5**
Agrigento, *Italy,* **62 E4**
Agua Prieta, *Mexico,* **26 C1**
Aguascalientes, *Mexico,* **26 D3**
Agulhas, Cape, *South Africa,* **72 C6**
Agulhas Negras, Mount, *Brazil,* **32 K4**
Ahaggar Mountains, *Algeria,* **68 G4**
Ahmadabad, *India,* **49 C6**
Ahvaz, *Iran,* **51 E5**
Aix-en-Provence, *France,* **61 F6**
Aizawl, *India,* **49 G6**
Ajaccio, *France,* **61 G6**
Ajdabiya, *Libya,* **66 F2**
Ajmer, *India,* **48 C5**
Akhisar, *Turkey,* **63 H4**
Akita, *Japan,* **47 P3**
Akjoujt, *Mauritania,* **68 C5**
Akola, *India,* **49 D6**
Aksaray, *Turkey,* **63 K4**
Aksu, *China,* **48 E2**
Alabama, *U.S.A., internal admin. area,* **25 J4**
Al Amarah, *Iraq,* **51 E5**
Aland Islands, *Finland,* **58 F3**
Alanya, *Turkey,* **63 J4**
Al Aqabah, *Jordan,* **51 C6**
Alaska, *U.S.A., internal admin. area,* **22 D2**
Alaska, Gulf of, *North America,* **22 E3**
Alaska Peninsula, *U.S.A.,* **22 D3**
Alaska Range, *U.S.A.,* **22 D2**
Alavus, *Finland,* **58 G3**
Al Ayn, *United Arab Emirates,* **51 G7**
Albacete, *Spain,* **61 D7**
Albania, *Europe, country,* **63 F3**
Albany, *Australia,* **38 C7**
Albany, *Georgia, U.S.A.,* **25 K4**
Albany, *New York, U.S.A., internal capital,* **25 M2**
Al Bayda, *Libya,* **66 F2**
Alberta, *Canada, internal admin. area,* **22 H3**
Albert, Lake, *Africa,* **71 F3**
Albino Point, *Angola,* **72 B3**
Alboran Island, *Spain,* **61 D7**
Alborg, *Denmark,* **59 D4**
Albuquerque, *U.S.A.,* **24 E3**
Aldabra Group, *Seychelles,* **73 J1**
Aleppo, *Syria,* **50 C4**
Alesund, *Norway,* **58 C3**
Aleutian Islands, *U.S.A.,* **23 A3**
Alexander Archipelago, *Canada,* **22 F3**
Alexander Bay, *South Africa,* **72 C5**
Alexandria, *Egypt,* **67 G2**
Algeciras, *Spain,* **61 C7**
Algeria, *Africa, country,* **68 F3**
Algiers, *Algeria, national capital,* **68 F1**
Al Hillah, *Iraq,* **50 D5**
Al Hoceima, *Morocco,* **68 E1**
Al Hudaydah, *Yemen,* **51 D9**
Ali Bayramli, *Azerbaijan,* **50 E4**
Alicante, *Spain,* **61 D7**
Alice Springs, *Australia,* **38 F4**
Aligarh, *India,* **48 D5**
Al Jawf, *Libya,* **66 F4**
Al Khums, *Libya,* **66 D2**
Al Kut, *Iraq,* **51 E5**
Allahabad, *India,* **48 E5**
Almaty, *Kazakhstan,* **48 D2**
Almeria, *Spain,* **61 D7**
Almetyevsk, *Russia,* **57 G3**
Almirante, *Panama,* **27 H6**
Al Mubarrez, *Saudi Arabia,* **51 E6**
Al Mukalla, *Yemen,* **51 E9**
Alor Setar, *Malaysia,* **42 B2**
Alps, *Europe,* **62 D2**
Al Qamishli, *Syria,* **50 D4**
Alta, *Norway,* **58 G1**
Altai Mountains, *Asia,* **46 D1**
Altamira, *Brazil,* **31 H4**
Altay, *China,* **48 F1**
Altay, *Mongolia,* **46 E1**
Altun Mountains, *China,* **48 G3**
Aluksne, *Latvia,* **59 H4**
Alytus, *Lithuania,* **59 H5**
Amadjuak Lake, *Canada,* **23 M2**
Amami, *Japan,* **47 L5**
Amarillo, *U.S.A.,* **24 F3**
Amazon, *South America,* **30 H4**
Amazon Delta, *Brazil,* **31 J3**
Ambanja, *Madagascar,* **73 J2**
Ambato, *Ecuador,* **30 C4**
Amber, Cape, *Madagascar,* **73 J2**
Ambilobe, *Madagascar,* **73 J2**
Ambon, *Indonesia,* **43 G4**
Ambositra, *Madagascar,* **73 J4**
American Samoa, *Oceania, dependency,* **36 F6**
America, United States of, *North America, country,* **24 F3**
Amiens, *France,* **60 E4**
Amman, *Jordan, national capital,* **51 C5**
Amravati, *India,* **49 D6**
Amritsar, *India,* **48 C4**
Amsterdam, *Netherlands, national capital,* **60 F3**
Am Timan, *Chad,* **66 F6**
Amu Darya, *Asia,* **50 H4**
Amundsen Gulf, *Canada,* **22 G1**
Amundsen Sea, *Antarctica,* **77 Q3**
Amur, *Asia,* **53 G3**
Anadyr, *Russia,* **53 J2**
Anadyr, Gulf of, *Asia,* **53 K2**
Analalava, *Madagascar,* **73 J2**
Anambas Islands, *Indonesia,* **42 C3**
Anchorage, *U.S.A.,* **22 E2**
Ancona, *Italy,* **62 E3**
Andaman Islands, *India,* **49 G8**
Andaman Sea, *Asia,* **44 C5**
Andara, *Namibia,* **72 D3**
Andes, *South America,* **32 E5**
Andorra, *Europe, country,* **61 E6**
Andorra la Vella, *Andorra, national capital,* **61 E6**
Andreanof Islands, *U.S.A.,* **23 B3**
Androka, *Madagascar,* **73 H5**
Andros, *The Bahamas,* **25 L6**
Aneto, Pico de, *Spain,* **61 E6**
Angel Falls, *Venezuela,* **30 F2**
Angers, *France,* **60 D5**
Angkor, *Cambodia,* **44 D5**
Angoche, *Mozambique,* **73 G3**
Angola, *Africa, country,* **72 C2**
Angra do Heroismo, *Azores,* **68 K10**
Angren, *Uzbekistan,* **48 C2**
Anguilla, *North America,* **26 M4**
Anjouan Island, *Comoros,* **73 H2**
Ankara, *Turkey, national capital,* **63 K3**
Annaba, *Algeria,* **68 G1**
An Najaf, *Iraq,* **51 D5**
Annapolis, *U.S.A., internal capital,* **25 L3**
An Nasiriyah, *Iraq,* **51 E5**
Anqing, *China,* **47 J4**
Anshan, *China,* **47 K2**
Antalaha, *Madagascar,* **73 K2**
Antalya, *Turkey,* **63 J4**
Antalya, Gulf of, *Turkey,* **63 J4**
Antananarivo, *Madagascar, national capital,* **73 J3**
Antarctica, **77 B4**
Antarctic Peninsula, *Antarctica,* **77 T2**
Anticosti Island, *Canada,* **23 N4**
Antigua and Barbuda, *North America, country,* **26 M4**
Antofagasta, *Chile,* **32 D4**
Antsalova, *Madagascar,* **73 H3**
Antsirabe, *Madagascar,* **73 J3**
Antsiranana, *Madagascar,* **73 J2**
Antwerp, *Belgium,* **60 F4**
Aomori, *Japan,* **47 P2**
Aoraki, *New Zealand,* **39 P8**
Apalachee Bay, *U.S.A.,* **25 K5**
Aparri, *Philippines,* **45 H4**
Apatity, *Russia,* **58 K2**
Apennines, *Italy,* **62 E3**
Apia, *Samoa, national capital,* **36 F6**
Appalachian Mountains, *U.S.A.,* **25 K3**
Aqsay, *Kazakhstan,* **57 G3**
Aqtau, *Kazakhstan,* **50 F3**
Aqtobe, *Kazakhstan,* **57 H3**
Arabian Desert, *Africa,* **67 H3**
Arabian Peninsula, *Asia,* **51 E7**
Arabian Sea, *Asia,* **51 G8**
Aracaju, *Brazil,* **31 L6**
Arad, *Romania,* **63 G2**
Arafura Sea, *Asia/Australasia,* **43 H5**
Araguaia, *Brazil,* **31 H6**
Araguaina, *Brazil,* **31 J5**
Arak, *Iran,* **50 E5**
Aral, *Kazakhstan,* **50 H2**
Aral Sea, *Asia,* **50 G2**
Arapiraca, *Brazil,* **31 L5**
Araraquara, *Brazil,* **32 J4**
Araure, *Venezuela,* **30 E2**
Arbil, *Iraq,* **50 D4**
Arctic Ocean, **75 A4**
Ardabil, *Iran,* **50 E4**
Arendal, *Norway,* **58 D4**
Arequipa, *Peru,* **30 D7**
Argentina, *South America, country,* **33 E7**
Argentino, Lake, *Argentina,* **33 D10**
Arhus, *Denmark,* **59 D4**
Arica, *Chile,* **32 D3**
Arica, Gulf of, *South America,* **30 D7**
Arizona, *U.S.A., internal admin. area,* **24 D4**
Arkansas, *U.S.A.,* **25 G3**
Arkansas, *U.S.A., internal admin. area,* **25 H4**
Arkhangelsk, *Russia,* **52 C2**
Armenia, *Asia, country,* **50 D3**
Armidale, *Australia,* **39 K6**
Arnhem, *Netherlands,* **60 F4**
Arnhem Land, *Australia,* **38 F2**
Arqalyq, *Kazakhstan,* **50 J1**
Ar Ramadi, *Iraq,* **50 D5**
Ar Raqqah, *Syria,* **50 C4**
Aruba, *North America,* **27 K5**
Aru Islands, *Indonesia,* **43 J5**
Arusha, *Tanzania,* **71 G4**
Arzamas, *Russia,* **56 E2**
Asahikawa, *Japan,* **47 P2**
Asansol, *India,* **49 F6**
Ashgabat, *Turkmenistan, national capital,* **50 G4**
Ashkhabad, *Turkmenistan, national capital,* **50 G4**
Asia, **19**
Asir, *Saudi Arabia,* **51 D7**
Asmara, *Eritrea, national capital,* **67 J5**
Assab, *Eritrea,* **67 K6**
As Sulaymaniyah, *Iraq,* **50 E4**
Assumption, *Seychelles,* **73 J1**
Astana, *Kazakhstan, national capital,* **52 D3**
Astove, *Seychelles,* **73 J2**
Astrakhan, *Russia,* **57 F4**
Asuncion, *Paraguay, national capital,* **32 G5**
Aswan, *Egypt,* **67 H4**
Aswan High Dam, *Egypt,* **67 H4**
Asyut, *Egypt,* **67 H3**
Atacama Desert, *Chile,* **32 E3**

Atalaia do Norte, *Brazil,* **30 D4**
Atar, *Mauritania,* **68 C4**
Atbarah, *Sudan,* **67 H5**
Atbasar, *Kazakhstan,* **50 J1**
Athabasca, *Canada,* **22 H3**
Athabasca, Lake, *Canada,* **22 J3**
Athens, *Greece, national capital,* **63 G4**
Atka Island, *U.S.A.,* **23 B3**
Atlanta, *U.S.A., internal capital,* **25 K4**
Atlantic City, *U.S.A.,* **25 M3**
Atlantic Ocean, 18
Atlas Mountains, *Africa,* **68 D2**
At Taif, *Saudi Arabia,* **51 D7**
Attapu, *Laos,* **44 E5**
Attu Island, *U.S.A.,* **23 A3**
Atyrau, *Kazakhstan,* **57 G4**
Auckland, *New Zealand,* **39 P7**
Augsburg, *Germany,* **60 G4**
Augusta, *U.S.A., internal capital,* **25 N2**
Aurangabad, *India,* **49 D7**
Austin, *U.S.A., internal capital,* **24 G4**
Australasia and Oceania, 19
Australia, *Australasia, country,* **38 E4**
Australian Capital Territory, *Australia, internal admin. area,* **39 J6**
Austria, *Europe, country,* **62 E2**
Awasa, *Ethiopia,* **71 G2**
Ayacucho, *Peru,* **30 D6**
Aydin, *Turkey,* **63 H4**
Ayers Rock, *Australia,* **38 F5**
Ayoun el Atrous, *Mauritania,* **69 D5**
Azerbaijan, *Asia, country,* **50 E3**
Azores, *Atlantic Ocean,* **68 K10**
Azov, Sea of, *Europe,* **63 K2**
Az Zarqa, *Jordan,* **51 C5**

b

Baardheere, *Somalia,* **71 H3**
Babahoyo, *Ecuador,* **30 C4**
Bab al Mandab, *Africa/Asia,* **67 K6**
Babruysk, *Belarus,* **59 J5**
Babuyan Islands, *Philippines,* **45 H4**
Babylon, *Iraq,* **50 D5**
Bacabal, *Brazil,* **31 K4**
Bacau, *Romania,* **63 H2**
Bac Lieu, *Vietnam,* **44 E6**
Bacolod, *Philippines,* **45 H5**
Badajoz, *Spain,* **61 C7**
Baffin Bay, *Canada,* **23 N1**
Baffin Island, *Canada,* **23 M2**
Bafoussam, *Cameroon,* **70 B2**
Bage, *Brazil,* **32 H6**
Baghdad, *Iraq, national capital,* **50 D5**
Bahamas, The, *North America, country,* **25 L5**
Bahawalpur, *Pakistan,* **48 C5**
Bahia, *Brazil,* **31 L6**
Bahia Blanca, *Argentina,* **33 F7**
Bahir Dar, *Ethiopia,* **71 G1**
Bahrain, *Asia, country,* **51 F6**
Baia Mare, *Romania,* **63 G2**
Baie-Comeau, *Canada,* **23 N4**
Baikal, Lake, *Russia,* **53 F3**
Bairiki, *Kiribati, national capital,* **36 E4**
Bakersfield, *U.S.A.,* **24 C3**
Baku, *Azerbaijan, national capital,* **50 E3**
Balakovo, *Russia,* **57 F3**
Balaton, Lake, *Hungary,* **59 F7**
Balbina Reservoir, *Brazil,* **31 G4**
Baldy Peak, *U.S.A.,* **24 E4**
Balearic Islands, *Spain,* **61 E7**
Bali, *Indonesia,* **42 E5**
Balikesir, *Turkey,* **63 H4**
Balikpapan, *Indonesia,* **42 E4**
Balkanabat, *Turkmenistan,* **50 F4**
Balkan Mountains, *Europe,* **63 G3**
Balkhash, Lake, *Kazakhstan,* **48 D1**
Balkuduk, *Kazakhstan,* **57 F4**
Balqash, *Kazakhstan,* **48 D1**
Balti, *Moldova,* **63 H2**
Baltic Sea, *Europe,* **59 F4**
Baltimore, *U.S.A.,* **25 L3**
Bamako, *Mali, national capital,* **69 D6**
Bamenda, *Cameroon,* **70 B2**
Bancs Providence, *Seychelles,* **73 K1**
Banda Aceh, *Indonesia,* **42 A2**
Bandar-e Abbas, *Iran,* **51 G6**
Bandar Seri Begawan, *Brunei, national capital,* **42 D2**
Banda Sea, *Indonesia,* **43 G5**
Bandundu, *Democratic Republic of Congo,* **70 C4**
Bandung, *Indonesia,* **42 C5**
Banfora, *Burkina Faso,* **69 E6**
Bangalore, *India,* **49 D8**
Bangassou, *Central African Republic,* **70 D3**
Bangka, *Indonesia,* **42 C4**
Bangkok, *Thailand, national capital,* **44 D5**
Bangladesh, *Asia, country,* **49 F6**
Bangor, *U.S.A.,* **25 N2**
Bangui, *Central African Republic, national capital,* **70 C3**
Bangweulu, Lake, *Zambia,* **72 E2**
Banja Luka, *Bosnia and Herzegovina,* **62 F2**
Banjarmasin, *Indonesia,* **42 D4**
Banjul, *The Gambia, national capital,* **69 B6**
Banks Island, *Canada,* **22 G1**
Banks Islands, *Vanuatu,* **39 N2**
Banska Bystrica, *Slovakia,* **59 F6**
Baoding, *China,* **47 J3**
Baoji, *China,* **46 G4**
Baotou, *China,* **46 G2**
Baqubah, *Iraq,* **50 D5**
Baranavichy, *Belarus,* **59 H5**
Barbacena, *Brazil,* **32 K4**
Barbados, *North America, country,* **26 N5**
Barcelona, *Spain,* **61 E6**
Barcelona, *Venezuela,* **30 F1**
Bareilly, *India,* **48 D5**
Barents Sea, *Europe,* **52 B2**
Bari, *Italy,* **62 F3**
Barinas, *Venezuela,* **30 D2**
Barkly Tableland, *Australia,* **38 G3**
Barnaul, *Russia,* **52 E3**
Barquisimeto, *Venezuela,* **30 E1**
Barra Falsa Point, *Mozambique,* **73 G4**
Barranquilla, *Colombia,* **30 D1**
Barra Point, *Mozambique,* **73 G4**
Barreiras, *Brazil,* **32 J2**
Barrow, Point, *U.S.A.,* **22 D1**
Barysaw, *Belarus,* **59 J5**
Basel, *Switzerland,* **62 C2**
Basra, *Iraq,* **51 E5**
Bassas da India, *Africa,* **73 G4**
Basse-Terre, *Guadeloupe,* **26 M4**
Basseterre, *St. Kitts and Nevis, national capital,* **26 M4**
Bass Strait, *Australia,* **38 J7**
Bastia, *France,* **61 G6**
Bata, *Equatorial Guinea,* **70 A3**
Batan Islands, *Philippines,* **45 H3**
Batdambang, *Cambodia,* **44 D5**
Bathurst, *Canada,* **23 N4**
Bathurst, *U.S.A.,* **25 N1**
Bathurst Island, *Canada,* **23 K1**
Batna, *Algeria,* **68 G1**
Baton Rouge, *U.S.A., internal capital,* **25 H4**
Batumi, *Georgia,* **50 D3**
Baturaja, *Indonesia,* **42 B4**
Bawku, *Ghana,* **69 E6**
Bayamo, *Cuba,* **27 J3**
Baydhabo, *Somalia,* **71 H3**
Bealanana, *Madagascar,* **73 J2**
Beaufort Sea, *North America,* **22 F1**
Beaufort West, *South Africa,* **72 D6**
Beaumont, *U.S.A.,* **25 H4**
Bechar, *Algeria,* **68 E2**
Beer Sheva, *Israel,* **51 B5**
Beijing, *China, national capital,* **47 J3**
Beira, *Mozambique,* **73 G3**
Beirut, *Lebanon, national capital,* **50 C5**
Bejaia, *Algeria,* **68 F1**
Bekescsaba, *Hungary,* **59 G7**
Bekily, *Madagascar,* **73 J4**
Belarus, *Europe, country,* **59 J5**
Belaya, *Russia,* **57 G2**
Belcher Islands, *Canada,* **23 L3**
Beledweyne, *Somalia,* **71 J3**
Belem, *Brazil,* **31 J4**
Belfast, *United Kingdom, internal capital,* **60 C3**
Belgaum, *India,* **49 C7**
Belgium, *Europe, country,* **60 E4**
Belgrade, *Serbia and Montenegro, national capital,* **63 G2**
Belitung, *Indonesia,* **42 C4**
Belize, *North America, country,* **26 G4**
Bellingham, *U.S.A.,* **24 B1**
Bellingshausen Sea, *Antarctica,* **77 R2**
Belmopan, *Belize, national capital,* **26 G4**
Belo Horizonte, *Brazil,* **32 K3**
Belomorsk, *Russia,* **58 K2**
Beloretsk, *Russia,* **57 H3**
Belo-Tsiribihina, *Madagascar,* **73 H3**
Bendigo, *Australia,* **38 H7**
Bengal, Bay of, *Asia,* **49 F7**
Benghazi, *Libya,* **66 F2**
Bengkulu, *Indonesia,* **42 B4**
Benguela, *Angola,* **72 B2**
Beni Mellal, *Morocco,* **68 D2**
Benin, *Africa, country,* **69 F6**
Benin, Bight of, *Africa,* **69 F7**
Benin City, *Nigeria,* **69 G7**
Beni Suef, *Egypt,* **67 H3**
Ben Nevis, *United Kingdom,* **60 C2**
Benoni, *South Africa,* **72 E5**
Berbera, *Somalia,* **71 J1**
Berberati, *Central African Republic,* **70 C3**
Berdyansk, *Ukraine,* **56 D4**
Berezniki, *Russia,* **57 H2**
Bergamo, *Italy,* **62 D2**
Bergen, *Norway,* **58 C3**
Bering Sea, *North America,* **22 C2**
Bering Strait, *U.S.A.,* **22 B2**
Berlin, *Germany, national capital,* **60 H3**
Bern, *Switzerland, national capital,* **62 C2**
Beroroha, *Madagascar,* **73 J4**
Bertoua, *Cameroon,* **70 B3**
Besalampy, *Madagascar,* **73 H3**
Besancon, *France,* **61 F5**
Bethel, *U.S.A.,* **22 C2**
Bethlehem, *South Africa,* **72 E5**
Betroka, *Madagascar,* **73 J4**
Beyneu, *Kazakhstan,* **50 G2**
Beysehir Lake, *Turkey,* **63 J4**
Beziers, *France,* **61 E6**
Bhagalpur, *India,* **48 F5**
Bhavnagar *India,* **49 C6**
Bhopal, *India,* **49 D6**
Bhutan, *Asia, country,* **48 G5**
Biak, *Indonesia,* **43 J4**
Bialystok, *Poland,* **59 G5**
Bida, *Nigeria,* **69 G7**
Biel, *Switzerland,* **62 C2**
Bielefeld, *Germany,* **60 G3**
Bien Hoa, *Vietnam,* **44 E5**
Bie Plateau, *Angola,* **72 B2**
Bignona, *Senegal,* **69 B6**
Bikaner, *India,* **48 C5**
Bila Tserkva, *Ukraine,* **59 J6**
Bilbao, *Spain,* **61 D6**
Bilhorod Dnistrovskyy, *Ukraine,* **56 C4**
Billings, *U.S.A.,* **24 E1**
Bindura, *Zimbabwe,* **72 F3**
Binga, *Zimbabwe,* **72 E3**
Bintulu, *Malaysia,* **42 D3**
Bioco, *Equatorial Guinea,* **70 A3**
Birao, *Central African Republic,* **70 D1**
Biratnagar, *Nepal,* **48 F5**
Birjand, *Iran,* **50 G5**
Birmingham, *United Kingdom,* **60 D3**
Birmingham, *U.S.A.,* **25 J4**
Birnin-Kebbi, *Nigeria,* **69 F6**
Biscay, Bay of, *Europe,* **61 C5**
Bishkek, *Kyrgyzstan, national capital,* **48 C2**
Bisho, *South Africa,* **72 E6**
Biskra, *Algeria,* **68 G2**
Bismarck, *U.S.A., internal capital,* **24 F1**
Bismarck Sea, *Papua New Guinea,* **43 L4**
Bissagos Archipelago, *Guinea-Bissau,* **69 B6**
Bissau, *Guinea-Bissau, national capital,* **69 B6**
Bitola, *Macedonia,* **63 G3**
Bitterfontein, *South Africa,* **72 C6**
Bizerte, *Tunisia,* **66 C1**
Blackpool, *United Kingdom,* **60 D3**
Black Sea, *Asia/Europe,* **52 B3**
Black Volta, *Africa,* **69 E6**
Blagoevgrad, *Bulgaria,* **63 G3**
Blagoveshchensk, *Russia,* **53 G3**
Blanca Bay, *Argentina,* **33 F7**
Blanc, Cape, *Africa,* **68 B4**
Blanc, Mont, *Europe,* **61 F5**
Blantyre, *Malawi,* **73 F3**
Blida, *Algeria,* **68 F1**
Bloemfontein, *South Africa, national capital,* **72 E5**
Blue Nile, *Africa,* **67 H6**
Bo, *Sierra Leone,* **69 C7**
Boa Vista, *Brazil,* **30 F3**
Boa Vista, *Cape Verde,* **69 M11**
Bobo Dioulasso, *Burkina Faso,* **69 E6**
Bodele Depression, *Africa,* **66 E5**
Boden, *Sweden,* **58 G2**
Bodo, *Norway,* **58 E2**
Bogor, *Indonesia,* **42 C5**
Bogota, *Colombia, national capital,* **30 D3**
Bohol, *Philippines,* **45 H6**
Boise, *U.S.A., internal capital,* **24 C2**
Bojnurd, *Iran,* **50 G4**
Boke, *Guinea,* **69 C6**
Bolivar Peak, *Venezuela,* **30 D2**
Bolivia, *South America, country,* **32 E3**
Bologna, *Italy,* **62 D2**
Bolzano, *Italy,* **62 D2**
Bombay, *India,* **49 C7**
Bondoukou, *Ivory Coast,* **69 E7**
Bongor, *Chad,* **70 C1**
Bonin Islands, *Japan,* **36 B2**
Bonn, *Germany,* **60 F4**
Boosaaso, *Somalia,* **71 J1**
Boothia, Gulf of, *Canada,* **23 K1**
Boothia Peninsula, *Canada,* **23 K1**
Bordeaux, *France,* **61 D5**
Bordj Bou Arreridj, *Algeria,* **68 F1**
Borlange, *Sweden,* **58 E3**
Borneo, *Asia,* **42 D4**
Bornholm, *Denmark,* **59 E5**
Borovichi, *Russia,* **58 K4**
Bosnia and Herzegovina, *Europe, country,* **62 F2**
Bosporus, *Turkey,* **63 J3**
Bossangoa, *Central African Republic,* **70 C2**
Bossembele, *Central African Republic,* **70 C2**
Bosten Lake, *China,* **48 F2**
Boston, *U.S.A., internal capital,* **25 M2**
Bothnia, Gulf of, *Europe,* **58 F3**
Botosani, *Romania,* **63 H2**
Botswana, *Africa, country,* **72 D4**
Bouake, *Ivory Coast,* **69 E7**
Bouar, *Central African Republic,* **70 C2**
Bougouni, *Mali,* **69 D6**
Boujdour, *Western Sahara,* **68 C3**
Bouna, *Ivory Coast,* **69 E7**
Bozoum, *Central African Republic,* **70 C2**
Braga, *Portugal,* **61 B6**
Braganca, *Brazil,* **31 J4**
Brahmapur, *India,* **49 E7**
Brahmaputra, *Asia,* **48 G5**
Braila, *Romania,* **63 H2**
Brandon, *Canada,* **23 K4**
Brandon, *U.S.A.,* **24 G1**
Brasilia, *Brazil, national capital,* **32 J3**
Brasov, *Romania,* **63 H2**
Bratislava, *Slovakia, national capital,* **59 F6**
Brazil, *South America, country,* **31 H5**
Brazilian Highlands, *Brazil,* **32 K2**
Brazzaville, *Congo, national capital,* **70 C4**
Bremen, *Germany,* **60 G3**
Bremerhaven, *Germany,* **60 G3**
Brescia, *Italy,* **62 D2**
Brest, *Belarus,* **59 G5**
Brest, *France,* **60 C4**
Bria, *Central African Republic,* **70 D2**
Bridgetown, *Barbados, national capital,* **26 N5**

Brisbane, *Australia, internal capital,* **39 K5**
Bristol, *United Kingdom,* **60 D4**
Bristol Bay, *U.S.A.,* **22 C3**
British Columbia, *Canada, internal admin. area,* **22 G3**
Brno, *Czech Republic,* **62 F1**
Broken Hill, *Australia,* **38 H6**
Brokopondo, *Surinam,* **31 G2**
Brooks Range, *U.S.A.,* **22 D2**
Brownsville, *U.S.A.,* **24 G5**
Bruges, *Belgium,* **60 E4**
Brunei, *Asia, country,* **42 D3**
Brussels, *Belgium, national capital,* **60 F4**
Bryansk, *Russia,* **56 C3**
Bucaramanga, *Colombia,* **30 D2**
Bucharest, *Romania, national capital,* **63 H2**
Budapest, *Hungary, national capital,* **59 F7**
Buenaventura, *Colombia,* **30 C3**
Buenos Aires, *Argentina, national capital,* **32 G6**
Buenos Aires, Lake, *South America,* **33 D9**
Buffalo, *U.S.A.,* **25 L2**
Buga, *Colombia,* **30 C3**
Buinsk, *Russia,* **57 F3**
Bujumbura, *Burundi, national capital,* **70 E4**
Bukavu, *Democratic Republic of Congo,* **70 E4**
Bulawayo, *Zimbabwe,* **72 E4**
Bulgan, *Mongolia,* **46 F1**
Bulgaria, *Europe, country,* **63 H3**
Bunbury, *Australia,* **38 C6**
Bundaberg, *Australia,* **39 K4**
Buon Me Thuot, *Vietnam,* **44 E5**
Buraydah, *Saudi Arabia,* **51 D6**
Burgas, *Bulgaria,* **63 H3**
Burgos, *Spain,* **61 D6**
Burkina Faso, *Africa, country,* **69 E6**
Burma, *Asia, country,* **44 C3**
Bursa, *Turkey,* **63 J3**
Buru, *Indonesia,* **43 G4**
Burundi, *Africa, country,* **70 E4**
Bushehr, *Iran,* **51 F6**
Buta, *Democratic Republic of Congo,* **70 D3**
Butare, *Rwanda,* **70 E4**
Butembo, *Democratic Republic of Congo,* **70 E3**
Buton, *Indonesia,* **43 F4**
Butuan, *Philippines,* **45 J6**
Buxoro, *Uzbekistan,* **48 A3**
Buzau, *Romania,* **63 H2**
Buzuluk, *Russia,* **57 G3**
Bydgoszcz, *Poland,* **59 F5**

C

Cabanatuan, *Philippines,* **45 H4**
Cabinda, *Angola, enclave,* **70 B5**
Cabonga Reservoir, *Canada,* **25 L1**
Cabora Bassa Reservoir, *Mozambique,* **72 F3**
Caceres, *Brazil,* **32 G3**
Caceres, *Colombia,* **30 C2**
Caceres, *Spain,* **61 C7**
Cachoeiro de Itapemirim, *Brazil,* **32 K4**
Cadiz, *Spain,* **61 C7**
Cadiz, Gulf of, *Europe,* **61 C7**
Caen, *France,* **60 D4**
Cagayan de Oro, *Philippines,* **45 H6**
Cagliari, *Italy,* **62 D4**
Caicara, *Venezuela,* **30 E2**
Cairns, *Australia,* **38 J3**
Cairo, *Egypt, national capital,* **67 H3**
Caiundo, *Angola,* **72 C3**
Cajamarca, *Peru,* **30 C5**
Calabar, *Nigeria,* **70 A2**
Calais, *France,* **60 E4**
Calama, *Chile,* **32 E4**
Calamian Group, *Philippines,* **45 G5**
Calapan, *Philippines,* **45 H5**
Calbayog, *Philippines,* **45 H5**
Calcutta, *India,* **49 F6**
Calgary, *Canada,* **22 H3**
Cali, *Colombia,* **30 C3**
Calicut, *India,* **49 D8**
California, *U.S.A., internal admin. area,* **24 C3**
California, Gulf of, *Mexico,* **26 B2**
Camaguey, *Cuba,* **27 J3**
Cambodia, *Asia, country,* **44 E5**
Cambridge, *United Kingdom,* **60 E3**
Cameroon, *Africa, country,* **70 B2**
Cameroon Mountain, *Cameroon,* **70 A3**
Cameta, *Brazil,* **31 J4**
Camiri, *Bolivia,* **32 F4**
Campeche, *Mexico,* **26 F4**
Campeche, Bay of, *Mexico,* **26 F3**
Campina Grande, *Brazil,* **31 L5**
Campinas, *Brazil,* **32 J4**
Campo Grande, *Brazil,* **32 H4**
Campos, *Brazil,* **32 K4**
Canada, *North America, country,* **22 J3**
Canadian, *U.S.A.,* **24 F3**
Canakkale, *Turkey,* **63 H3**
Canary Islands, *Atlantic Ocean,* **68 B3**
Canaveral, Cape, *U.S.A.,* **25 K5**
Canberra, *Australia, national capital,* **39 J7**
Cancun, *Mexico,* **27 G3**
Cangombe, *Angola,* **72 D2**
Cannes, *France,* **61 F6**
Cantabrian Mountains, *Spain,* **61 C6**
Can Tho, *Vietnam,* **44 E6**
Canton, *China,* **47 H6**
Cape Coast, *Ghana,* **69 E7**
Cape Town, *South Africa, national capital,* **72 C6**
Cape Verde, *Atlantic Ocean, country,* **69 L11**
Cape York Peninsula, *Australia,* **38 H2**
Cap-Haitien, *Haiti,* **27 K4**
Caprivi Strip, *Namibia,* **72 D3**
Caracas, *Venezuela, national capital,* **30 E1**
Cardiff, *United Kingdom, internal capital,* **60 D4**
Caribbean Sea, *North/South America,* **27 J4**
Carlisle, *United Kingdom,* **60 D3**
Carnarvon, *Australia,* **38 B4**
Carnarvon, *South Africa,* **72 D6**
Carnot, Cape, *Australia,* **38 G7**
Caroline Islands, *Federated States of Micronesia,* **36 B4**
Carpathian Mountains, *Europe,* **59 H7**
Carpentaria, Gulf of, *Australia,* **38 G2**
Carson City, *U.S.A., internal capital,* **24 C3**
Cartagena, *Colombia,* **30 C1**
Cartagena, *Spain,* **61 D7**
Carthage, *Tunisia,* **66 D1**
Cartwright, *Canada,* **23 P3**
Caruaru, *Brazil,* **31 L5**
Casablanca, *Morocco,* **68 D2**
Cascade Range, *U.S.A.,* **24 B2**
Cascais, *Portugal,* **61 B7**
Cascavel, *Brazil,* **32 H4**
Casper, *U.S.A.,* **24 E2**
Caspian Depression, *Asia,* **50 F2**
Caspian Sea, *Asia,* **57 G4**
Castellon de la Plana, *Spain,* **61 D7**
Castelo Branco, *Portugal,* **61 C7**
Castries, *St. Lucia, national capital,* **26 M5**
Catamarca, *Argentina,* **32 E5**
Catania, *Italy,* **62 E4**
Catanzaro, *Italy,* **62 F4**
Cat Island, *The Bahamas,* **25 L6**
Caucasus Mountains, *Asia/Europe,* **50 D3**
Caxias do Sul, *Brazil,* **32 H5**
Cayenne, *French Guiana, national capital,* **31 H3**
Cayman Islands, *North America,* **27 H4**
Cebu, *Philippines,* **45 H5**
Cedar Lake *Canada,* **22 J3**
Cedar Rapids, *U.S.A.,* **25 H2**
Cedros Island, *Mexico,* **26 A2**
Ceduna, *Australia,* **38 F6**
Celaya, *Mexico,* **26 D3**
Celebes, *Indonesia,* **43 F4**
Celebes Sea, *Asia,* **45 H7**
Celtic Sea, *Europe,* **60 C4**
Central African Republic, *Africa, country,* **70 C2**
Central Cordillera, *Peru,* **30 C5**
Central Russian Uplands, *Russia,* **56 D3**
Central Siberian Plateau, *Russia,* **53 F2**
Central Sierras, *Spain,* **61 D6**
Ceram, *Indonesia,* **43 G4**
Ceram Sea, *Indonesia,* **43 G4**
Cerro de Pasco, *Peru,* **30 C6**
Cesis, *Latvia,* **59 H4**
Ceske Budejovice, *Czech Republic,* **62 E1**
Ceuta, *Africa,* **61 C8**
Chacabuco, *Argentina,* **32 F6**
Chad, *Africa, country,* **66 E5**
Chad, Lake, *Africa,* **66 D6**
Chala, *Peru,* **30 D7**
Chalan Kanoa, *Northern Marianas,* **36 B3**
Chalkida, *Greece,* **63 G4**
Challapata, *Bolivia,* **32 E3**
Chalon-sur-Saone, *France,* **61 F5**
Chanaral, *Chile,* **32 D5**
Chandigarh, *India,* **48 D4**
Chandrapur, *India,* **49 D7**
Changchun, *China,* **47 L2**
Changde, *China,* **46 H5**
Changhua, *Taiwan,* **47 K6**
Chang Jiang, *China,* **47 J4**
Changsha, *China,* **47 H5**
Changzhi, *China,* **47 H3**
Chania, *Greece,* **63 G5**
Channel Islands, *Europe,* **60 D4**
Channel Islands, *U.S.A.,* **24 C4**
Chapaev, *Kazakhstan,* **57 G3**
Charagua, *Bolivia,* **32 F3**
Charleroi, *Belgium,* **60 F4**
Charleston, *South Carolina, U.S.A.,* **25 L4**
Charleston, *West Virginia, U.S.A., internal capital,* **25 K3**
Charlotte, *U.S.A.,* **25 K3**
Charlottesville, *U.S.A.,* **25 L3**
Charlottetown, *Canada, internal capital,* **23 N4**
Chatham Islands, *New Zealand,* **39 R8**
Chattanooga, *U.S.A.,* **25 J3**
Chavuma, *Zambia,* **72 D2**
Cheboksary, *Russia,* **57 F2**
Chech Erg, *Africa,* **68 E3**
Cheju, *South Korea,* **47 L4**
Chelyabinsk, *Russia,* **57 J2**
Chemnitz, *Germany,* **60 H4**
Chengdu, *China,* **46 F4**
Chennai, *India,* **49 E8**
Chenzhou, *China,* **47 H5**
Cherbourg, *France,* **60 D4**
Cherepovets, *Russia,* **56 D2**
Cherkasy, *Ukraine,* **56 C4**
Chernihiv, *Ukraine,* **56 C3**
Chernivtsi, *Ukraine,* **59 H6**
Chesterfield Islands, *New Caledonia,* **39 M3**
Cheyenne, *U.S.A., internal capital,* **24 F2**
Chiang Mai, *Thailand,* **44 C4**
Chicago, *U.S.A.,* **25 J2**
Chiclayo, *Peru,* **30 C5**
Chico, *U.S.A.,* **24 B3**
Chicoutimi, *Canada,* **23 M4**
Chidley, Cape, *Canada,* **23 N2**
Chifeng, *China,* **47 J2**
Chigubo, *Mozambique,* **73 F4**
Chihli, Gulf of, *China,* **47 J3**
Chihuahua, *Mexico,* **26 C2**
Chile, *South America, country,* **32 D6**
Chillan, *Chile,* **33 D7**
Chiloe Island, *Chile,* **33 C8**
Chilung, *Taiwan,* **47 K5**
Chilwa, Lake, *Africa,* **73 G3**
Chimanimani, *Zimbabwe,* **73 F3**
Chimbote, *Peru,* **30 C5**
China, *Asia, country,* **46 E3**
Chincha Alta, *Peru,* **30 C6**
Chingola, *Zambia,* **72 E2**
Chinhoyi, *Zimbabwe,* **72 F3**
Chios, *Greece,* **63 H4**
Chipata, *Zambia,* **73 F2**
Chiredzi, *Zimbabwe,* **72 F4**
Chisinau, *Moldova, national capital,* **59 J2**
Chittagong, *Bangladesh,* **49 G6**
Chongjin, *North Korea,* **47 L2**
Chongju, *South Korea,* **47 L3**
Chongqing, *China,* **46 G5**
Chonos Archipelago, *Chile,* **33 C8**
Chott el Jerid, *Tunisia,* **66 C2**
Christchurch, *New Zealand,* **39 P8**
Christmas Island, *Asia,* **42 C6**
Chukchi Sea, *Arctic Ocean,* **75 B2**
Chulucanas, *Peru,* **30 B5**
Chumphon, *Thailand,* **44 C5**
Churchill, *Canada,* **23 K3**
Churchill Falls, *Canada,* **23 N3**
Cienfuegos, *Cuba,* **27 H3**
Cilacap, *Indonesia,* **42 C5**
Cincinnati, *U.S.A.,* **25 K3**
Ciudad Bolivar, *Venezuela,* **30 F2**
Ciudad del Carmen, *Mexico,* **26 F4**
Ciudad del Este, *Paraguay,* **32 H5**
Ciudad Guayana, *Venezuela,* **30 F2**
Ciudad Juarez, *Mexico,* **26 C1**
Ciudad Obregon, *Mexico,* **26 C2**
Ciudad Real, *Spain,* **61 D7**
Ciudad Victoria, *Mexico,* **26 E3**
Clark Hill Lake, *U.S.A.,* **25 K4**
Clermont-Ferrand, *France,* **61 E5**
Cleveland, *U.S.A.,* **25 K2**
Cluj-Napoca, *Romania,* **63 G2**
Coast Mountains, *Canada,* **22 F3**
Coast Ranges, *U.S.A.,* **24 B2**
Coats Land, *Antarctica,* **77 A3**
Coatzacoalcos, *Mexico,* **26 F4**
Cobija, *Bolivia,* **32 E2**
Cochabamba, *Bolivia,* **32 E3**
Cochin, *India,* **49 D9**
Cocos Island, *Costa Rica,* **27 G6**
Cod, Cape, *U.S.A.,* **25 N2**
Coeur d'Alene, *U.S.A.,* **24 C1**
Coiba Island, *Panama,* **27 H6**
Coihaique, *Chile,* **33 D9**
Coimbatore, *India,* **49 D8**
Coimbra, *Portugal,* **61 B6**
Colima, *Mexico,* **26 D4**
Cologne, *Germany,* **60 F4**
Colombia, *South America, country,* **30 D3**
Colombo, *Sri Lanka, national capital,* **49 D9**
Colon, *Panama,* **27 J6**
Colorado, *Argentina,* **33 F7**
Colorado, *U.S.A.,* **24 D4**
Colorado, *U.S.A., internal admin. area,* **24 E3**
Colorado Plateau, *U.S.A.,* **24 D3**
Colorado Springs, *U.S.A.,* **24 F3**
Columbia, *U.S.A.,* **24 C1**
Columbia, *U.S.A., internal capital,* **25 K4**
Columbine, Cape, *South Africa,* **72 C6**
Columbus, *U.S.A., internal capital,* **25 K3**
Colwyn Bay, *United Kingdom,* **60 D3**
Communism Peak, *Tajikistan,* **48 C3**
Como, Lake, *Italy,* **62 D2**
Comodoro Rivadavia, *Argentina,* **33 E9**
Comoros, *Africa, country,* **73 H2**
Conakry, *Guinea, national capital,* **69 C7**
Concepcion, *Bolivia,* **32 F3**
Concepcion, *Chile,* **33 D7**
Concepcion, *Paraguay,* **32 G4**
Concord, *U.S.A., internal capital,* **25 M2**
Concordia, *Argentina,* **32 G6**
Congo, *Africa,* **70 C4**
Congo, *Africa, country,* **70 C4**
Congo, Democratic Republic of, *Africa, country,* **70 D4**
Connecticut, *U.S.A., internal admin. area,* **25 M2**
Con Son, *Vietnam,* **44 E6**
Constanta, *Romania,* **63 J2**
Constantine, *Algeria,* **68 G1**
Cook Islands, *Oceania,* **36 G7**
Cook, Mount, *New Zealand,* **39 P8**
Cook Strait, *New Zealand,* **39 P8**
Copenhagen, *Denmark, national capital,* **59 E5**
Copiapo, *Chile,* **32 D5**

Coquimbo, *Chile,* **32 D5**
Coral Sea, *Oceania,* **39 K2**
Coral Sea Islands Territory, *Oceania, dependency,* **39 K3**
Cordoba, *Argentina,* **32 F6**
Cordoba, *Spain,* **61 C7**
Corfu, *Greece,* **63 F4**
Cork, *Ireland,* **60 B4**
Corner Brook, *Canada,* **23 P4**
Coro, *Venezuela,* **30 E1**
Coropuna, Mount, *Peru,* **30 D6**
Corpus Christi, *U.S.A.,* **24 G5**
Corrientes, *Argentina,* **32 G5**
Corsica, *France,* **61 G6**
Corum, *Turkey,* **63 K3**
Corumba, *Brazil,* **32 G3**
Cosenza, *Italy,* **62 F4**
Cosmoledo Group, *Seychelles,* **73 J1**
Costa Rica, *North America, country,* **27 G6**
Cotonou, *Benin,* **69 F7**
Cottbus, *Germany,* **60 H4**
Cradock, *South Africa,* **72 E6**
Craiova, *Romania,* **63 G2**
Cravo Norte, *Colombia,* **30 D2**
Crete, *Greece,* **63 H5**
Criciuma, *Brazil,* **32 J5**
Crimea, *Ukraine,* **63 K2**
Cristobal Colon, *Colombia,* **30 D1**
Croatia, *Europe, country,* **62 F2**
Cruzeiro do Sul, *Brazil,* **30 D5**
Cuamba, *Mozambique,* **73 G2**
Cuangar, *Angola,* **72 C3**
Cuango, *Africa,* **72 C1**
Cuanza, *Angola,* **72 C2**
Cuba, *North America, country,* **27 J3**
Cucuta, *Colombia,* **30 D2**
Cuenca, *Ecuador,* **30 C4**
Cuiaba, *Brazil,* **32 G3**
Culiacan, *Mexico,* **26 C3**
Cumana, *Venezuela,* **30 F1**
Cumberland Peninsula, *Canada,* **23 N2**
Cunene, *Africa,* **72 C3**
Curitiba, *Brazil,* **32 J5**
Cusco, *Peru,* **30 D6**
Cuttack, *India,* **49 F6**
Cuxhaven, *Germany,* **60 G3**
Cyclades, *Greece,* **63 H4**
Cyprus, *Asia, country,* **63 J5**
Cyrene, *Libya,* **66 F2**
Czech Republic, *Europe, country,* **62 E1**
Czestochowa, *Poland,* **59 F6**

d

Dabeiba, *Colombia,* **30 C2**
Dagupan, *Philippines,* **45 H4**
Dahlak Archipelago, *Eritrea,* **67 K5**
Dakar, *Senegal, national capital,* **69 B6**
Dal, *Sweden,* **58 F3**
Da Lat, *Vietnam,* **44 E5**
Dali, *China,* **46 F5**
Dalian, *China,* **47 K3**
Dallas, *U.S.A.,* **25 G4**
Daloa, *Ivory Coast,* **69 D7**
Damascus, *Syria, national capital,* **50 C5**
Damavand, *Iran,* **50 F4**
Damongo, *Ghana,* **69 E7**
Da Nang, *Vietnam,* **44 E4**
Dandong, *China,* **47 K2**
Danube, *Europe,* **59 F7**
Danube, Mouths of the, *Europe,* **63 J2**
Daqing, *China,* **47 L1**
Darbhanga, *India,* **48 F5**
Dar es Salaam, *Tanzania, national capital,* **71 G5**
Darien, Gulf of, *Colombia,* **30 C2**
Darjeeling, *India,* **48 F5**
Darling, *Australia,* **38 H6**
Darnah, *Libya,* **66 F2**
Darwin, *Australia, internal capital,* **38 F2**
Darwin, Mount, *Zimbabwe,* **72 F3**
Dasht-e Kavir, *Iran,* **50 F5**
Dasoguz, *Turkmenistan,* **50 G3**
Datong, *China,* **47 H2**
Daugavpils, *Latvia,* **59 H5**
Davangere, *India,* **49 D8**
Davao, *Philippines,* **45 J6**
David, *Panama,* **27 H6**
Davis Strait, *Canada,* **23 P2**
Dawson, *Canada,* **22 F2**
Dayr az Zawr, *Syria,* **50 D4**
Daytona Beach, *U.S.A.,* **25 K5**
De Aar, *South Africa,* **72 D6**
Dease Lake, *Canada,* **22 G3**
Death Valley, *U.S.A.,* **24 C3**
Debrecen, *Hungary,* **59 G7**
Debre Zeyit, *Ethiopia,* **71 G2**
Deccan Plateau, *India,* **49 D7**
Delaware, *U.S.A., internal admin. area,* **25 L3**
Delgado, Cape, *Mozambique,* **73 H2**
Delhi, *India,* **48 D5**
Del Rio, *U.S.A.,* **24 F5**
Democratic Republic of Congo, *Africa, country,* **70 D4**
Denizli, *Turkey,* **63 J4**
Denmark, *Europe, country,* **59 D5**
Denpasar, *Indonesia,* **42 E5**
D'Entrecasteaux Islands, *Papua New Guinea,* **43 M5**
Denver, *U.S.A., internal capital,* **24 E3**
Dera Ghazi Khan, *Pakistan,* **48 C4**
Derbent, *Russia,* **50 E3**
Dese, *Ethiopia,* **71 G1**
Des Moines, *U.S.A., internal capital,* **25 H2**
Desna, *Europe,* **56 C3**
Detroit, *U.S.A.,* **25 K2**
Devon Island, *Canada,* **23 L1**
Devonport, *Australia,* **38 J8**
Dhaka, *Bangladesh, national capital,* **49 G6**
Dhamar, *Yemen,* **51 D9**
Dhule, *India,* **49 C6**
Dibrugarh, *India,* **48 G5**
Dijon, *France,* **61 F5**
Dikhil, *Djibouti,* **67 K6**
Dili, *East Timor, national capital,* **43 G5**
Dilolo, *Democratic Republic of Congo,* **70 D6**
Dinaric Alps, *Europe,* **62 E2**
Dire Dawa, *Ethiopia,* **71 H2**
Divo, *Ivory Coast,* **69 D7**
Diyarbakir, *Turkey,* **50 D4**
Djado Plateau, *Africa,* **66 D4**
Djambala, *Congo,* **70 B4**
Djelfa, *Algeria,* **68 F2**
Djema, *Central African Republic,* **70 E2**
Djemila, *Algeria,* **68 G1**
Djibouti, *Africa, country,* **67 K6**
Djibouti, *Djibouti, national capital,* **67 K6**
Djougou, *Benin,* **69 F7**
Dnieper, *Europe,* **56 C4**
Dniester, *Europe,* **59 H6**
Dniprodzerzhynsk, *Ukraine,* **56 C4**
Dnipropetrovsk, *Ukraine,* **56 D4**
Doba, *Chad,* **70 C2**
Dobrich, *Bulgaria,* **63 H3**
Dodecanese, *Greece,* **63 H4**
Dodoma, *Tanzania, national capital,* **71 G5**
Doha, *Qatar, national capital,* **51 F6**
Dolak, *Indonesia,* **43 J5**
Dolores, *Argentina,* **33 G7**
Dominica, *North America, country,* **26 M4**
Dominican Republic, *North America, country,* **27 L3**
Don, *Russia,* **56 E4**
Dondo, *Angola,* **72 B1**
Donets, *Europe,* **56 D4**
Donetsk, *Ukraine,* **56 D4**
Dongting Lake, *China,* **47 H5**
Dori, *Burkina Faso,* **69 E6**
Dosso, *Niger,* **69 F6**
Douala, *Cameroon,* **70 A3**
Douglas, *South Africa,* **72 D5**
Dourados, *Brazil,* **32 H4**
Douro, *Europe,* **61 C6**
Dover, *United Kingdom,* **60 E4**
Dover, *U.S.A., internal capital,* **25 L3**
Dover, Strait of, *Europe,* **60 E4**
Drakensberg, *South Africa,* **72 E6**
Drake Passage, *South America,* **33 E11**
Drammen, *Norway,* **58 D4**
Dresden, *Germany,* **60 H4**
Drobeta-Turnu Severin, *Romania,* **63 G2**
Dryden, *Canada,* **23 K4**
Dubai, *United Arab Emirates,* **51 G6**
Dubawnt Lake, *Canada,* **22 J2**
Dubbo, *Australia,* **39 J6**
Dublin, *Ireland, national capital,* **60 C3**
Dubrovnik, *Croatia,* **63 F3**
Duisburg, *Germany,* **60 F4**
Duitama, *Colombia,* **30 D2**
Duluth, *U.S.A.,* **25 H1**
Dumaguete, *Philippines,* **45 H6**
Dundee, *United Kingdom,* **60 D2**
Dunedin, *New Zealand,* **39 P9**
Durango, *Mexico,* **26 D3**
Durazno, *Uruguay,* **32 G6**
Durban, *South Africa,* **72 E5**
Durres, *Albania,* **63 E3**
Dushanbe, *Tajikistan, national capital,* **48 B3**
Dusseldorf, *Germany,* **60 F4**
Dzhankoy, *Ukraine,* **63 K2**
Dzungarian Basin, *China,* **48 F1**

e

East Antarctica, *Antarctica,* **77 E3**
East Cape, *New Zealand,* **39 Q7**
East China Sea, *Asia,* **47 K5**
Easter Island, *Pacific Ocean,* **37 N7**
Eastern Cordillera, *Colombia,* **30 D3**
Eastern Cordillera, *Peru,* **30 D6**
Eastern Ghats, *India,* **49 D8**
Eastern Sierra Madre, *Mexico,* **26 D2**
East Falkland, *Falkland Islands,* **33 G10**
East London, *South Africa,* **72 E6**
East Siberian Sea, *Russia,* **53 J2**
East Timor, *Asia, country,* **43 G5**
Ebolowa, *Cameroon,* **70 B3**
Ebro, *Spain,* **61 D6**
Ecuador, *South America, country,* **30 B4**
Edinburgh, *United Kingdom, internal capital,* **60 D2**
Edirne, *Turkey,* **63 H3**
Edmonton, *Canada, internal capital,* **22 H3**
Edmundston, *Canada,* **23 N4**
Edward, Lake, *Africa,* **70 E4**
Edwards Plateau, *U.S.A.,* **24 F4**
Efate, *Vanuatu,* **39 N3**
Egypt, *Africa, country,* **67 G3**
Eindhoven, *Netherlands,* **60 F4**
Elat, *Israel,* **51 B6**
Elazig, *Turkey,* **50 C4**
Elba, *Italy,* **62 D3**
Elbasan, *Albania,* **63 G3**
Elbe, *Europe,* **60 G3**
Elbrus, Mount, *Russia,* **50 D3**
Elche, *Spain,* **61 D7**
Eldorado, *Argentina,* **32 H5**
Eldoret, *Kenya,* **71 G3**
Elephant Island, *Atlantic Ocean,* **33 H12**
Eleuthera, *The Bahamas,* **25 L5**
El Fasher, *Sudan,* **67 G6**
Elgon, Mount, *Uganda,* **71 F3**
El Hierro, *Canary Islands,* **68 B3**
Elista, *Russia,* **50 D2**
El Jadida, *Morocco,* **68 D2**
El Jem, *Tunisia,* **66 D1**
Ellesmere Island, *Canada,* **75 R3**
Ellsworth Land, *Antarctica,* **77 R3**
El Mansura, *Egypt,* **67 H2**
El Minya, *Egypt,* **67 H3**
El Obeid, *Sudan,* **67 H6**
El Oued, *Algeria,* **68 G2**
El Paso, *U.S.A.,* **24 E4**
El Salvador, *North America, country,* **26 G5**
Embi, *Kazakhstan,* **50 G2**
Emi Koussi, *Chad,* **66 E4**
Empty Quarter, *Asia,* **51 E8**
Encarnacion, *Paraguay,* **32 G5**
Ende, *Indonesia,* **43 F5**
Enderby Land, *Antarctica,* **77 E3**
Engels, *Russia,* **57 F3**
England, *United Kingdom, internal admin. area,* **60 D3**
English Channel, *Europe,* **60 D4**
Ennedi Plateau, *Africa,* **66 F5**
Enschede, *Netherlands,* **60 F3**
Entebbe, *Uganda,* **71 F3**
Enugu, *Nigeria,* **69 G7**
Ephesus, *Turkey,* **63 H4**
Equatorial Guinea, *Africa, country,* **70 A3**
Erenhot, *China,* **46 H2**
Erfurt, *Germany,* **60 G4**
Erie, *U.S.A.,* **25 K2**
Erie, Lake, *U.S.A.,* **25 K2**
Eritrea, *Africa, country,* **67 J5**
Er Rachidia, *Morocco,* **68 E2**
Ershovka, *Kazakhstan,* **57 K3**
Erzurum, *Turkey,* **50 D4**
Esbjerg, *Denmark,* **59 D5**
Esfahan, *Iran,* **50 F5**
Eskilstuna, *Sweden,* **58 F4**
Eskisehir, *Turkey,* **63 J4**
Esmeraldas, *Ecuador,* **30 C3**
Esperance, *Australia,* **38 D6**
Espinosa, *Brazil,* **32 K2**
Espiritu Santo, *Vanuatu,* **39 N3**
Espoo, *Finland,* **58 H3**
Espungabera, *Mozambique,* **73 F4**
Esquel, *Argentina,* **33 D8**
Essaouira, *Morocco,* **68 D2**
Es Semara, *Western Sahara,* **68 C3**
Essen, *Germany,* **60 F4**
Estevan, *Canada,* **22 J4**
Estonia, *Europe, country,* **58 H4**
Ethiopia, *Africa, country,* **71 G2**
Ethiopian Highlands, *Ethiopia,* **71 G1**
Etna, Mount, *Italy,* **62 E4**
Etosha Pan, *Namibia,* **72 C3**
Euboea, *Greece,* **63 G4**
Eugene, *U.S.A.,* **24 B2**
Eugenia, Point, *Mexico,* **26 A2**
Euphrates, *Asia,* **51 E5**
Europa Island, *Africa,* **73 H4**
Europe, 19
Evansville, *U.S.A.,* **25 J3**
Everest, Mount, *Asia,* **48 F5**
Everglades, The, *U.S.A.,* **25 K5**
Evora, *Portugal,* **61 C7**
Evry, *France,* **60 E4**
Exeter, *United Kingdom,* **60 D4**
Eyl, *Somalia,* **71 J2**
Eyre, Lake, *Australia,* **38 G5**

f

Fada-Ngourma, *Burkina Faso,* **69 F6**
Fairbanks, *U.S.A.,* **22 E2**
Faisalabad, *Pakistan,* **48 C4**
Fakfak, *Indonesia,* **43 H4**
Falkland Islands, *Atlantic Ocean,* **33 F10**
Farasan Islands, *Saudi Arabia,* **51 D8**
Farewell, Cape, *New Zealand,* **39 P8**
Fargo, *U.S.A.,* **25 G1**
Fargona, *Uzbekistan,* **48 C2**
Farmington, *U.S.A.,* **24 E3**
Faro, *Portugal,* **61 C7**
Farquhar Group, *Seychelles,* **73 K1**
Faxafloi, *Iceland,* **58 N2**
Faya-Largeau, *Chad,* **66 E5**
Federated States of Micronesia, *Oceania, country,* **36 C4**
Feira de Santana, *Brazil,* **32 L2**
Feodosiya, *Ukraine,* **63 K2**
Fernandina, *Ecuador,* **30 N10**
Ferrara, *Italy,* **62 D2**
Fes, *Morocco,* **68 E2**
Fianarantsoa, *Madagascar,* **73 J4**
Fiji, *Oceania, country,* **39 Q3**
Finland, *Europe, country,* **58 H2**
Finland, Gulf of, *Europe,* **58 H4**
Flagstaff, *U.S.A.,* **24 D3**
Flensburg, *Germany,* **60 G3**
Flinders Island, *Australia,* **39 J7**
Flin Flon, *Canada,* **22 J3**
Florence, *Italy,* **62 D3**

Florencia, *Colombia,* **30 C3**
Flores, *Azores,* **68 J10**
Flores, *Indonesia,* **43 F5**
Flores Sea, *Indonesia,* **43 F5**
Floresta, *Brazil,* **31 L5**
Floriano, *Brazil,* **31 K5**
Florianopolis, *Brazil,* **32 J5**
Florida, *U.S.A., internal admin. area,* **25 K5**
Florida Keys, *U.S.A.,* **25 K6**
Florida, Straits of, *North America,* **25 K6**
Focsani, *Romania,* **63 H2**
Foggia, *Italy,* **62 E3**
Fogo, *Cape Verde,* **69 M12**
Fomboni, *Comoros,* **73 H2**
Formosa, *Argentina,* **32 G5**
Fort Albany, *Canada,* **23 L3**
Fortaleza, *Brazil,* **31 L4**
Fort Chipewyan, *Canada,* **22 H3**
Fort-de-France, *Martinique,* **26 M5**
Fort Lauderdale, *U.S.A.,* **25 K5**
Fort McMurray, *Canada,* **22 H3**
Fort Nelson, *Canada,* **22 G3**
Fort Peck Lake, *U.S.A.,* **24 E1**
Fort Providence, *Canada,* **22 H2**
Fort St. John, *Canada,* **22 G3**
Fort Severn, *Canada,* **23 L3**
Fort Vermilion, *Canada,* **22 H3**
Fort Wayne, *U.S.A.,* **25 J2**
Fort Worth, *U.S.A.,* **24 G4**
Foumban, *Cameroon,* **70 B2**
Foxe Basin, *Canada,* **23 M2**
Foxe Peninsula, *Canada,* **23 M2**
Fox Islands, *U.S.A.,* **23 C3**
Foz do Cunene, *Angola,* **72 B3**
Foz do Iguacu, *Brazil,* **32 H5**
France, *Europe, country,* **61 E5**
Franceville, *Gabon,* **70 B4**
Francistown, *Botswana,* **72 E4**
Frankfort, *U.S.A., internal capital,* **25 K3**
Frankfurt, *Germany,* **60 G4**
Franz Josef Land, *Russia,* **52 C1**
Fraser Island, *Australia,* **39 K5**
Fredericton, *Canada, internal capital,* **23 N4**
Fredrikstad, *Norway,* **58 D4**
Freeport City, *The Bahamas,* **25 L5**
Freetown, *Sierra Leone, national capital,* **69 C7**
Freiburg, *Germany,* **60 F4**
French Guiana, *South America, dependency,* **31 H3**
French Polynesia, *Oceania, dependency,* **37 J6**
Fresno, *U.S.A.,* **24 C3**
Frisian Islands, *Europe,* **60 F3**
Froya, *Norway,* **58 D3**
Fuerteventura, *Canary Islands,* **68 B3**
Fuji, Mount, *Japan,* **47 N3**
Fukui, *Japan,* **47 N3**
Fukuoka, *Japan,* **47 M4**
Fukushima, *Japan,* **47 P3**
Funafuti, *Tuvalu, national capital,* **36 E5**
Funchal, *Madeira,* **68 B2**
Furnas Reservoir, *Brazil,* **32 J4**
Fushun, *China,* **47 K2**
Fuxin, *China,* **47 K2**
Fyn, *Denmark,* **59 D5**

g

Gabes, *Tunisia,* **66 D2**
Gabes, Gulf of, *Africa,* **66 D2**
Gabon, *Africa, country,* **70 B4**
Gaborone, *Botswana, national capital,* **72 E4**
Gafsa, *Tunisia,* **66 C2**
Gagnoa, *Ivory Coast,* **69 D7**
Gairdner, Lake, *Australia,* **38 F6**
Galapagos Islands, *Ecuador,* **30 N9**
Galati, *Romania,* **63 J2**
Galdhopiggen, *Norway,* **58 D3**
Galle, *Sri Lanka,* **49 E9**
Gallinas, Cape, *Colombia,* **30 D1**
Galveston, *U.S.A.,* **25 H5**
Galway, *Ireland,* **60 B3**
Gambela, *Ethiopia,* **71 F2**
Gambia, The, *Africa, country,* **69 B6**
Ganca, *Azerbaijan,* **50 E3**
Gander, *Canada,* **23 P4**
Ganges, *Asia,* **48 E5**
Ganges, Mouths of the, *Asia,* **49 F6**
Ganzhou, *China,* **47 H5**
Gao, *Mali,* **69 F5**
Garda, Lake, *Italy,* **62 D2**
Garissa, *Kenya,* **71 G4**
Garonne, *France,* **61 E5**
Garoua, *Cameroon,* **70 B2**
Gaspe, *Canada,* **23 N4**
Gatchina, *Russia,* **58 J4**
Gavle, *Sweden,* **58 F3**
Gaza, *Israel,* **51 B5**
Gaziantep, *Turkey,* **50 C4**
Gdansk, *Poland,* **59 F5**
Gdansk, Gulf of, *Poland,* **59 F5**
Gdynia, *Poland,* **59 F5**
Gedaref, *Sudan,* **67 J6**
Geelong, *Australia,* **38 H7**
Gejiu, *China,* **46 F6**
Gemena, *Democratic Republic of Congo,* **70 C3**
General Roca, *Argentina,* **33 E7**
General Santos, *Philippines,* **45 J6**
General Villegas, *Argentina,* **32 F7**
Geneva, *Switzerland,* **62 C2**
Geneva, Lake, *Europe,* **62 C2**
Genoa, *Italy,* **62 D2**
Genoa, Gulf of, *Italy,* **62 D2**
Gent, *Belgium,* **60 E4**
Georgetown, *Guyana, national capital,* **31 G2**
George Town, *Malaysia,* **42 B2**
Georgia, *Asia, country,* **50 D3**
Georgia, *U.S.A., internal admin. area,* **25 K4**
Gera, *Germany,* **60 H4**
Geraldton, *Australia,* **38 B5**
Gerlachovsky stit, *Slovakia,* **59 G6**
Germany, *Europe, country,* **60 G4**
Gerona, *Spain,* **61 E6**
Ghadamis, *Libya,* **66 C2**
Ghana, *Africa, country,* **69 E7**
Ghardaia, *Algeria,* **68 F2**
Gharyan, *Libya,* **66 D2**
Ghat, *Libya,* **66 D3**
Gibraltar, *Europe,* **61 C7**
Gibson Desert, *Australia,* **38 E4**
Gijon, *Spain,* **61 C6**
Gilbert Islands, *Kiribati,* **36 E5**
Gilgit, *Pakistan,* **48 C3**
Girardeau, Cape, *U.S.A.,* **25 J3**
Giza, Pyramids of, *Egypt,* **67 H3**
Gladstone, *Australia,* **39 K4**
Glama, *Norway,* **58 D3**
Glasgow, *United Kingdom,* **60 C3**
Glazov, *Russia,* **57 G2**
Glorioso Islands, *Africa,* **73 J2**
Gloucester, *United Kingdom,* **60 D4**
Gobabis, *Namibia,* **72 C4**
Gobi Desert, *Asia,* **46 F2**
Gochas, *Namibia,* **72 C4**
Godavari, *India,* **49 D7**
Gode, *Ethiopia,* **71 H2**
Goiania, *Brazil,* **32 J3**
Gold Coast, *Australia,* **39 K5**
Golmud, *China,* **48 G3**
Goma, *Democratic Republic of Congo,* **70 E4**
Gonaives, *Haiti,* **27 K4**
Gonder, *Ethiopia,* **71 G1**
Gongga Shan, *China,* **46 F5**
Good Hope, Cape of, *South Africa,* **72 C6**
Goose Lake, *U.S.A.,* **24 B2**
Gorakhpur, *India,* **49 E5**
Gorgan, *Iran,* **50 F4**
Gori, *Georgia,* **50 D3**
Gorki Reservoir, *Russia,* **56 E2**
Gorontalo, *Indonesia,* **43 F3**
Gorzow Wielkopolski, *Poland,* **59 E5**
Gothenburg, *Sweden,* **59 E4**
Gotland, *Sweden,* **59 F4**
Gottingen, *Germany,* **60 G4**
Gouin Reservoir, *Canada,* **25 L1**
Goundam, *Mali,* **69 E5**
Governador Valadares, *Brazil,* **32 K3**
Graaff-Reinet, *South Africa,* **72 D6**
Grafton, *Australia,* **39 K5**
Grahamstown, *South Africa,* **72 E6**
Granada, *Spain,* **61 D7**
Gran Canaria, *Canary Islands,* **68 B3**
Gran Chaco, *South America,* **32 F4**
Grand Bahama, *The Bahamas,* **25 L5**
Grand Canal, *China,* **47 J4**
Grand Canyon, *U.S.A.,* **24 D3**
Grand Comoro, *Comoros,* **73 H2**
Grande Bay, *Argentina,* **33 E10**
Grande Prairie, *Canada,* **22 H3**
Grand Forks, *U.S.A.,* **25 G1**
Grand Island, *U.S.A.,* **24 G2**
Grand Junction, *U.S.A.,* **24 E3**
Grand Rapids, *Canada,* **23 K3**
Grand Rapids, *U.S.A.,* **25 J2**
Grand Teton, *U.S.A.,* **24 D2**
Graskop, *South Africa,* **72 F5**
Graz, *Austria,* **62 E2**
Great Australian Bight, *Australia,* **38 F6**
Great Barrier Reef, *Australia,* **38 J3**
Great Basin, *U.S.A.,* **24 C2**
Great Bear Lake, *Canada,* **22 G2**
Great Dividing Range, *Australia,* **39 J6**
Great Eastern Erg, *Algeria,* **68 G3**
Greater Antilles, *North America,* **27 J4**
Greater Khingan Range, *China,* **47 J1**
Greater Sunda Islands, *Asia,* **42 C4**
Great Falls, *U.S.A.,* **24 D1**
Great Inagua, *The Bahamas,* **27 K3**
Great Karoo, *South Africa,* **72 D6**
Great Plains, *U.S.A.,* **24 F2**
Great Rift Valley, *Africa,* **71 F5**
Great Salt Desert, *Iran,* **50 F5**
Great Salt Lake, *U.S.A.,* **24 D2**
Great Salt Lake Desert, *U.S.A.,* **24 D2**
Great Sandy Desert, *Australia,* **38 D4**
Great Slave Lake, *Canada,* **22 H2**
Great Victoria Desert, *Australia,* **38 D5**
Great Wall of China, *China,* **46 F3**
Great Western Erg, *Algeria,* **68 E2**
Greece, *Europe, country,* **63 G4**
Green Bay, *U.S.A.,* **25 J2**
Greenland, *North America, dependency,* **75 P3**
Greenland Sea, *Atlantic Ocean,* **75 M3**
Greensboro, *U.S.A.,* **25 L3**
Greenville, *U.S.A.,* **25 H4**
Grenada, *North America, country,* **26 M5**
Grenoble, *France,* **61 F5**
Griffith, *Australia,* **38 J6**
Groningen, *Netherlands,* **60 F3**
Groot, *South Africa,* **72 D6**
Groote Eylandt, *Australia,* **38 G2**
Grossglockner, *Austria,* **62 E2**
Groznyy, *Russia,* **50 E3**
Grudziadz, *Poland,* **59 F5**
Grunau, *Namibia,* **72 C5**
Grytviken, *South Georgia,* **33 L10**
Guadalajara, *Mexico,* **26 D3**
Guadalquivir, *Spain,* **61 C7**
Guadalupe Island, *Mexico,* **26 A2**
Guadeloupe, *North America,* **26 M4**
Guadiana, *Europe,* **61 C7**
Gualeguaychu, *Argentina,* **32 G6**
Guam, *Oceania,* **36 B3**
Guangzhou, *China,* **47 H6**
Guantanamo, *Cuba,* **27 J3**
Guarapuava, *Brazil,* **32 H5**
Guardafui, Cape, *Somalia,* **71 K1**
Guatemala, *North America, country,* **26 F4**
Guatemala City, *Guatemala, national capital,* **26 F5**
Guaviare, *Colombia,* **30 E3**
Guayaquil, *Ecuador,* **30 C4**
Guayaquil, Gulf of, *Ecuador,* **30 B4**
Gueckedou, *Guinea,* **69 C7**
Guelma, *Algeria,* **62 C4**
Guiana Highlands, *Venezuela,* **30 E2**
Guilin, *China,* **46 H5**
Guinea, *Africa, country,* **69 C6**
Guinea-Bissau, *Africa, country,* **69 B6**
Guinea, Gulf of, *Africa,* **69 F8**
Guiria, *Venezuela,* **30 F1**
Guiyang, *China,* **46 G5**
Gujranwala, *Pakistan,* **48 C4**
Gujrat, *Pakistan,* **48 C4**
Gulbarga, *India,* **49 D7**
Gulf, The, *Asia,* **51 F6**
Gulu, *Uganda,* **71 F3**
Gunnbjorns Mountain, *Greenland,* **75 N2**
Gunung Kerinci, *Indonesia,* **42 B4**
Gunung Tahan, *Malaysia,* **42 B3**
Gurupi, *Brazil,* **32 J2**
Gusau, *Nigeria,* **69 G6**
Guwahati, *India,* **48 G5**
Guyana, *South America, country,* **31 G2**
Gwalior, *India,* **48 D5**
Gweru, *Zimbabwe,* **72 E3**
Gympie, *Australia,* **39 K5**
Gyor, *Hungary,* **59 F7**

h

Haapsalu, *Estonia,* **58 G4**
Haarlem, *Netherlands,* **60 F3**
Hadhramaut, *Yemen,* **51 E9**
Ha Giang, *Vietnam,* **44 E3**
Hague, The, *Netherlands, national capital,* **60 F3**
Haifa, *Israel,* **50 B5**
Haikou, *China,* **46 H6**
Hail, *Saudi Arabia,* **51 D6**
Hailar, *China,* **47 J1**
Hainan, *China,* **46 H7**
Hai Phong, *Vietnam,* **44 E3**
Haiti, *North America, country,* **27 K4**
Hakodate, *Japan,* **47 P2**
Halifax, *Canada, internal capital,* **23 N4**
Halmahera, *Indonesia,* **43 G3**
Halmstad, *Sweden,* **59 E4**
Hamadan, *Iran,* **50 E5**
Hamah, *Syria,* **50 C4**
Hamamatsu, *Japan,* **47 N4**
Hamburg, *Germany,* **60 G3**
Hameenlinna, *Finland,* **58 H3**
Hamhung, *North Korea,* **47 L3**
Hami, *China,* **48 G2**
Hamilton, *Canada,* **23 M4**
Hamilton, *New Zealand,* **39 Q7**
Hammerfest, *Norway,* **58 G1**
Handan, *China,* **47 H3**
Hangzhou, *China,* **47 K4**
Hannover, *Germany,* **60 G3**
Hanoi, *Vietnam, national capital,* **44 E3**
Happy Valley-Goose Bay, *Canada,* **23 N3**
Haradh, *Saudi Arabia,* **51 E7**
Harare, *Zimbabwe, national capital,* **72 F3**
Harbin, *China,* **47 L1**
Harer, *Ethiopia,* **71 H2**
Hargeysa, *Somalia,* **71 H2**
Harney Basin, *U.S.A.,* **24 C2**
Harper, *Liberia,* **69 D8**
Harrisburg, *U.S.A., internal capital,* **25 L2**
Harrismith, *South Africa,* **72 E5**
Hartford, *U.S.A., internal capital,* **25 M2**
Hatteras, Cape, *U.S.A.,* **25 L3**
Hattiesburg, *U.S.A.,* **25 J4**
Hat Yai, *Thailand,* **44 D6**
Hauki Lake, *Finland,* **58 J3**
Havana, *Cuba, national capital,* **27 H3**
Hawaii, *Pacific Ocean, internal admin. area,* **25 P7**
Hawaiian Islands, *Pacific Ocean,* **25 P7**
Hebrides, *United Kingdom,* **60 C2**
Hefei, *China,* **47 J4**
Hegang, *China,* **47 M1**
Hejaz, *Saudi Arabia,* **51 C6**
Helena, *U.S.A., internal capital,* **24 D1**
Helmand, *Asia,* **48 B4**
Helsingborg, *Sweden,* **59 E4**
Helsinki, *Finland, national capital,* **58 H3**
Hengyang, *China,* **46 H5**
Henzada, *Burma,* **44 C4**
Herat, *Afghanistan,* **48 A4**
Hermosillo, *Mexico,* **26 B2**
Hiiumaa, *Estonia,* **58 G4**
Hilo, *U.S.A.,* **25 P8**

Himalayas, *Asia,* **48 E4**
Hindu Kush, *Asia,* **48 B3**
Hinton, *Canada,* **22 H3**
Hiroshima, *Japan,* **47 M4**
Hispaniola, *North America,* **27 K4**
Hitra, *Norway,* **58 D3**
Hobart, *Australia, internal capital,* **38 J8**
Ho Chi Minh City, *Vietnam,* **44 E5**
Hohhot, *China,* **46 H2**
Hokkaido, *Japan,* **47 P2**
Holguin, *Cuba,* **27 J3**
Homs, *Syria,* **50 C5**
Homyel, *Belarus,* **59 J5**
Honduras, *North America, country,* **27 G4**
Honduras, Gulf of, *North America,* **27 G4**
Honefoss, *Norway,* **58 D3**
Hong Kong, *China,* **47 H6**
Honiara, *Solomon Islands, national capital,* **36 D5**
Honolulu, *U.S.A., internal capital,* **25 P7**
Honshu, *Japan,* **47 N3**
Horlivka, *Ukraine,* **56 D4**
Hormuz, Strait of, *Asia,* **51 G6**
Horn, Cape, *Chile,* **33 D11**
Horn Lake, *Sweden,* **58 F2**
Hotan, *China,* **48 D3**
Hotazel, *South Africa,* **72 D5**
Houston, *U.S.A.,* **25 G5**
Hradec Kralove, *Czech Republic,* **62 E1**
Hrodna, *Belarus,* **59 G5**
Huacrachuco, *Peru,* **30 C5**
Huaihua, *China,* **46 H5**
Huambo, *Angola,* **72 C2**
Huancayo, *Peru,* **30 C6**
Huang He, *China,* **47 H3**
Huanuco, *Peru,* **30 C5**
Huascaran, Mount, *Peru,* **30 C5**
Hubli, *India,* **49 D7**
Hudiksvall, *Sweden,* **58 F3**
Hudson Bay, *Canada,* **23 L3**
Hudson Strait, *Canada,* **23 M2**
Hue, *Vietnam,* **44 E4**
Huelva, *Spain,* **61 C7**
Hull, *United Kingdom,* **60 D3**
Hulun Lake, *China,* **47 J1**
Hungary, *Europe, country,* **59 F7**
Huntsville, *Canada,* **23 M4**
Huntsville, *U.S.A.,* **25 J4**
Hurghada, *Egypt,* **67 H3**
Huron, Lake, *U.S.A.,* **25 K2**
Hvannadalshnukur, *Iceland,* **58 P2**
Hwange, *Zimbabwe,* **72 E3**
Hyderabad, *India,* **49 D7**
Hyderabad, *Pakistan,* **48 B5**
Hyesan, *North Korea,* **47 L2**

i

Iasi, *Romania,* **63 H2**
Ibadan, *Nigeria,* **69 F7**
Ibague, *Colombia,* **30 C3**
Ibarra, *Ecuador,* **30 C3**
Ibb, *Yemen,* **51 D9**
Iberian Mountains, *Spain,* **61 D6**
Ibiza, *Spain,* **61 E7**
Ica, *Peru,* **30 C6**
Iceland, *Europe, country,* **58 P2**
Idaho, *U.S.A., internal admin. area,* **24 C2**
Idaho Falls, *U.S.A.,* **24 D2**
Ierapetra, *Greece,* **63 H5**
Iguacu Falls, *South America,* **32 H5**
Ihosy, *Madagascar,* **73 J4**
Ikopa, *Madagascar,* **73 J3**
Ilagan, *Philippines,* **45 H4**
Ilebo, *Democratic Republic of Congo,* **70 D4**
Ilheus, *Brazil,* **32 L2**
Iliamna Lake, *U.S.A.,* **22 D2**
Iligan, *Philippines,* **45 H6**
Illapel, *Chile,* **32 D6**
Illimani, Mount, *Bolivia,* **32 E3**
Illinois, *U.S.A., internal admin. area,* **25 J2**
Illizi, *Algeria,* **68 G3**
Ilmen, Lake, *Russia,* **58 J4**
Iloilo, *Philippines,* **45 H5**
Ilonga, *Tanzania,* **71 G5**
Ilorin, *Nigeria,* **69 F7**
Imperatriz, *Brazil,* **31 J5**
Imphal, *India,* **49 G6**
Inari, Lake, *Finland,* **58 H1**
Inchon, *South Korea,* **47 L3**
Indals, *Sweden,* **58 E3**
Inderbor, *Kazakhstan,* **57 G4**
India, *Asia, country,* **49 D6**
Indiana, *U.S.A., internal admin. area,* **25 J2**
Indianapolis, *U.S.A., internal capital,* **25 J3**
Indian Ocean, 19
Indonesia, *Asia, country,* **42 C5**
Indore, *India,* **49 D6**
Indus, *Asia,* **48 B5**
Ingolstadt, *Germany,* **60 G4**
Inhambane, *Mozambique,* **73 G4**
Inner Mongolia, *China,* **47 H2**
Innsbruck, *Austria,* **62 D2**
Inukjuak, *Canada,* **23 M3**
Inuvik, *Canada,* **22 F2**
Invercargill, *New Zealand,* **39 N9**
Inyangani, *Zimbabwe,* **73 F3**
Ioannina, *Greece,* **63 G4**
Ionian Sea, *Europe,* **63 F4**
Iowa, *U.S.A., internal admin. area,* **25 H2**
Ipiales, *Colombia,* **30 C3**
Ipoh, *Malaysia,* **42 B3**
Ipswich, *United Kingdom,* **60 E3**
Iqaluit, *Canada, internal capital,* **23 N2**
Iquique, *Chile,* **32 D4**
Iquitos, *Peru,* **30 D4**
Irakleio, *Greece,* **63 H5**
Iran, *Asia, country,* **50 F5**
Iranshahr, *Iran,* **51 H6**
Iraq, *Asia, country,* **50 D5**
Irbid, *Jordan,* **50 C5**
Ireland, *Europe, country,* **60 B3**
Iringa, *Tanzania,* **71 G5**
Irish Sea, *Europe,* **60 C3**
Irkutsk, *Russia,* **53 F3**
Irrawaddy, *Burma,* **44 C4**
Irrawaddy, Mouths of the, *Burma,* **44 B4**
Irtysh, *Asia,* **52 D3**
Isabela, *Ecuador,* **30 N10**
Isafjordhur, *Iceland,* **58 N2**
Isiro, *Democratic Republic of Congo,* **70 E3**
Islamabad, *Pakistan, national capital,* **48 C4**
Isle of Man, *Europe,* **60 C3**
Isle of Wight, *United Kingdom,* **60 D4**
Ismailia, *Egypt,* **67 H2**
Isoka, *Zambia,* **73 F2**
Isparta, *Turkey,* **63 J4**
Israel, *Asia, country,* **51 B5**
Issyk, Lake, *Kyrgyzstan,* **48 D2**
Istanbul, *Turkey,* **63 J3**
Itaituba, *Brazil,* **31 G4**
Itajai, *Brazil,* **32 J5**
Italy, *Europe, country,* **62 D2**
Itapetininga, *Brazil,* **32 J4**
Ivano-Frankivsk, *Ukraine,* **59 H6**
Ivanovo, *Russia,* **56 E2**
Ivdel, *Russia,* **57 J1**
Ivory Coast, *Africa, country,* **69 D7**
Ivujivik, *Canada,* **23 M2**
Izhevsk, *Russia,* **57 G2**
Izmir, *Turkey,* **63 H4**

j

Jabalpur, *India,* **49 D6**
Jackson, *Mississippi, U.S.A., internal capital,* **25 H4**
Jackson, *Tennessee, U.S.A.,* **25 J3**
Jacksonville, *U.S.A.,* **25 K4**
Jaen, *Spain,* **61 D7**
Jaffna, *Sri Lanka,* **49 E9**
Jaipur, *India,* **48 D5**
Jakarta, *Indonesia, national capital,* **42 C5**
Jalalabad, *Afghanistan,* **48 C4**
Jalal-Abad, *Kyrgyzstan,* **48 C2**
Jamaica, *North America, country,* **27 J4**
Jambi, *Indonesia,* **42 B4**
James Bay, *Canada,* **23 L3**
Jamestown, *U.S.A.,* **25 L2**
Jammu, *India,* **48 C4**
Jammu and Kashmir, *Asia,* **48 D4**
Jamnagar, *India,* **49 C6**
Jamshedpur, *India,* **49 F6**
Japan, *Asia, country,* **47 N3**
Japan, Sea of, *Asia,* **47 M2**
Japura, *Brazil,* **30 E4**
Jatai, *Brazil,* **32 H3**
Java, *Indonesia,* **42 C5**
Java Sea, *Indonesia,* **42 C5**
Jayapura, *Indonesia,* **43 K4**
Jedda, *Saudi Arabia,* **51 C7**
Jefferson City, *U.S.A., internal capital,* **25 H3**
Jekabpils, *Latvia,* **59 H4**
Jelgava, *Latvia,* **59 G4**
Jember, *Indonesia,* **42 D5**
Jerba, *Tunisia,* **66 D2**
Jerez de la Frontera, *Spain,* **61 C7**
Jerusalem, *Israel, national capital,* **51 C5**
Jhansi, *India,* **48 D5**
Jiamusi, *China,* **47 M1**
Jilin, *China,* **47 L2**
Jima, *Ethiopia,* **71 G2**
Jinhua, *China,* **47 J5**
Jining, *China,* **47 J3**
Jinja, *Uganda,* **71 F3**
Jinzhou, *China,* **47 K2**
Jixi, *China,* **47 M1**
Jizzax, *Uzbekistan,* **48 B2**
Joao Pessoa, *Brazil,* **31 M5**
Jodhpur, *India,* **48 C5**
Johannesburg, *South Africa,* **72 E5**
Johnston Atoll, *Oceania,* **36 G3**
Johor Bahru, *Malaysia,* **42 B3**
Jolo, *Philippines,* **45 H6**
Jonesboro, *U.S.A.,* **25 H3**
Jonkoping, *Sweden,* **59 E4**
Jordan, *Asia, country,* **51 C5**
Jorhat, *India,* **48 G5**
Jos, *Nigeria,* **70 A2**
Juan de Nova, *Africa,* **73 H3**
Juazeiro, *Brazil,* **31 K5**
Juazeiro do Norte, *Brazil,* **31 L5**
Juba, *Africa,* **71 H3**
Juba, *Sudan,* **71 F3**
Juchitan, *Mexico,* **26 E4**
Juiz de Fora, *Brazil,* **32 K4**
Juliaca, *Peru,* **30 D7**
Juneau, *U.S.A., internal capital,* **22 F3**
Jurmala, *Latvia,* **59 G4**
Jurua, *Brazil,* **30 E5**
Jutland, *Europe,* **59 D4**
Jyvaskyla, *Finland,* **58 H3**

k

K2, *Asia,* **48 D3**
Kaamanen, *Finland,* **58 H1**
Kabinda, *Democratic Republic of Congo,* **70 D5**
Kabul, *Afghanistan, national capital,* **48 B4**
Kabunda, *Democratic Republic of Congo,* **70 E6**
Kabwe, *Zambia,* **72 E2**
Kadoma, *Zimbabwe,* **72 E3**
Kaduna, *Nigeria,* **69 G6**
Kaedi, *Mauritania,* **69 C5**
Kafakumba, *Democratic Republic of Congo,* **70 D5**
Kafue, *Zambia,* **72 E3**
Kagoshima, *Japan,* **47 M4**
Kahramanmaras, *Turkey,* **50 C4**
Kahului, *U.S.A.,* **25 P7**
Kainji Reservoir, *Nigeria,* **69 F6**
Kairouan, *Tunisia,* **66 D1**
Kajaani, *Finland,* **58 H2**
Kakhovske Reservoir, *Ukraine,* **56 C4**
Kalahari Desert, *Africa,* **72 D4**
Kalamata, *Greece,* **63 G4**
Kalemie, *Democratic Republic of Congo,* **70 E5**
Kalgoorlie, *Australia,* **38 D6**
Kaliningrad, *Russia,* **59 G5**
Kalisz, *Poland,* **59 F6**
Kalkrand, *Namibia,* **72 C4**
Kalmar, *Sweden,* **59 F4**
Kaluga, *Russia,* **56 D3**
Kamanjab, *Namibia,* **72 B3**
Kama Reservoir, *Russia,* **57 H2**
Kamativi, *Zimbabwe,* **72 E3**
Kamchatka Peninsula, *Russia,* **53 H3**
Kamenka, *Russia,* **56 E3**
Kamina, *Democratic Republic of Congo,* **70 E5**
Kamloops, *Canada,* **22 G3**
Kampala, *Uganda, national capital,* **71 F3**
Kampong Cham, *Cambodia,* **44 E5**
Kampong Chhnang, *Cambodia,* **44 D5**
Kampong Saom, *Cambodia,* **44 D5**
Kamyanets-Podilskyy, *Ukraine,* **59 H6**
Kamyshin, *Russia,* **56 F3**
Kananga, *Democratic Republic of Congo,* **70 D5**
Kanazawa, *Japan,* **47 N3**
Kandahar, *Afghanistan,* **48 B4**
Kandalaksha, *Russia,* **58 K2**
Kandi, *Benin,* **69 F6**
Kandy, *Sri Lanka,* **49 E9**
Kang, *Botswana,* **72 D4**
Kangaroo Island, *Australia,* **38 G7**
Kanggye, *North Korea,* **47 L2**
Kankan, *Guinea,* **69 D6**
Kano, *Nigeria,* **66 C6**
Kanpur, *India,* **48 E5**
Kansas, *U.S.A., internal admin. area,* **24 G3**
Kansas City, *U.S.A.,* **25 H3**
Kanye, *Botswana,* **72 E4**
Kaohsiung, *Taiwan,* **47 K6**
Kaolack, *Senegal,* **69 B6**
Kara-Balta, *Kyrgyzstan,* **48 C2**
Karabuk, *Turkey,* **63 K3**
Karachi, *Pakistan,* **49 B6**
Karaj, *Iran,* **50 F4**
Karakol, *Kyrgyzstan,* **48 D2**
Karakorum Range, *Asia,* **48 D3**
Kara Kum Desert, *Turkmenistan,* **50 G3**
Karaman, *Turkey,* **63 K4**
Karamay, *China,* **48 E1**
Kara Sea, *Russia,* **52 D2**
Kariba, *Zimbabwe,* **72 E3**
Kariba, Lake, *Africa,* **72 E3**
Karibib, *Namibia,* **72 C4**
Karimata Strait, *Indonesia,* **42 C4**
Karlovac, *Croatia,* **62 E2**
Karlovy Vary, *Czech Republic,* **62 E1**
Karlshamn, *Sweden,* **59 E4**
Karlsruhe, *Germany,* **60 G4**
Karlstad, *Sweden,* **58 E4**
Karmoy, *Norway,* **58 C4**
Karonga, *Malawi,* **73 F1**
Karora, *Eritrea,* **67 J5**
Karpathos, *Greece,* **63 H5**
Karratha, *Australia,* **38 C4**
Kasai, *Africa,* **70 C4**
Kasama, *Zambia,* **72 F2**
Kashi, *China,* **48 D3**
Kassala, *Sudan,* **67 J5**
Kassel, *Germany,* **60 G4**
Kasungu, *Malawi,* **73 F2**
Kataba, *Zambia,* **72 E3**
Kathmandu, *Nepal, national capital,* **48 F5**
Katiola, *Ivory Coast,* **69 D7**
Katowice, *Poland,* **59 F6**
Katsina, *Nigeria,* **69 G6**
Kattegat, *Europe,* **59 D4**
Kauai, *U.S.A.,* **25 P7**
Kaukau Veld, *Africa,* **72 C4**
Kaunas, *Lithuania,* **59 G5**
Kavala, *Greece,* **63 H3**
Kawambwa, *Zambia,* **72 E1**
Kayes, *Mali,* **69 C6**
Kayseri, *Turkey,* **50 C4**
Kazakhstan, *Asia, country,* **52 C3**
Kazan, *Russia,* **57 F2**
Kaztalovka, *Kazakhstan,* **57 F4**
Kebnekaise, *Sweden,* **58 F2**
Kecskemet, *Hungary,* **59 F7**
Kedougou, *Senegal,* **69 C6**
Keetmanshoop, *Namibia,* **72 C5**

Kefallonia, *Greece,* **63 F4**
Keflavik, *Iceland,* **58 N2**
Kelowna, *Canada,* **22 H4**
Kempten, *Germany,* **60 G5**
Kendari, *Indonesia,* **43 F4**
Kenema, *Sierra Leone,* **69 C7**
Kenhardt, *South Africa,* **72 D5**
Kenitra, *Morocco,* **68 D2**
Kenora, *Canada,* **23 K4**
Kentucky, *U.S.A., internal admin. area,* **25 J3**
Kentucky Lake, *U.S.A.,* **25 J3**
Kenya, *Africa, country,* **71 G3**
Kenya, Mount, *Kenya,* **71 G4**
Kerch, *Ukraine,* **63 L2**
Kerema, *Papua New Guinea,* **43 L5**
Keren, *Eritrea,* **67 J5**
Kerkenah Islands, *Tunisia,* **66 D2**
Kermadec Islands, *New Zealand,* **39 Q6**
Kerman, *Iran,* **51 G5**
Kermanshah, *Iran,* **50 E5**
Key West, *U.S.A.,* **25 K6**
Khabarovsk, *Russia,* **53 G3**
Khanka, Lake, *Asia,* **47 M2**
Kharkiv, *Ukraine,* **56 D3**
Khartoum, *Sudan, national capital,* **67 H5**
Kherson, *Ukraine,* **56 C4**
Khmelnytskyy, *Ukraine,* **59 H6**
Khon Kaen, *Thailand,* **44 D4**
Khorugh, *Tajikistan,* **48 C3**
Khouribga, *Morocco,* **68 D2**
Khujand, *Tajikistan,* **48 B2**
Khulna, *Bangladesh,* **49 F6**
Kidal, *Mali,* **68 F5**
Kiel, *Germany,* **60 G3**
Kielce, *Poland,* **59 G6**
Kiev, *Ukraine, national capital,* **59 J6**
Kievske Reservoir, *Ukraine,* **56 C3**
Kiffa, *Mauritania,* **69 C5**
Kigali, *Rwanda, national capital,* **71 F4**
Kigoma, *Tanzania,* **70 E4**
Kikwit, *Democratic Republic of Congo,* **70 C5**
Kilimanjaro, *Africa,* **71 G4**
Kilwa, *Democratic Republic of Congo,* **70 E5**
Kimberley, *South Africa,* **72 D5**
Kimberley Plateau, *Australia,* **38 E3**
Kimchaek, *North Korea,* **47 L2**
Kindia, *Guinea,* **69 C6**
Kindu, *Democratic Republic of Congo,* **70 E4**
Kineshma, *Russia,* **56 E2**
King George Island, *Atlantic Ocean,* **33 G12**
Kingisepp, *Russia,* **58 J4**
King Island, *Australia,* **38 H7**
Kings Peak, *U.S.A.,* **24 D2**
Kingston, *Canada,* **23 M4**
Kingston, *Jamaica, national capital,* **27 J4**
Kingstown, *St. Vincent and the Grenadines, national capital,* **26 M5**
King William Island, *Canada,* **23 K2**
Kinkala, *Congo,* **70 B4**
Kinshasa, *Democratic Republic of Congo, national capital,* **70 C4**
Kipushi, *Democratic Republic of Congo,* **70 E6**
Kiribati, *Oceania, country,* **36 F5**
Kirikkale, *Turkey,* **63 K4**
Kirinyaga, *Kenya,* **71 G4**
Kirishi, *Russia,* **58 K4**
Kirkenes, *Norway,* **58 J1**
Kirkland Lake, *Canada,* **23 L4**
Kirkuk, *Iraq,* **50 D4**
Kirkwall, *United Kingdom,* **60 D2**
Kirov, *Russia,* **57 F2**
Kirovohrad, *Ukraine,* **56 C4**
Kiruna, *Sweden,* **58 G2**
Kisangani, *Democratic Republic of Congo,* **70 E3**
Kisii, *Kenya,* **71 F4**
Kismaayo, *Somalia,* **71 H4**
Kisumu, *Kenya,* **71 F4**
Kita, *Mali,* **69 D6**
Kitakyushu, *Japan,* **47 M4**
Kitale, *Kenya,* **71 G3**
Kitwe, *Zambia,* **72 E2**
Kiuruvesi, *Finland,* **58 H3**
Kivu, Lake, *Africa,* **70 E4**
Klagenfurt, *Austria,* **62 E2**
Klaipeda, *Lithuania,* **59 G5**
Klar, *Europe,* **58 E3**
Klintsy, *Russia,* **59 K5**
Knittelfeld, *Austria,* **62 E2**
Knoxville, *U.S.A.,* **25 K3**
Kobar Sink, *Ethiopia,* **67 K6**
Koblenz, *Germany,* **60 F4**
Kochi, *India,* **49 D9**
Kodiak Island, *U.S.A.,* **22 D3**
Koforidua, *Ghana,* **69 E7**
Kohtla-Jarve, *Estonia,* **58 H4**
Kokkola, *Finland,* **58 G3**
Kokshetau, *Kazakhstan,* **50 J1**
Kola Peninsula, *Russia,* **58 L2**
Kolda, *Senegal,* **69 C6**
Kolding, *Denmark,* **59 D5**
Kolhapur, *India,* **49 C7**
Kolkata, *India,* **49 F6**
Kolomna, *Russia,* **56 D2**
Kolwezi, *Democratic Republic of Congo,* **70 E6**
Kolyma Range, *Russia,* **53 H2**
Komsomolets, *Kazakhstan,* **57 J3**
Komsomolsk, *Russia,* **53 G3**
Konduz, *Afghanistan,* **48 B3**
Kongur Shan, *China,* **48 D3**
Konosha, *Russia,* **56 E1**
Konya, *Turkey,* **63 K4**
Korce, *Albania,* **63 G3**
Korea Bay, *Asia,* **47 K3**
Korea Strait, *Asia,* **47 L4**
Korhogo, *Ivory Coast,* **69 D7**
Korla, *China,* **48 F2**
Koror, *Palau, national capital,* **36 A4**
Korosten, *Ukraine,* **59 J6**
Kosciuszko, Mount, *Australia,* **39 J7**
Kosice, *Slovakia,* **59 G6**
Kosti, *Sudan,* **67 H6**
Kostomuksha, *Russia,* **58 J2**
Kostroma, *Russia,* **56 E2**
Koszalin, *Poland,* **59 F5**
Kota, *India,* **48 D5**
Kota Bharu, *Malaysia,* **42 B2**
Kota Kinabalu, *Malaysia,* **42 E2**
Kotka, *Finland,* **58 H3**
Kotlas, *Russia,* **57 F1**
Koudougou, *Burkina Faso,* **69 E6**
Koutiala, *Mali,* **69 D6**
Kouvola, *Finland,* **58 H3**
Kovel, *Ukraine,* **59 H6**
Kozhikode, *India,* **49 D8**
Kragujevac, *Serbia and Montenegro,* **63 G2**
Krakatoa, *Indonesia,* **42 C5**
Krakow, *Poland,* **59 G6**
Kraljevo, *Serbia and Montenegro,* **63 G3**
Kramatorsk, *Ukraine,* **56 D4**
Kranj, *Slovenia,* **62 E2**
Krasnodar, *Russia,* **50 C2**
Krasnoyarsk, *Russia,* **52 E3**
Kremenchuk, *Ukraine,* **56 C4**
Kremenchukske Reservoir, *Ukraine,* **56 C4**
Krishna, *India,* **49 D7**
Kristiansand, *Norway,* **58 C4**
Kristiansund, *Norway,* **58 C3**
Krong Kaoh Kong, *Cambodia,* **44 D5**
Kroonstad, *South Africa,* **72 E5**
Krugersdorp, *South Africa,* **72 E5**
Kryvyy Rih, *Ukraine,* **56 C4**
Kuala Lumpur, *Malaysia, national capital,* **42 B3**
Kuala Terengganu, *Malaysia,* **42 B2**
Kuantan, *Malaysia,* **42 B3**
Kuching, *Malaysia,* **42 D3**
Kuhmo, *Finland,* **58 J2**
Kuito, *Angola,* **72 C2**
Kulob, *Tajikistan,* **48 B3**
Kumamoto, *Japan,* **47 M4**
Kumanovo, *Macedonia,* **63 G3**
Kumasi, *Ghana,* **69 E7**
Kumba, *Cameroon,* **70 A3**
Kumo, *Nigeria,* **66 D6**
Kunlun Mountains, *China,* **48 E3**
Kunming, *China,* **46 F5**
Kuopio, *Finland,* **58 H2**
Kupang, *Indonesia,* **43 F6**
Kuressaare, *Estonia,* **59 G4**
Kurgan, *Russia,* **57 K2**
Kurikka, *Finland,* **58 G3**
Kuril Islands, *Russia,* **53 H3**
Kursk, *Russia,* **56 D3**
Kushiro, *Japan,* **47 P2**
Kutahya, *Turkey,* **63 J4**
Kutaisi, *Georgia,* **50 D3**
Kutch, Rann of, *India,* **49 B6**
Kuujjuaq, *Canada,* **23 N3**
Kuusamo, *Finland,* **58 J2**
Kuwait, *Asia, country,* **51 E6**
Kuwait City, *Kuwait, national capital,* **51 E6**
Kuybyshev Reservoir, *Russia,* **57 F3**
Kuyto, Lake, *Russia,* **58 K2**
Kuytun, *China,* **48 F2**
Kwangju, *South Korea,* **47 L3**
Kyoga, Lake, *Uganda,* **71 F3**
Kyoto, *Japan,* **47 N3**
Kyrenia, *Cyprus,* **63 K5**
Kyrgyzstan, *Asia, country,* **48 C2**
Kythira, *Greece,* **63 G4**
Kyushu, *Japan,* **47 M4**
Kyzyl, *Russia,* **52 E3**

L

Laayoune, *Western Sahara, national capital,* **68 C3**
Labe, *Guinea,* **69 C6**
Labrador City, *Canada,* **23 N3**
Labrador Sea, *North America,* **23 P2**
La Chorrera, *Colombia,* **30 D4**
La Coruna, *Spain,* **61 B6**
Ladoga, Lake, *Russia,* **58 J3**
Ladysmith, *South Africa,* **72 E5**
Lae, *Papua New Guinea,* **43 L5**
Lagdo Reservoir, *Cameroon,* **70 B2**
La Gomera, *Canary Islands,* **68 B3**
Lagos, *Nigeria,* **69 F7**
Lagos, *Portugal,* **61 B7**
La Grande Reservoir, *Canada,* **23 M3**
Lagunillas, *Venezuela,* **30 D1**
Lahat, *Indonesia,* **42 B4**
Lahore, *Pakistan,* **48 C4**
Lahti, *Finland,* **58 H3**
Lai, *Chad,* **70 C2**
La Libertad, *Ecuador,* **30 B4**
Lambarene, *Gabon,* **70 B4**
Lamia, *Greece,* **63 G4**
Lancaster Sound, *Canada,* **23 L1**
Land's End, *United Kingdom,* **60 C4**
Langanes, *Iceland,* **58 Q2**
Langsa, *Indonesia,* **42 A3**
Lansing, *U.S.A., internal capital,* **25 K2**
Lanzarote, *Canary Islands,* **68 C3**
Lanzhou, *China,* **46 F3**
Laoag, *Philippines,* **45 H4**
Lao Cai, *Vietnam,* **44 D3**
La Oroya, *Peru,* **30 C6**
Laos, *Asia, country,* **44 D4**
La Palma, *Canary Islands,* **68 B3**
La Palma, *Panama,* **27 J6**
La Paz, *Bolivia, national capital,* **32 E3**
La Paz, *Mexico,* **26 B3**
La Perouse Strait, *Asia,* **47 P1**
Lapland, *Europe,* **58 H1**
La Plata, *Argentina,* **32 G6**
Lappeenranta, *Finland,* **58 J3**
Laptev Sea, *Russia,* **53 G2**
Larache, *Morocco,* **68 D1**
Laredo, *U.S.A.,* **24 G5**
La Rioja, *Argentina,* **32 E5**
Larisa, *Greece,* **63 G4**
Larkana, *Pakistan,* **48 B5**
Larnaca, *Cyprus,* **63 K5**
La Rochelle, *France,* **61 D5**
La Romana, *Dominican Republic,* **27 L4**
Larvik, *Norway,* **58 D4**
Lashio, *Burma,* **44 C3**
Lastoursville, *Gabon,* **70 B4**
Las Vegas, *U.S.A.,* **24 C3**
Latakia, *Syria,* **50 C4**
Latvia, *Europe, country,* **59 H4**
Launceston, *Australia,* **38 J8**
Lausanne, *Switzerland,* **62 C2**
Lautoka, *Fiji,* **39 Q3**
Lebanon, *Asia, country,* **50 C5**
Lecce, *Italy,* **63 F3**
Ledo, Cape, *Angola,* **72 B1**
Leeds, *United Kingdom,* **60 D3**
Leeuwarden, *Netherlands,* **60 F3**
Leeuwin, Cape, *Australia,* **38 B6**
Leeward Islands, *North America,* **26 M4**
Legaspi, *Philippines,* **45 H5**
Legnica, *Poland,* **59 F6**
Le Havre, *France,* **60 E4**
Leipzig, *Germany,* **60 H4**
Leiria, *Portugal,* **61 B7**
Le Mans, *France,* **60 E4**
Lena, *Russia,* **53 G2**
Leon, *Mexico,* **26 D3**
Leon, *Nicaragua,* **27 G5**
Leon, *Spain,* **61 C6**
Leonardville, *Namibia,* **72 C4**
Lerida, *Spain,* **61 E6**
Lerwick, *United Kingdom,* **60 D1**
Les Cayes, *Haiti,* **27 K4**
Leshan, *China,* **46 F5**
Leskovac, *Serbia and Montenegro,* **63 G3**
Lesotho, *Africa, country,* **72 E5**
Lesser Antilles, *North America,* **26 M5**
Lesser Sunda Islands, *Indonesia,* **42 E5**
Lesvos, *Greece,* **63 H4**
Lethbridge, *Canada,* **22 H4**
Leticia, *Brazil,* **30 E4**
Lewiston, *U.S.A.,* **24 C1**
Lexington, *U.S.A.,* **25 K3**
Lhasa, *China,* **48 G5**
Lhokseumawe, *Indonesia,* **42 A2**
Lianyungang, *China,* **47 J4**
Liaoyuan, *China,* **47 L2**
Liberec, *Czech Republic,* **62 E1**
Liberia, *Africa, country,* **69 D7**
Liberia, *Costa Rica,* **27 G5**
Libreville, *Gabon, national capital,* **70 A3**
Libya, *Africa, country,* **66 E3**
Libyan Desert, *Africa,* **66 F3**
Lichinga, *Mozambique,* **73 G2**
Lida, *Belarus,* **59 H5**
Lidkoping, *Sweden,* **58 E4**
Liechtenstein, *Europe, country,* **62 D2**
Liege, *Belgium,* **60 F4**
Lieksa, *Finland,* **58 J3**
Liepaja, *Latvia,* **59 G4**
Ligurian Sea, *Europe,* **62 C3**
Likasi, *Democratic Republic of Congo,* **70 E6**
Lille, *France,* **60 E4**
Lillehammer, *Norway,* **58 D3**
Lilongwe, *Malawi, national capital,* **73 F2**
Lima, *Peru, national capital,* **30 C6**
Limassol, *Cyprus,* **63 K5**
Limerick, *Ireland,* **60 B3**
Limnos, *Greece,* **56 C3**
Limoges, *France,* **61 E5**
Limon, *Costa Rica,* **27 H5**
Limpopo, *Africa,* **72 F4**
Linares, *Chile,* **33 D7**
Linchuan, *China,* **47 J5**
Lincoln, *U.S.A., internal capital,* **25 G2**
Lindi, *Tanzania,* **71 G6**
Line Islands, *Kiribati,* **37 H4**
Linhares, *Brazil,* **32 K3**
Linkoping, *Sweden,* **58 E4**
Linz, *Austria,* **62 E1**
Lions, Gulf of, *Europe,* **61 F6**
Lipari Islands, *Italy,* **62 E4**
Lipetsk, *Russia,* **56 D3**
Lisbon, *Portugal, national capital,* **61 B7**
Lithuania, *Europe, country,* **59 G5**
Little Andaman, *India,* **49 G8**
Little Rock, *U.S.A., internal capital,* **25 H4**
Liuzhou, *China,* **46 G6**

Liverpool, *United Kingdom,* **60 D3**
Livingstone, *Zambia,* **72 E3**
Livorno, *Italy,* **62 D3**
Liwale, *Tanzania,* **71 G5**
Ljubljana, *Slovenia, national capital,* **62 E2**
Llanos, *South America,* **30 D2**
Lloydminster, *Canada,* **22 J3**
Lobamba, *Lesotho, national capital,* **72 F5**
Lodz, *Poland,* **59 F6**
Lofoten, *Norway,* **58 E1**
Logan, Mount, *Canada,* **22 F2**
Logrono, *Spain,* **61 D6**
Loire, *France,* **60 E5**
Loja, *Ecuador,* **30 C4**
Lokan Reservoir, *Finland,* **58 H2**
Lolland, *Denmark,* **59 D5**
Lombok, *Indonesia,* **42 E5**
Lome, *Togo, national capital,* **69 F7**
London, *Canada,* **23 L4**
London, *United Kingdom, national capital,* **60 D4**
Londonderry, *United Kingdom,* **60 C3**
Londrina, *Brazil,* **32 H4**
Long Island, *The Bahamas,* **25 L6**
Long Xuyen, *Vietnam,* **44 E5**
Lopez, Cape, *Gabon,* **70 A4**
Lop Lake, *China,* **48 G2**
Lord Howe Island, *Australia,* **39 L6**
Los Angeles, *Chile,* **33 D7**
Los Angeles, *U.S.A.,* **24 C4**
Los Mochis, *Mexico,* **26 C2**
Louangphrabang, *Laos,* **44 D4**
Loubomo, *Congo,* **70 B4**
Louga, *Senegal,* **69 B5**
Louisiana, *U.S.A., internal admin. area,* **25 H4**
Lower California, *Mexico,* **26 B2**
Loyalty Islands, *New Caledonia,* **39 N4**
Luacano, *Angola,* **72 D2**
Luanda, *Angola, national capital,* **72 B1**
Luangwa, *Africa,* **72 F2**
Luanshya, *Zambia,* **72 E2**
Lubango, *Angola,* **72 B2**
Lubbock, *U.S.A.,* **24 F4**
Lublin, *Poland,* **59 G6**
Lubny, *Ukraine,* **56 C3**
Lubumbashi, *Democratic Republic of Congo,* **70 E6**
Lucena, *Philippines,* **45 H5**
Lucerne, *Switzerland,* **62 D2**
Lucira, *Angola,* **72 B2**
Lucknow, *India,* **48 E5**
Luderitz, *Namibia,* **72 C5**
Ludhiana, *India,* **48 D4**
Ludza, *Latvia,* **59 H4**
Luena, *Angola,* **72 C2**
Luganville, *Vanuatu,* **39 N3**
Lugo, *Spain,* **61 C6**
Luhansk, *Ukraine,* **56 D4**
Luiana, *Angola,* **72 D3**
Lukulu, *Zambia,* **72 D2**
Lumbala Kaquengue, *Angola,* **72 D2**
Lumbala Nguimbo, *Angola,* **72 D2**
Lundazi, *Zambia,* **73 F2**
Lupilichi, *Mozambique,* **73 G2**
Lusaka, *Zambia, national capital,* **72 E3**
Lutsk, *Ukraine,* **59 H6**
Luxembourg, *Europe, country,* **60 F4**
Luxembourg, *Luxembourg, national capital,* **60 F4**
Luxor, *Egypt,* **67 H3**
Luzhou, *China,* **46 G5**
Luzon, *Philippines,* **45 H4**
Luzon Strait, *Philippines,* **45 H4**
Lviv, *Ukraine,* **59 H6**
Lyon, *France,* **61 F5**
Lysychansk, *Ukraine,* **56 D4**

m

Maan, *Jordan,* **51 C5**
Maastricht, *Netherlands,* **60 F4**
Macae, *Brazil,* **32 K4**
Macapa, *Brazil,* **31 H3**
Macau, *China,* **47 H6**
Macedonia, *Europe, country,* **63 G3**
Maceio, *Brazil,* **31 L5**
Machakos, *Kenya,* **71 G4**
Machala, *Ecuador,* **30 C4**
Machu Picchu, *Peru,* **30 D6**
Mackay, *Australia,* **39 J4**
Mackenzie, *Canada,* **22 G2**
Mackenzie Bay, *Canada,* **22 F2**
Mackenzie Mountains, *Canada,* **22 F2**
Macon, *U.S.A.,* **25 K4**
Madagascar, *Africa, country,* **73 J4**
Madang, *Papua New Guinea,* **43 L5**
Madeira, *Atlantic Ocean,* **68 B2**
Madeira, *Brazil,* **30 F5**
Madingou, *Congo,* **70 B4**
Madison, *U.S.A., internal capital,* **25 J2**
Madras, *India,* **49 E8**
Madrid, *Spain, national capital,* **61 D6**
Madurai, *India,* **49 D9**
Maevatanana, *Madagascar,* **73 J3**
Mafeteng, *Lesotho,* **72 E5**
Mafia Island, *Tanzania,* **71 H5**
Magadan, *Russia,* **53 H3**
Magangue, *Colombia,* **30 D2**
Magdalena, *Bolivia,* **32 F2**
Magdeburg, *Germany,* **60 G3**
Magellan, Strait of, *South America,* **33 E10**
Magnitogorsk, *Russia,* **57 H3**
Mahajanga, *Madagascar,* **73 J3**
Mahalapye, *Botswana,* **72 E4**
Mahilyow, *Belarus,* **59 J5**
Mahon, *Spain,* **61 F7**
Maiduguri, *Nigeria,* **66 D6**
Mai-Ndombe, Lake, *Democratic Republic of Congo,* **70 C4**
Maine, *U.S.A., internal admin. area,* **25 N1**
Maine, Gulf of, *U.S.A.,* **25 N2**
Maio, *Cape Verde,* **69 M11**
Majorca, *Spain,* **61 E7**
Majuro, *Marshall Islands, national capital,* **36 E4**
Makarikari, *Botswana,* **72 D4**
Makassar Strait, *Indonesia,* **43 E4**
Makeni, *Sierra Leone,* **69 C7**
Makgadikgadi Pans, *Botswana,* **72 D4**
Makhachkala, *Russia,* **50 E3**
Makkovik, *Canada,* **23 P3**
Makokou, *Gabon,* **70 B3**
Makumbako, *Tanzania,* **71 F5**
Makurdi, *Nigeria,* **70 A2**
Mala, *Peru,* **30 C6**
Malabo, *Equatorial Guinea, national capital,* **70 A3**
Maladzyechna, *Belarus,* **59 H5**
Malaga, *Spain,* **61 C7**
Malaimbandy, *Madagascar,* **73 J4**
Malakal, *Sudan,* **71 F2**
Malakula, *Vanuatu,* **39 N3**
Malang, *Indonesia,* **42 D5**
Malanje, *Angola,* **72 C1**
Malar, Lake, *Sweden,* **58 F4**
Malatya, *Turkey,* **50 C4**
Malawi, *Africa, country,* **73 F2**
Malawi, Lake, *Africa,* **71 F6**
Malaysia, *Asia, country,* **42 B2**
Maldives, *Asia, country,* **49 C9**
Male, *Maldives, national capital,* **49 C10**
Malegaon, *India,* **49 C6**
Mali, *Africa, country,* **68 E5**
Malindi, *Kenya,* **71 H4**
Malmo, *Sweden,* **59 E5**
Malpelo Island, *Colombia,* **30 B3**
Malta, *Europe, country,* **62 E4**
Mamoudzou, *Mayotte,* **73 J2**
Mamuno, *Botswana,* **72 D4**
Man, *Ivory Coast,* **69 D7**
Manado, *Indonesia,* **43 F3**
Managua, *Nicaragua, national capital,* **27 G5**
Manakara, *Madagascar,* **73 J4**
Manama, *Bahrain, national capital,* **51 F6**
Manaus, *Brazil,* **31 G4**
Manchester, *United Kingdom,* **60 D3**
Manchuria, *China,* **47 K2**
Mandalay, *Burma,* **44 C3**
Mandera, *Kenya,* **71 H3**
Mandritsara, *Madagascar,* **73 J3**
Mandurah, *Australia,* **38 C6**
Mangalore, *India,* **49 C8**
Mania, *Madagascar,* **73 J3**
Manicouagan Reservoir, *Canada,* **23 N3**
Manila, *Philippines, national capital,* **45 H5**
Manisa, *Turkey,* **63 H4**
Man, Isle of, *Europe,* **60 C3**
Manitoba, *Canada, internal admin. area,* **23 K3**
Manitoba, Lake, *Canada,* **23 K3**
Manizales, *Colombia,* **30 C2**
Manja, *Madagascar,* **73 H4**
Mannar, *Sri Lanka,* **49 E9**
Mannar, Gulf of, *Asia,* **49 D9**
Mannheim, *Germany,* **60 G4**
Mansa, *Zambia,* **72 E2**
Manta, *Ecuador,* **30 B4**
Manzhouli, *China,* **53 F3**
Mao, *Chad,* **66 E6**
Maoke Range, *Indonesia,* **43 J4**
Maputo, *Mozambique, national capital,* **73 F5**
Maraba, *Brazil,* **31 J5**
Maracaibo, *Venezuela,* **30 D1**
Maracaibo, Lake, *Venezuela,* **30 D2**
Maracay, *Venezuela,* **30 E1**
Maradi, *Niger,* **66 C6**
Maranon, *Peru,* **30 C4**
Marathon, *Canada,* **23 L4**
Mar del Plata, *Argentina,* **33 G7**
Margarita Island, *Venezuela,* **30 F1**
Margherita Peak, *Africa,* **70 E3**
Marib, *Yemen,* **51 E8**
Maribor, *Slovenia,* **62 E2**
Marie Byrd Land, *Antarctica,* **77 Q3**
Mariental, *Namibia,* **72 C4**
Marijampole, *Lithuania,* **59 G5**
Marilia, *Brazil,* **32 J4**
Marimba, *Angola,* **72 C1**
Mariupol, *Ukraine,* **56 D4**
Marka, *Somalia,* **71 H3**
Marmara, Sea of, *Turkey,* **63 J3**
Maroantsetra, *Madagascar,* **73 J3**
Maroua, *Cameroon,* **70 B1**
Marquesas Islands, *French Polynesia,* **37 K5**
Marrakech, *Morocco,* **68 D2**
Marra, Mount, *Sudan,* **66 F6**
Marsa Matruh, *Egypt,* **67 G2**
Marseille, *France,* **61 F6**
Marshall Islands, *Oceania, country,* **36 D3**
Martapura, *Indonesia,* **42 D4**
Martinique, *North America,* **26 M5**
Mary, *Turkmenistan,* **50 H4**
Maryland, *U.S.A., internal admin. area,* **25 L3**
Masaka, *Uganda,* **71 F4**
Masasi, *Tanzania,* **71 G6**
Masbate, *Philippines,* **45 H5**
Maseru, *Lesotho, national capital,* **72 E5**
Mashhad, *Iran,* **50 G4**
Masirah Island, *Oman,* **51 G7**
Massachusetts, *U.S.A., internal admin. area,* **25 M2**
Massangena, *Mozambique,* **73 F4**
Massawa, *Eritrea,* **67 J5**
Massif Central, *France,* **61 E5**
Massinga, *Mozambique,* **73 G4**
Masvingo, *Zimbabwe,* **72 F4**
Matagalpa, *Nicaragua,* **27 G5**
Matala, *Angola,* **72 B2**
Matamoros, *Mexico,* **26 E2**
Matanzas, *Cuba,* **27 H3**
Mataram, *Indonesia,* **42 E5**
Mataro, *Spain,* **61 E6**
Matehuala, *Mexico,* **26 D3**
Mato Grosso, Plateau of, *Brazil,* **31 G6**
Matsuyama, *Japan,* **47 M4**
Maturin, *Venezuela,* **30 F2**
Maui, *U.S.A.,* **25 P7**
Maun, *Botswana,* **72 D3**
Mauritania, *Africa, country,* **68 C5**
Mauritius, *Indian Ocean, country,* **73 L3**
Mavinga, *Angola,* **72 D3**
Mayotte, *Africa,* **73 J2**
Mazar-e Sharif, *Afghanistan,* **48 B3**
Mazatlan, *Mexico,* **26 C3**
Mazyr, *Belarus,* **59 J5**
Mbabane, *Swaziland, national capital,* **72 F5**
Mbala, *Zambia,* **72 F1**
Mbale, *Uganda,* **71 F3**
Mbandaka, *Democratic Republic of Congo,* **70 C3**
Mbarara, *Uganda,* **71 F4**
Mbeya, *Tanzania,* **71 F5**
Mbuji-Mayi, *Democratic Republic of Congo,* **70 D5**
McClintock Channel, *Canada,* **22 J1**
McClure Strait, *Canada,* **22 G1**
McKinley, Mount, *U.S.A.,* **22 D2**
Mead, Lake, *U.S.A.,* **24 D3**
Mecca, *Saudi Arabia,* **51 C7**
Mecula, *Mozambique,* **73 G2**
Medan, *Indonesia,* **42 A3**
Medellin, *Colombia,* **30 C2**
Medford, *U.S.A.,* **24 B2**
Medina, *Saudi Arabia,* **51 C7**
Mediterranean Sea, *Africa/Europe,* **19**
Medvezhyegorsk, *Russia,* **58 K3**
Meerut, *India,* **48 D5**
Meiktila, *Burma,* **44 C3**
Meizhou, *China,* **47 J6**
Mekele, *Ethiopia,* **71 G1**
Meknes, *Morocco,* **68 D2**
Mekong, *Asia,* **44 E5**
Melaka, *Malaysia,* **42 B3**
Melamo, Cape, *Mozambique,* **73 H2**
Melanesia, *Oceania,* **36 D5**
Melbourne, *Australia, internal capital,* **38 H7**
Melilla, *Africa,* **61 D7**
Melitopol, *Ukraine,* **56 D4**
Melo, *Uruguay,* **32 H6**
Melville Island, *Australia,* **38 F2**
Melville Island, *Canada,* **22 H1**
Melville Peninsula, *Canada,* **23 L2**
Memphis, *U.S.A.,* **25 J3**
Mendoza, *Argentina,* **32 E6**
Menongue, *Angola,* **72 C2**
Mentawai Islands, *Indonesia,* **42 A4**
Menzel Bourguiba, *Tunisia,* **66 C1**
Mergui, *Burma,* **44 C5**
Mergui Archipelago, *Burma,* **44 C5**
Merida, *Mexico,* **26 G3**
Meridian, *U.S.A.,* **25 J4**
Merlo, *Argentina,* **32 E6**
Mersin, *Turkey,* **50 B4**
Meru, *Kenya,* **71 G3**
Messina, *Italy,* **62 E4**
Messina, *South Africa,* **72 F4**
Metz, *France,* **60 F4**
Mexicali, *Mexico,* **26 A1**
Mexico, *North America, country,* **26 D3**
Mexico City, *Mexico, national capital,* **26 E4**
Mexico, Gulf of, *North America,* **26 F3**
Mexico, Plateau of, *Mexico,* **26 D2**
Miami, *U.S.A.,* **25 K5**
Michigan, *U.S.A., internal admin. area,* **25 J2**
Michigan, Lake, *U.S.A.,* **25 J2**
Michurinsk, *Russia,* **56 E3**
Micronesia, *Oceania,* **36 C4**
Micronesia, Federated States of, *Oceania, country,* **36 C4**
Middlesbrough, *United Kingdom,* **60 D3**
Midway Islands, *Pacific Ocean,* **36 F2**
Mikkeli, *Finland,* **58 H3**
Milan, *Italy,* **62 D2**
Milange, *Mozambique,* **73 G3**
Mildura, *Australia,* **38 H6**
Milwaukee, *U.S.A.,* **25 J2**
Minas, *Uruguay,* **32 G6**
Mindanao, *Philippines,* **45 H6**
Mindelo, *Cape Verde,* **69 M11**
Mindoro, *Philippines,* **45 H5**
Mingacevir, *Azerbaijan,* **50 E3**
Minna, *Nigeria,* **69 G7**

Minneapolis, *U.S.A.,* **25 H2**
Minnesota, *U.S.A., internal admin. area,* **25 G1**
Minorca, *Spain,* **61 E6**
Minot, *U.S.A.,* **24 F1**
Minsk, *Belarus, national capital,* **59 H5**
Miri, *Malaysia,* **42 D3**
Mirim Lake, *Brazil,* **32 H6**
Miskolc, *Hungary,* **59 G6**
Misool, *Indonesia,* **43 H4**
Misratah, *Libya,* **66 E2**
Mississippi, *U.S.A.,* **25 H4**
Mississippi, *U.S.A., internal admin. area,* **25 H4**
Mississippi Delta, *U.S.A.,* **25 J5**
Missoula, *U.S.A.,* **24 D1**
Missouri, *U.S.A.,* **24 G2**
Missouri, *U.S.A., internal admin. area,* **25 H3**
Mistassini, Lake, *Canada,* **23 M3**
Mitwaba, *Democratic Republic of Congo,* **70 E5**
Mkushi, *Zambia,* **72 E2**
Mmabatho, *South Africa,* **72 E5**
Moanda, *Gabon,* **70 B4**
Mobile, *U.S.A.,* **25 J4**
Mochudi, *Botswana,* **72 E4**
Mocuba, *Mozambique,* **73 G3**
Modena, *Italy,* **62 D2**
Mogadishu, *Somalia, national capital,* **71 J3**
Mogao Caves, *China,* **46 E2**
Mohilla Island, *Comoros,* **73 H2**
Mo i Rana, *Norway,* **58 E2**
Mojave Desert, *U.S.A.,* **24 C4**
Moldova, *Europe, country,* **63 J2**
Moldoveanu, Mount, *Romania,* **56 C4**
Molepolole, *Botswana,* **72 E4**
Mollendo, *Peru,* **30 D7**
Molokai, *U.S.A.,* **25 P7**
Molopo, *Africa,* **72 D5**
Molucca Sea, *Indonesia,* **43 F4**
Mombasa, *Kenya,* **71 G4**
Monaco, *Europe, country,* **61 F6**
Monastir, *Tunisia,* **66 D1**
Monchegorsk, *Russia,* **58 K2**
Monclova, *Mexico,* **26 D2**
Moncton, *Canada,* **23 N4**
Mongo, *Chad,* **66 E6**
Mongolia, *Asia, country,* **46 F1**
Mongu, *Zambia,* **72 D3**
Monrovia, *Liberia, national capital,* **69 C7**
Montalvo, *Ecuador,* **30 C4**
Montana, *U.S.A., internal admin. area,* **24 E1**
Montauban, *France,* **61 E5**
Montego Bay, *Jamaica,* **27 J4**
Monterrey, *Mexico,* **26 D2**
Montes Claros, *Brazil,* **32 K3**
Montevideo, *Uruguay, national capital,* **32 G6**
Montgomery, *U.S.A., internal capital,* **25 J4**
Montpelier, *U.S.A., internal capital,* **25 M2**
Montpellier, *France,* **61 E6**
Montreal, *Canada,* **23 M4**
Montserrat, *North America,* **26 M4**
Monywa, *Burma,* **44 C3**
Moose Jaw, *Canada,* **22 J3**
Mopti, *Mali,* **69 E6**
Moree, *Australia,* **39 J5**
Morelia, *Mexico,* **26 D4**
Morocco, *Africa, country,* **68 D2**
Morogoro, *Tanzania,* **71 G5**
Morombe, *Madagascar,* **73 H4**
Moroni, *Comoros, national capital,* **73 H2**
Morotai, *Indonesia,* **43 G3**
Morpara, *Brazil,* **32 K2**
Moscow, *Russia, national capital,* **56 D2**
Moshi, *Tanzania,* **71 G4**
Mosquitos, Gulf of, *North America,* **27 H5**
Mossendjo, *Congo,* **70 B4**
Mossoro, *Brazil,* **31 L5**
Most, *Czech Republic,* **62 E1**
Mostaganem, *Algeria,* **68 F1**
Mostar, *Bosnia and Herzegovina,* **62 F3**
Mosul, *Iraq,* **50 D4**
Moulmein, *Burma,* **44 C4**
Moundou, *Chad,* **70 C2**
Mount Gambier, *Australia,* **38 H7**
Mount Hagen, *Papua New Guinea,* **43 K5**
Mount Isa, *Australia,* **38 G4**
Mount Li, *China,* **46 G4**
Moyale, *Ethiopia,* **71 G3**
Moyobamba, *Peru,* **30 C5**
Mozambique, *Africa, country,* **73 F3**
Mozambique, *Mozambique,* **73 H3**
Mozambique Channel, *Africa,* **73 G4**
Mpika, *Zambia,* **72 F2**
Mtwara, *Tanzania,* **71 H6**
Mudanjiang, *China,* **47 L2**
Mueda, *Mozambique,* **73 G2**
Mufulira, *Zambia,* **72 E2**
Multan, *Pakistan,* **48 C4**
Mumbai, *India,* **49 C7**
Mumbue, *Angola,* **72 C2**
Munhango, *Angola,* **72 C2**
Munich, *Germany,* **60 G4**
Munster, *Germany,* **60 F4**
Murcia, *Spain,* **61 D7**
Murmansk, *Russia,* **58 K1**
Murom, *Russia,* **56 E2**
Murray, *Australia,* **38 G6**
Murzuq, *Libya,* **66 D3**
Muscat, *Oman, national capital,* **51 G7**
Mutare, *Zimbabwe,* **73 F3**
Mutoko, *Zimbabwe,* **72 F3**
Mutsamudu, *Comoros,* **73 H2**
Mutshatsha, *Democratic Republic of Congo,* **70 D6**
Mwali, *Comoros,* **73 H2**
Mwanza, *Tanzania,* **71 F4**
Mwene-Ditu, *Democratic Republic of Congo,* **70 D5**
Mweru, Lake, *Africa,* **72 E1**
Mwinilunga, *Zambia,* **72 D2**
Myanmar, *Asia, country,* **44 C3**
Myitkyina, *Burma,* **44 C2**
Mykolayiv, *Ukraine,* **56 C4**
Mysore, *India,* **49 D8**
Mzuzu, *Malawi,* **73 F2**

n

Naberezhnyye Chelny, *Russia,* **57 G2**
Nabeul, *Tunisia,* **62 D4**
Nacala, *Mozambique,* **73 H2**
Nador, *Morocco,* **61 D8**
Naga, *Philippines,* **45 H5**
Nagasaki, *Japan,* **47 L4**
Nagoya, *Japan,* **47 N3**
Nagpur, *India,* **49 D6**
Nain, *Canada,* **23 N3**
Nairobi, *Kenya, national capital,* **71 G4**
Najran, *Saudi Arabia,* **51 D8**
Nakhodka, *Russia,* **47 M2**
Nakhon Ratchasima, *Thailand,* **44 D5**
Nakhon Sawan, *Thailand,* **44 D4**
Nakhon Si Thammarat, *Thailand,* **44 D6**
Nakuru, *Kenya,* **71 G4**
Nalchik, *Russia,* **50 D3**
Namangan, *Uzbekistan,* **48 C2**
Namib Desert, *Africa,* **72 B3**
Namibe, *Angola,* **72 B3**
Namibia, *Africa, country,* **72 C4**
Nam Lake, *China,* **48 G4**
Nampo, *North Korea,* **47 L3**
Nampula, *Mozambique,* **73 G3**
Namsos, *Norway,* **58 D2**
Namur, *Belgium,* **60 F4**
Nanaimo, *Canada,* **22 G4**
Nanchang, *China,* **47 J5**
Nancy, *France,* **60 F4**
Nanded, *India,* **49 D7**
Nanjing, *China,* **47 J4**
Nanning, *China,* **46 G6**
Nanping, *China,* **47 J5**
Nantes, *France,* **61 D5**
Napier, *New Zealand,* **39 Q7**
Naples, *Italy,* **62 E3**
Narmada, *India,* **49 C6**
Narva, *Estonia,* **58 J4**
Narvik, *Norway,* **58 F1**
Nashik, *India,* **49 C6**
Nashville, *U.S.A., internal capital,* **25 J3**
Nasi Lake, *Finland,* **58 G3**
Nassau, *The Bahamas, national capital,* **25 L5**
Nasser, Lake, *Egypt,* **67 H4**
Natal, *Brazil,* **31 L5**
Natitingou, *Benin,* **69 F6**
Natuna Islands, *Indonesia,* **42 C3**
Nauru, *Oceania, country,* **36 D5**
Navapolatsk, *Belarus,* **59 J5**
Navoiy, *Uzbekistan,* **48 B2**
Nawabshah, *Pakistan,* **48 B5**
Naxcivan, *Azerbaijan,* **50 E4**
Nazca, *Peru,* **30 D6**
Nazret, *Ethiopia,* **71 G2**
Ndalatando, *Angola,* **72 B1**
Ndele, *Central African Republic,* **70 D2**
Ndjamena, *Chad, national capital,* **66 E6**
Ndola, *Zambia,* **72 E2**
Near Islands, *U.S.A.,* **23 A3**
Nebraska, *U.S.A., internal admin. area,* **24 F2**
Necochea, *Argentina,* **33 G7**
Negombo, *Sri Lanka,* **49 D9**
Negro, *Brazil,* **30 F4**
Negro, Cape, *Peru,* **30 B5**
Negros, *Philippines,* **45 H6**
Neiva, *Colombia,* **30 C3**
Nekemte, *Ethiopia,* **71 G2**
Nellore, *India,* **49 E8**
Nelson, *New Zealand,* **39 P8**
Nelspruit, *South Africa,* **72 F5**
Nema, *Mauritania,* **69 D5**
Neman, *Europe,* **59 G5**
Nepal, *Asia, country,* **48 E5**
Netherlands, *Europe, country,* **60 F3**
Netherlands Antilles, *North America, dependency,* **27 L5**
Nettilling Lake, *Canada,* **23 M2**
Neuquen, *Argentina,* **33 E7**
Nevada, *U.S.A., internal admin. area,* **24 C3**
Nevers, *France,* **61 E5**
New Amsterdam, *Guyana,* **31 G2**
Newark, *U.S.A.,* **25 M2**
New Britain, *Papua New Guinea,* **43 M5**
New Brunswick, *Canada, internal admin. area,* **23 N4**
New Caledonia, *Oceania,* **39 M4**
Newcastle, *Australia,* **39 K6**
Newcastle upon Tyne, *United Kingdom,* **60 D3**
New Delhi, *India, national capital,* **48 D5**
Newfoundland, *Canada,* **23 P4**
Newfoundland, *Canada, internal admin. area,* **23 N3**
New Guinea, *Asia/Oceania,* **43 J4**
New Hampshire, *U.S.A., internal admin. area,* **25 M2**
New Ireland, *Papua New Guinea,* **43 M4**
New Jersey, *U.S.A., internal admin. area,* **25 M3**
New Mexico, *U.S.A., internal admin. area,* **24 E4**
New Orleans, *U.S.A.,* **25 J5**
New Plymouth, *New Zealand,* **39 P7**
Newport, *United Kingdom,* **60 D4**
New Siberia Islands, *Russia,* **53 H2**
New South Wales, *Australia, internal admin. area,* **38 H6**
New York, *U.S.A.,* **25 M2**
New York, *U.S.A., internal admin. area,* **25 M2**
New Zealand, *Australasia, country,* **39 Q8**
Ngami, Lake, *Botswana,* **72 D4**
Ngaoundere, *Cameroon,* **70 B2**
Ngoma, *Zambia,* **72 E3**
Nha Trang, *Vietnam,* **44 E5**
Niagara Falls, *North America,* **23 M4**
Niamey, *Niger, national capital,* **69 F6**
Nias, *Indonesia,* **42 A3**
Nicaragua, *North America, country,* **27 G5**
Nicaragua, Lake, *Nicaragua,* **27 H5**
Nice, *France,* **61 F6**
Nicobar Islands, *India,* **49 G9**
Nicosia, *Cyprus, national capital,* **63 K5**
Nieuw Nickerie, *Surinam,* **31 G2**
Niger, *Africa,* **69 G7**
Niger, *Africa, country,* **66 D5**
Niger Delta, *Nigeria,* **69 G8**
Nigeria, *Africa, country,* **69 F7**
Niigata, *Japan,* **47 N3**
Nikopol, *Ukraine,* **56 C4**
Niksic, *Serbia and Montenegro,* **63 F3**
Nile, *Africa,* **67 H3**
Nile Delta, *Egypt,* **67 H2**
Nimes, *France,* **61 F6**
Ningbo, *China,* **47 K5**
Niono, *Mali,* **69 D6**
Nioro du Sahel, *Mali,* **69 D5**
Nipigon, Lake, *Canada,* **23 L4**
Nis, *Serbia and Montenegro,* **63 G3**
Nitra, *Slovakia,* **59 F6**
Niue, *Oceania,* **36 G6**
Nizhniy Novgorod, *Russia,* **56 E2**
Nizhniy Tagil, *Russia,* **57 H2**
Njazidja, *Comoros,* **73 H2**
Njinjo, *Tanzania,* **71 G5**
Nkongsamba, *Cameroon,* **70 A3**
Nogales, *Mexico,* **26 B1**
Nokaneng, *Botswana,* **72 D3**
Norfolk Island, *Australia,* **39 N5**
Norilsk, *Russia,* **52 E2**
Norrkoping, *Sweden,* **58 F4**
North America, **18**
North Bay, *Canada,* **23 M4**
North Cape, *New Zealand,* **39 P6**
North Cape, *Norway,* **58 J1**
North Carolina, *U.S.A., internal admin. area,* **25 K3**
North Dakota, *U.S.A., internal admin. area,* **24 F1**
Northern Ireland, *United Kingdom, internal admin. area,* **60 C3**
Northern Mariana Islands, *Oceania,* **36 B3**
Northern Territory, *Australia, internal admin. area,* **38 F3**
North European Plain, *Russia,* **56 C2**
North Frisian Islands, *Europe,* **60 F3**
North Island, *New Zealand,* **39 Q7**
North Korea, *Asia, country,* **47 L2**
North Sea, *Europe,* **60 E2**
North West Cape, *Australia,* **38 B4**
Northwest Territories, *Canada, internal admin. area,* **22 G2**
Norway, *Europe, country,* **58 D3**
Norwegian Sea, *Europe,* **58 C2**
Norwich, *United Kingdom,* **60 E3**
Nosy Be, *Madagascar,* **73 J2**
Nosy Boraha, *Madagascar,* **73 J3**
Nottingham, *United Kingdom,* **60 D3**
Nouadhibou, *Mauritania,* **68 B4**
Nouakchott, *Mauritania, national capital,* **68 B5**
Noumea, *New Caledonia,* **39 N4**
Nova Iguacu, *Brazil,* **32 K4**
Nova Mambone, *Mozambique,* **73 G4**
Novara, *Italy,* **62 D2**
Nova Scotia, *Canada, internal admin. area,* **23 N4**
Novaya Zemlya, *Russia,* **52 C2**
Novgorod, *Russia,* **58 J4**
Novi Sad, *Serbia and Montenegro,* **63 F2**
Novocherkassk, *Russia,* **56 E4**
Novo Mesto, *Slovenia,* **62 E2**
Novorossiysk, *Russia,* **50 C3**
Novosibirsk, *Russia,* **52 E3**
Novyy Urengoy, *Russia,* **52 D2**
Nubian Desert, *Africa,* **67 H4**
Nueva Loja, *Ecuador,* **30 C3**
Nukualofa, *Tonga, national capital,* **36 F7**
Nukus, *Uzbekistan,* **50 G3**
Nullarbor Plain, *Australia,* **38 E6**
Nunavut, *Canada, internal admin. area,* **23 K2**
Nungo, *Mozambique,* **73 G2**
Nunivak Island, *U.S.A.,* **22 C3**
Nuqui, *Colombia,* **30 C2**

Nuremberg, *Germany,* **60 G4**
Nyala, *Sudan,* **66 F6**
Nyasa, Lake, *Africa,* **71 F6**
Nyeri, *Kenya,* **71 G4**
Nykobing, *Denmark,* **59 D5**
Nzerekore, *Guinea,* **69 D7**
Nzwani, *Comoros,* **73 H2**

O

Oahu, *U.S.A.,* **25 P7**
Oaxaca, *Mexico,* **26 E4**
Ob, *Russia,* **52 D2**
Obi, *Indonesia,* **43 G4**
Obninsk, *Russia,* **56 D2**
Obo, *Central African Republic,* **70 E2**
Odda, *Norway,* **58 C3**
Odemis, *Turkey,* **63 J4**
Odense, *Denmark,* **59 D5**
Oder, *Europe,* **59 E5**
Odesa, *Ukraine,* **56 C4**
Odienne, *Ivory Coast,* **69 D7**
Ogbomoso, *Nigeria,* **69 F7**
Ogden, *U.S.A.,* **24 D2**
Ohio, *U.S.A.,* **25 J3**
Ohio, *U.S.A., internal admin. area,* **25 K2**
Ojinaga, *Mexico,* **26 D2**
Ojos del Salado, Mount, *South America,* **32 E5**
Oka, *Russia,* **56 E2**
Okahandja, *Namibia,* **72 C4**
Okaukuejo, *Namibia,* **72 C3**
Okavango, *Africa,* **72 D3**
Okavango Swamp, *Botswana,* **72 D3**
Okayama, *Japan,* **47 M4**
Okeechobee, Lake, *U.S.A.,* **25 K5**
Okhotsk, Sea of, *Asia,* **53 H3**
Okinawa, *Japan,* **47 L5**
Oklahoma, *U.S.A., internal admin. area,* **24 G4**
Oklahoma City, *U.S.A., internal capital,* **24 G3**
Oktyabrskiy, *Russia,* **57 G3**
Oland, *Sweden,* **59 F4**
Olavarria, *Argentina,* **33 F7**
Olbia, *Italy,* **62 D3**
Oleksandriya, *Ukraine,* **56 C4**
Ollague, *Chile,* **32 E4**
Olomouc, *Czech Republic,* **62 F1**
Olongapo, *Philippines,* **45 H5**
Olsztyn, *Poland,* **59 G5**
Olympia, *U.S.A., internal capital,* **24 B1**
Olympus, Mount, *Greece,* **63 G3**
Omaha, *U.S.A.,* **25 G2**
Oman, *Asia, country,* **51 G7**
Oman, Gulf of, *Asia,* **51 G7**
Omdurman, *Sudan,* **67 H5**
Omsk, *Russia,* **52 D3**
Ondangwa, *Namibia,* **72 C3**
Onega, Lake, *Russia,* **58 K3**
Onitsha, *Nigeria,* **69 G7**
Ontario, *Canada, internal admin. area,* **23 L3**
Ontario, Lake, *U.S.A.,* **25 L2**
Opochka, *Russia,* **59 J4**
Opole, *Poland,* **59 F6**
Oporto, *Portugal,* **61 B6**
Oppdal, *Norway,* **58 D3**
Opuwo, *Namibia,* **72 B3**
Oradea, *Romania,* **63 G2**
Oral, *Kazakhstan,* **57 G3**
Oran, *Algeria,* **68 E1**
Orange, *Africa,* **72 C5**
Orange, Cape, *Brazil,* **31 H3**
Orapa, *Botswana,* **72 E4**
Orebro, *Sweden,* **58 E4**
Oregon, *U.S.A., internal admin. area,* **24 B2**
Orel, *Russia,* **56 D3**
Orenburg, *Russia,* **57 H3**
Orense, *Spain,* **61 C6**
Orinoco, *Venezuela,* **30 F2**
Orinoco Delta, *Venezuela,* **30 F2**
Oristano, *Italy,* **62 D4**
Orizaba, *Mexico,* **26 E4**
Orkney, *South Africa,* **72 E5**
Orkney Islands, *United Kingdom,* **60 D2**
Orlando, *U.S.A.,* **25 K5**
Orleans, *France,* **60 E5**
Orsha, *Belarus,* **59 J5**
Orsk, *Russia,* **57 H3**
Oruro, *Bolivia,* **32 E3**
Osaka, *Japan,* **47 N4**
Osh, *Kyrgyzstan,* **48 C2**
Osijek, *Croatia,* **63 F2**
Oskarshamn, *Sweden,* **59 F4**
Oslo, *Norway, national capital,* **58 D4**
Osnabruck, *Germany,* **60 G3**
Osorno, *Chile,* **33 D8**
Ostersund, *Sweden,* **58 E3**
Ostrava, *Czech Republic,* **63 F1**
Otavi, *Namibia,* **72 C3**
Otjiwarongo, *Namibia,* **72 C4**
Ottawa, *Canada, national capital,* **23 M4**
Ouadda, *Central African Republic,* **70 D2**
Ouagadougou, *Burkina Faso, national capital,* **69 E6**
Ouahigouya, *Burkina Faso,* **69 E6**
Ouargla, *Algeria,* **68 G2**
Ouarzazate, *Morocco,* **68 D2**
Oudtshoorn, *South Africa,* **72 D6**
Ouesso, *Congo,* **70 C3**
Oujda, *Morocco,* **68 E2**
Oulu, *Finland,* **58 H2**
Oulu Lake, *Finland,* **58 H2**
Ovalle, *Chile,* **32 D6**
Oviedo, *Spain,* **61 C6**
Owando, *Congo,* **70 C4**
Owen Sound, *Canada,* **23 L4**
Owo, *Nigeria,* **69 G7**
Oxford, *United Kingdom,* **60 D4**
Oyem, *Gabon,* **70 B3**
Ozark Plateau, *U.S.A.,* **25 H3**

P

Paarl, *South Africa,* **72 C6**
Pacasmayo, *Peru,* **30 C5**
Pacific Ocean, **18**
Padang, *Indonesia,* **42 B4**
Pafuri, *Mozambique,* **72 F4**
Pagadian, *Philippines,* **45 H6**
Paijanne Lake, *Finland,* **58 H3**
Pakistan, *Asia, country,* **48 B5**
Pakxe, *Laos,* **44 E4**
Palangkaraya, *Indonesia,* **42 D4**
Palau, *Oceania, country,* **36 A4**
Palawan, *Philippines,* **45 G6**
Palembang, *Indonesia,* **42 B4**
Palencia, *Spain,* **61 C6**
Palermo, *Italy,* **62 E4**
Palikir, *Federated States of Micronesia, national capital,* **36 C4**
Palk Strait, *Asia,* **49 D9**
Palma, *Mozambique,* **73 H2**
Palma, *Spain,* **61 E7**
Palmas, Cape, *Africa,* **69 D8**
Palmyra Atoll, *Oceania,* **36 G4**
Palopo, *Indonesia,* **43 F4**
Palu, *Indonesia,* **43 E4**
Pampas, *Argentina,* **33 F7**
Pamplona, *Colombia,* **30 D2**
Pamplona, *Spain,* **61 D6**
Panama, *North America, country,* **27 H6**
Panama Canal, *Panama,* **27 J6**
Panama City, *Panama, national capital,* **27 J6**
Panama, Gulf of, *North America,* **27 J6**
Panay, *Philippines,* **45 H5**
Panevezys, *Lithuania,* **59 H5**
Pangkalpinang, *Indonesia,* **42 C4**
Panjgur, *Pakistan,* **48 A5**
Pantelleria, *Italy,* **62 E4**
Panzhihua, *China,* **46 F5**
Papeete, *French Polynesia,* **37 J6**
Paphos, *Cyprus,* **63 K5**
Papua, Gulf of, *Papua New Guinea,* **43 K5**
Papua New Guinea, *Oceania, country,* **43 L5**
Paracel Islands, *Asia,* **45 F4**
Paraguaipoa, *Venezuela,* **30 D1**
Paraguay, *South America,* **32 G4**
Paraguay, *South America, country,* **32 F4**
Parakou, *Benin,* **69 F7**
Paramaribo, *Surinam, national capital,* **31 G2**
Parana, *South America,* **32 G6**
Paranagua, *Brazil,* **32 J5**
Parepare, *Indonesia,* **43 E4**
Paris, *France, national capital,* **60 E4**
Parma, *Italy,* **62 D2**
Parnaiba, *Brazil,* **31 K4**
Parnu, *Estonia,* **58 H4**
Parry Islands, *Canada,* **22 J1**
Pasadena, *U.S.A.,* **24 C4**
Passo Fundo, *Brazil,* **32 H5**
Pasto, *Colombia,* **30 C3**
Patagonia, *Argentina,* **33 E9**
Pathein, *Burma,* **44 B4**
Patna, *India,* **48 F5**
Patos de Minas, *Brazil,* **32 J3**
Patos Lagoon, *Brazil,* **32 H6**
Patra, *Greece,* **63 G4**
Pattaya, *Thailand,* **44 D5**
Pau, *France,* **61 D6**
Pavlodar, *Kazakhstan,* **52 D3**
Paysandu, *Uruguay,* **32 G6**
Peace River, *Canada,* **22 H3**
Pecos, *U.S.A.,* **24 F4**
Pecs, *Hungary,* **59 F7**
Pedro Juan Caballero, *Paraguay,* **32 G4**
Pegu, *Burma,* **44 C4**
Peipus, Lake, *Europe,* **58 H4**
Peiraias, *Greece,* **63 G4**
Pekanbaru, *Indonesia,* **42 B3**
Pelagian Islands, *Italy,* **62 E5**
Peleng, *Indonesia,* **43 F4**
Pelotas, *Brazil,* **32 H6**
Pematangsiantar, *Indonesia,* **42 A3**
Pemba, *Mozambique,* **73 H2**
Pemba Island, *Tanzania,* **71 G5**
Penang, *Malaysia,* **42 B2**
Penas, Gulf of, *Chile,* **33 C9**
Pennsylvania, *U.S.A., internal admin. area,* **25 L2**
Pensacola, *U.S.A.,* **25 J4**
Penza, *Russia,* **56 F3**
Penzance, *United Kingdom,* **60 C4**
Peoria, *U.S.A.,* **25 J2**
Pereira, *Colombia,* **30 C3**
Perm, *Russia,* **57 H2**
Perpignan, *France,* **61 E6**
Persepolis, *Iran,* **51 F6**
Persian Gulf, *Asia,* **51 F6**
Perth, *Australia, internal capital,* **38 C6**
Peru, *South America, country,* **30 C5**
Perugia, *Italy,* **62 E3**
Pescara, *Italy,* **62 E3**
Peshawar, *Pakistan,* **48 C4**
Petauke, *Zambia,* **72 F2**
Petra, *Jordan,* **51 C5**
Petrolina, *Brazil,* **31 K5**
Petropavlovsk-Kamchatskiy, *Russia,* **53 H3**
Petrozavodsk, *Russia,* **58 K3**
Philadelphia, *U.S.A.,* **25 L3**
Philippines, *Asia, country,* **45 J5**
Philippine Sea, *Asia,* **45 H5**
Phitsanulok, *Thailand,* **44 D4**
Phnom Penh, *Cambodia, national capital,* **44 D5**
Phoenix, *U.S.A., internal capital,* **24 D4**
Phongsali, *Laos,* **44 D3**
Piatra Neamt, *Romania,* **63 H2**
Pica, *Chile,* **32 E4**
Pico, *Azores,* **68 K10**
Pielis Lake, *Finland,* **58 J3**
Pierre, *U.S.A., internal capital,* **24 F2**
Pietermaritzburg, *South Africa,* **72 F5**
Pietersburg, *South Africa,* **72 E4**
Pihlaja Lake, *Finland,* **58 J3**
Pik Pobedy, *Asia,* **48 E2**
Pilcomayo, *South America,* **32 F4**
Pilsen, *Czech Republic,* **62 E1**
Pinar del Rio, *Cuba,* **27 H3**
Pindus Mountains, *Greece,* **63 G4**
Pingdingshan, *China,* **47 H4**
Pinsk, *Belarus,* **59 H5**
Pisa, *Italy,* **62 D3**
Pitcairn Islands, *Oceania,* **37 L7**
Pitesti, *Romania,* **63 H2**
Pittsburgh, *U.S.A.,* **25 L2**
Piura, *Peru,* **30 B5**
Platte, *U.S.A.,* **24 F2**
Pleven, *Bulgaria,* **63 H3**
Plock, *Poland,* **59 F5**
Ploiesti, *Romania,* **63 H2**
Plovdiv, *Bulgaria,* **63 H3**
Plumtree, *Zimbabwe,* **72 E4**
Plymouth, *United Kingdom,* **60 C4**
Po, *Italy,* **62 D2**
Pocos de Caldas, *Brazil,* **32 J4**
Podgorica, *Serbia and Montenegro,* **56 C4**
Podolsk, *Russia,* **56 D2**
Pointe-Noire, *Congo,* **70 B4**
Poitiers, *France,* **61 E5**
Pokhara, *Nepal,* **48 E5**
Poland, *Europe, country,* **59 F6**
Polatsk, *Belarus,* **59 J5**
Poltava, *Ukraine,* **56 C4**
Polynesia, *Oceania,* **36 G5**
Pompeii, *Italy,* **62 E3**
Ponta Delgada, *Azores,* **68 K10**
Ponta Pora, *Brazil,* **32 G4**
Pontianak, *Indonesia,* **42 C3**
Poole, *United Kingdom,* **60 D4**
Poopo, Lake, *Bolivia,* **32 E3**
Popayan, *Colombia,* **30 C3**
Porbandar, *India,* **49 B6**
Pori, *Finland,* **58 G3**
Porlamar, *Venezuela,* **26 M5**
Port-au-Prince, *Haiti, national capital,* **27 K4**
Port Blair, *India,* **49 G8**
Port Elizabeth, *South Africa,* **72 E6**
Port-Gentil, *Gabon,* **70 A4**
Port Harcourt, *Nigeria,* **69 G8**
Port Hardy, *Canada,* **22 G3**
Port Hedland, *Australia,* **38 C4**
Portland, *Australia,* **38 H7**
Portland, *Maine, U.S.A.,* **25 M2**
Portland, *Oregon, U.S.A.,* **24 B1**
Port Louis, *Mauritius, national capital,* **73 L4**
Port Macquarie, *Australia,* **39 K6**
Port McNeill, *Canada,* **22 G3**
Port Moresby, *Papua New Guinea, national capital,* **43 L5**
Porto Alegre, *Brazil,* **32 H5**
Port-of-Spain, *Trinidad and Tobago, national capital,* **26 M5**
Porto-Novo, *Benin, national capital,* **69 F7**
Porto-Vecchio, *France,* **61 G6**
Porto Velho, *Brazil,* **30 F5**
Port Said, *Egypt,* **67 H2**
Portsmouth, *United Kingdom,* **60 D4**
Port Sudan, *Sudan,* **67 J5**
Portugal, *Europe, country,* **61 B7**
Port-Vila, *Vanuatu, national capital,* **39 N3**
Porvenir, *Chile,* **33 D10**
Posadas, *Argentina,* **32 G5**
Poti, *Georgia,* **50 D3**
Potiskum, *Nigeria,* **66 D6**
Potosi, *Bolivia,* **32 E3**
Potsdam, *Germany,* **60 H3**
Poyang Lake, *China,* **47 J5**
Poznan, *Poland,* **59 F5**
Prachuap Khiri Khan, *Thailand,* **44 C5**
Prague, *Czech Republic, national capital,* **62 E1**
Praia, *Cape Verde, national capital,* **69 M12**
Presidente Prudente, *Brazil,* **32 H4**
Presov, *Slovakia,* **59 G6**
Pretoria, *South Africa, national capital,* **72 E5**
Preveza, *Greece,* **63 G4**
Prieska, *South Africa,* **72 D5**
Prilep, *Macedonia,* **63 G3**
Prince Albert, *Canada,* **22 J3**
Prince Edward Island, *Canada, internal admin. area,* **23 N4**
Prince George, *Canada,* **22 G3**

Prince of Wales Island, *Canada,* **23 K1**
Prince Rupert, *Canada,* **22 F3**
Principe, *Sao Tome and Principe,* **69 G8**
Pripet, *Europe,* **59 J6**
Pripet Marshes, *Europe,* **59 H5**
Pristina, *Serbia and Montenegro,* **63 G3**
Providence, *Seychelles,* **73 K1**
Providence, *U.S.A., internal capital,* **25 M2**
Providence, Cape, *New Zealand,* **39 N9**
Provo, *U.S.A.,* **24 D2**
Prudhoe Bay, *U.S.A.,* **22 E1**
Pskov, *Russia,* **59 J4**
Pskov, Lake, *Europe,* **58 J4**
Pucallpa, *Peru,* **30 D5**
Puebla, *Mexico,* **26 E4**
Pueblo, *U.S.A.,* **24 F3**
Puerto Ayora, *Ecuador,* **30 N10**
Puerto Cabezas, *Nicaragua,* **27 H5**
Puerto Deseado, *Argentina,* **33 E9**
Puerto Inirida, *Colombia,* **30 E3**
Puertò Leguizamo, *Colombia,* **30 D4**
Puerto Maldonado, *Peru,* **30 E6**
Puerto Montt, *Chile,* **33 D8**
Puerto Natales, *Chile,* **33 D10**
Puerto Paez, *Venezuela,* **30 E2**
Puerto Princesa, *Philippines,* **45 G6**
Puerto Rico, *North America,* **26 L4**
Puerto Suarez, *Bolivia,* **32 G3**
Puerto Vallarta, *Mexico,* **26 C3**
Pula, *Croatia,* **62 E2**
Pulog, Mount, *Philippines,* **45 H4**
Puncak Jaya, *Indonesia,* **43 J4**
Pune, *India,* **49 C7**
Puno, *Peru,* **30 D7**
Punta Arenas, *Chile,* **33 D10**
Puntarenas, *Costa Rica,* **27 H5**
Purus, *Brazil,* **30 E5**
Pusan, *South Korea,* **47 L3**
Pushkin, *Russia,* **58 J4**
Puula Lake, *Finland,* **58 H3**
Pweto, *Democratic Republic of Congo,* **70 E5**
Pya, Lake, *Russia,* **58 J2**
Pye, *Burma,* **44 C4**
Pyinmana, *Burma,* **44 C4**
Pyongyang, *North Korea, national capital,* **47 L3**
Pyramids of Giza, *Egypt,* **67 H3**
Pyrenees, *Europe,* **61 D6**
Pyrgos, *Greece,* **63 G4**

q

Qaidam Basin, *China,* **48 G3**
Qaraghandy, *Kazakhstan,* **52 D3**
Qatar, *Asia, country,* **51 F6**
Qattara Depression, *Egypt,* **67 G3**
Qazvin, *Iran,* **50 E4**
Qena, *Egypt,* **67 H3**
Qingdao, *China,* **47 K3**
Qinghai Lake, *China,* **46 F3**
Qinhuangdao, *China,* **47 J3**
Qiqihar, *China,* **47 K1**
Qom, *Iran,* **50 F5**
Qostanay, *Kazakhstan,* **57 J3**
Quanzhou, *China,* **47 J6**
Quebec, *Canada, internal admin. area,* **23 M3**
Quebec, *Canada, internal capital,* **23 M4**
Queen Charlotte Islands, *Canada,* **22 F3**
Queen Elizabeth Islands, *Canada,* **22 H1**
Queen Maud Land, *Antarctica,* **77 C3**
Queensland, *Australia, internal admin. area,* **38 H4**
Quelimane, *Mozambique,* **73 G3**
Quellon, *Chile,* **33 D8**
Quetta, *Pakistan,* **48 B4**
Quevedo, *Ecuador,* **30 C4**
Quezaltenango, *Guatemala,* **26 F4**
Quezon City, *Philippines,* **45 H5**
Quibdo, *Colombia,* **30 C2**
Quillabamba, *Peru,* **30 D6**
Quimper, *France,* **60 C5**
Quincy, *U.S.A.,* **25 H3**
Qui Nhon, *Vietnam,* **44 E5**
Quirima, *Angola,* **72 C2**
Quito, *Ecuador, national capital,* **30 C4**
Qurghonteppa, *Tajikistan,* **48 B3**
Qyzylorda, *Kazakhstan,* **50 J3**

r

Raahe, *Finland,* **58 H2**
Rabat, *Morocco, national capital,* **68 D2**
Rabaul, *Papua New Guinea,* **43 M4**
Rabnita, *Moldova,* **63 J2**
Radisson, *Canada,* **23 M3**
Radom, *Poland,* **59 G6**
Ragusa, *Italy,* **62 E4**
Rahimyar Khan, *Pakistan,* **48 C5**
Rainier, Mount, *U.S.A.,* **24 B1**
Raipur, *India,* **49 E6**
Rajahmundry, *India,* **49 E7**
Rajkot, *India,* **49 C6**
Rajshahi, *Bangladesh,* **49 F6**
Rakops, *Botswana,* **72 D4**
Raleigh, *U.S.A., internal capital,* **25 L3**
Ralik Islands, *Marshall Islands,* **36 D3**
Ramnicu Valcea, *Romania,* **63 H2**
Rancagua, *Chile,* **32 D6**
Ranchi, *India,* **49 F6**
Randers, *Denmark,* **59 D4**
Rangoon, *Burma, national capital,* **44 C4**
Rangpur, *Bangladesh,* **48 F5**
Rapid City, *U.S.A.,* **24 F2**
Ras Dashen, *Ethiopia,* **71 G1**
Rasht, *Iran,* **50 E4**
Ratak Islands, *Marshall Islands,* **36 E3**
Rat Islands, *U.S.A.,* **23 A3**
Rauma, *Finland,* **58 G3**
Ravenna, *Italy,* **62 E2**
Rawson, *Argentina,* **33 E8**
Rechytsa, *Belarus,* **59 J5**
Recife, *Brazil,* **31 M5**
Reconquista, *Argentina,* **32 G5**
Red, *Asia,* **46 F6**
Red, *U.S.A.,* **25 G4**
Red Deer, *Canada,* **22 H3**
Redding, *U.S.A.,* **24 B2**
Red Sea, *Africa/Asia,* **67 J4**
Regensburg, *Germany,* **60 H4**
Regina, *Canada, internal capital,* **22 J3**
Regina, *French Guiana,* **31 H3**
Rehoboth, *Namibia,* **72 C4**
Reims, *France,* **60 F4**
Reindeer Lake, *Canada,* **22 J3**
Rennell Island, *Solomon Islands,* **39 M2**
Rennes, *France,* **60 D4**
Reno, *U.S.A.,* **24 C3**
Reunion, *Indian Ocean,* **73 L4**
Revelstoke, *Canada,* **22 H3**
Revillagigedo Islands, *Mexico,* **26 B4**
Reykjavik, *Iceland, national capital,* **58 N2**
Rhine, *Europe,* **60 F4**
Rhode Island, *U.S.A., internal admin. area,* **25 M2**
Rhodes, *Greece,* **63 J4**
Rhone, *Europe,* **61 F5**
Riau Islands, *Indonesia,* **42 B3**
Ribeirao Preto, *Brazil,* **32 J4**
Riberalta, *Bolivia,* **32 E2**
Richards Bay, *South Africa,* **72 F5**
Richmond, *U.S.A., internal capital,* **25 L3**
Riga, *Latvia, national capital,* **59 H4**
Riga, Gulf of, *Europe,* **59 G4**
Rijeka, *Croatia,* **62 E2**
Rimini, *Italy,* **62 E2**
Rio Branco, *Brazil,* **30 E5**
Rio Cuarto, *Argentina,* **32 F6**
Rio de Janeiro, *Brazil,* **32 K4**
Rio Gallegos, *Argentina,* **33 E10**
Rio Grande, *Argentina,* **33 E10**
Rio Grande, *Brazil,* **32 H6**
Rio Grande, *U.S.A.,* **24 F5**
Riohacha, *Colombia,* **30 D1**
Rivas, *Nicaragua,* **27 G5**
Rivera, *Uruguay,* **32 G6**
Riverside, *U.S.A.,* **24 C4**
Rivne, *Ukraine,* **59 H6**
Riyadh, *Saudi Arabia, national capital,* **51 E7**
Roanoke, *U.S.A.,* **25 L3**
Robson, Mount, *Canada,* **22 H3**
Rochester, *U.S.A.,* **25 L2**
Rockford, *U.S.A.,* **25 J2**
Rockhampton, *Australia,* **39 K4**
Rocky Mountains, *U.S.A.,* **24 D1**
Romania, *Europe, country,* **63 G2**
Rome, *Italy, national capital,* **62 E3**
Rondonopolis, *Brazil,* **32 H3**
Ronne, *Denmark,* **59 E5**
Ronne Ice Shelf, *Antarctica,* **77 S3**
Roraima, Mount, *South America,* **30 F2**
Rosario, *Argentina,* **32 F6**
Roseau, *Dominica, national capital,* **26 M4**
Roslavl, *Russia,* **59 K5**
Ross Ice Shelf, *Antarctica,* **77 M4**
Rosso, *Mauritania,* **69 B5**
Ross Sea, *Antarctica,* **77 M3**
Rostock, *Germany,* **60 H3**
Rostov, *Russia,* **56 D4**
Roti, *Indonesia,* **43 F6**
Rotorua, *Australia,* **39 Q7**
Rotterdam, *Netherlands,* **60 F4**
Rouen, *France,* **60 E4**
Rovaniemi, *Finland,* **58 H2**
Roxas, *Philippines,* **45 H5**
Rub al Khali, *Asia,* **51 E8**
Rudnyy, *Kazakhstan,* **57 J3**
Rufino, *Argentina,* **32 F6**
Rufunsa, *Zambia,* **72 E3**
Rukwa, Lake, *Tanzania,* **71 F5**
Rundu, *Namibia,* **72 C3**
Rurrenabaque, *Bolivia,* **32 E2**
Ruse, *Bulgaria,* **63 H3**
Russia, *Asia/Europe, country,* **52 E3**
Ruvuma, *Africa,* **71 G6**
Rwanda, *Africa, country,* **70 E4**
Ryazan, *Russia,* **56 D3**
Rybinsk, *Russia,* **56 D2**
Rybinsk Reservoir, *Russia,* **56 D2**
Rybnik, *Poland,* **59 F6**
Ryukyu Islands, *Japan,* **47 L5**
Rzeszow, *Poland,* **59 G6**
Rzhev, *Russia,* **56 C2**

s

Saarbrucken, *Germany,* **60 F4**
Saarijarvi, *Finland,* **58 H3**
Sabha, *Libya,* **66 D3**
Sabzevar, *Iran,* **50 G4**
Sacramento, *U.S.A., internal capital,* **24 B3**
Sadah, *Yemen,* **51 E8**
Safi, *Morocco,* **68 D2**
Sahara, *Africa,* **66 C5**
Saharanpur, *India,* **48 D5**
Sahel, *Africa,* **66 C6**
Sahiwal, *Pakistan,* **48 C4**
Saida, *Algeria,* **68 F2**
Saigon, *Vietnam,* **44 E5**
Saimaa Lake, *Finland,* **58 H3**
St. Andrew, Cape, *Madagascar,* **73 H3**
St. Denis, *Reunion,* **73 L4**
St. Etienne, *France,* **61 F5**
St. Francis, Cape, *South Africa,* **72 D6**
St. George, *U.S.A.,* **24 D3**
St. George's, *Grenada, national capital,* **26 M5**
St. Helier, *Channel Islands,* **60 D4**
Saint John, *Canada,* **23 N4**
St. John's, *Antigua and Barbuda, national capital,* **26 M4**
St. John's, *Canada, internal capital,* **23 P4**
St. Kitts and Nevis, *North America, country,* **26 M4**
St. Lawrence, *Canada,* **23 M4**
St. Lawrence, Gulf of, *Canada,* **23 N4**
St. Lawrence Island, *U.S.A.,* **22 B2**
St. Louis, *Senegal,* **69 B5**
St. Louis, *U.S.A.,* **25 H3**
St. Lucia, *North America, country,* **26 M5**
St. Lucia, Cape, *South Africa,* **73 F5**
St. Malo, *France,* **60 D4**
St. Martha, Cape, *Angola,* **72 B2**
St. Martin, *North America,* **26 M4**
St. Mary, Cape, *Madagascar,* **73 J5**
St. Paul, *U.S.A., internal capital,* **25 H1**
St. Petersburg, *Russia,* **58 J4**
St. Petersburg, *U.S.A.,* **25 K5**
St. Pierre, *Seychelles,* **73 J1**
St. Pierre and Miquelon, *North America,* **23 P4**
St. Polten, *Austria,* **62 E1**
St. Vincent and the Grenadines, *North America, country,* **26 M5**
St. Vincent, Cape, *Portugal,* **61 B7**
Sakhalin, *Russia,* **53 H3**
Saki, *Azerbaijan,* **50 E3**
Saki, *Nigeria,* **69 F7**
Sakishima Islands, *Japan,* **47 K6**
Sal, *Cape Verde,* **69 M11**
Salado, *Argentina,* **32 F5**
Salalah, *Oman,* **51 F8**
Salamanca, *Spain,* **61 C6**
Salem, *India,* **49 D8**
Salem, *U.S.A., internal capital,* **24 B1**
Salerno, *Italy,* **62 E3**
Salihorsk, *Belarus,* **59 H5**
Salinas, *U.S.A.,* **24 B3**
Salta, *Argentina,* **32 E4**
Saltillo, *Mexico,* **26 D2**
Salt Lake City, *U.S.A., internal capital,* **24 D2**
Salto, *Uruguay,* **32 G6**
Salton Sea, *U.S.A.,* **24 C4**
Salvador, *Brazil,* **31 L6**
Salween, *Asia,* **44 C4**
Salzburg, *Austria,* **62 E2**
Samar, *Philippines,* **45 J5**
Samara, *Russia,* **57 G3**
Samarinda, *Indonesia,* **42 E4**
Samarqand, *Uzbekistan,* **48 B3**
Sambalpur, *India,* **49 E6**
Samoa, *Oceania, country,* **36 F6**
Sampwe, *Democratic Republic of Congo,* **70 E5**
Sam Rayburn Reservoir, *U.S.A.,* **25 H4**
Samsun, *Turkey,* **50 C3**
San, *Mali,* **69 E6**
Sana, *Yemen, national capital,* **51 D8**
Sanandaj, *Iran,* **50 E4**
San Andres Island, *Colombia,* **27 H5**
San Antonio, *U.S.A.,* **24 G5**
San Antonio, Cape, *Argentina,* **33 G7**
San Antonio Oeste, *Argentina,* **33 F8**
San Cristobal, *Ecuador,* **30 P10**
San Cristobal, *Venezuela,* **30 D2**
Sandakan, *Malaysia,* **43 E2**
San Diego, *U.S.A.,* **24 C4**
Sandoway, *Burma,* **44 B4**
San Fernando, *Chile,* **32 D6**
San Fernando de Apure, *Venezuela,* **30 E2**
San Francisco, *Argentina,* **32 F6**
San Francisco, *U.S.A.,* **24 B3**
San Francisco, Cape, *Ecuador,* **30 B3**
Sangihe Islands, *Indonesia,* **43 G3**
San Jorge, Gulf of, *Argentina,* **33 E9**
San Jose, *Costa Rica, national capital,* **27 H6**
San Jose, *U.S.A.,* **24 B3**
San Jose de Chiquitos, *Bolivia,* **32 F3**
San Jose del Guaviare, *Colombia,* **30 D3**
San Juan, *Argentina,* **32 E6**
San Juan, *Puerto Rico,* **26 L4**
San Julian, *Argentina,* **33 E9**
Sanliurfa, *Turkey,* **50 C4**
San Lucas, Cape, *Mexico,* **26 B3**
San Luis, *Argentina,* **32 E6**
San Luis Obispo, *U.S.A.,* **24 B3**
San Luis Potosi, *Mexico,* **26 D3**
San Marino, *Europe, country,* **62 E3**
San Matias, Gulf of, *Argentina,* **33 F8**
San Miguel de Tucuman, *Argentina,* **32 E5**
San Nicolas de los Arroyos, *Argentina,* **32 F6**
San Pedro, *Ivory Coast,* **69 D8**
San Pedro de Atacama, *Chile,* **32 E4**
San Rafael, *Argentina,* **32 E6**
San Remo, *Italy,* **62 C3**
San Salvador, *Ecuador,* **30 N10**
San Salvador, *El Salvador, national capital,* **26 G5**

San Salvador de Jujuy, *Argentina,* **32 E4**
San Sebastian, *Spain,* **61 D6**
Santa Clara, *Cuba,* **27 H3**
Santa Cruz, *Bolivia,* **32 F3**
Santa Cruz, *Ecuador,* **30 N10**
Santa Cruz Islands, *Solomon Islands,* **39 N2**
Santa Elena, *Venezuela,* **30 F3**
Santa Fe, *Argentina,* **32 F6**
Santa Fe, *U.S.A., internal capital,* **24 E3**
Santa Maria, *Brazil,* **32 H5**
Santa Marta, *Colombia,* **30 D1**
Santander, *Spain,* **61 D6**
Santarem, *Brazil,* **31 H4**
Santa Rosa, *Argentina,* **33 F7**
Santiago, *Chile, national capital,* **32 D6**
Santiago, *Dominican Republic,* **27 K4**
Santiago, *Panama,* **27 H6**
Santiago de Compostela, *Spain,* **61 B6**
Santiago de Cuba, *Cuba,* **27 J3**
Santiago del Estero, *Argentina,* **32 F5**
Santo Antao, *Cape Verde,* **69 L11**
Santo Domingo, *Dominican Republic, national capital,* **27 L4**
Santo Domingo de los Colorados, *Ecuador,* **30 C4**
San Valentin, Mount, *Chile,* **33 D9**
Sanya, *China,* **46 G7**
Sao Francisco, *Brazil,* **31 L5**
Sao Jose do Rio Preto, *Brazil,* **32 J4**
Sao Luis, *Brazil,* **31 K4**
Sao Miguel, *Azores,* **68 K10**
Sao Nicolau, *Cape Verde,* **69 M11**
Sao Paulo, *Brazil,* **32 J4**
Sao Roque, Cape, *Brazil,* **31 L4**
Sao Tiago, *Cape Verde,* **69 M11**
Sao Tome, *Sao Tome and Principe, national capital,* **69 G8**
Sao Tome and Principe, *Africa, country,* **69 G8**
Sapporo, *Japan,* **47 P2**
Saqqara, *Egypt,* **67 H3**
Sarajevo, *Bosnia and Herzegovina, national capital,* **63 F3**
Saransk, *Russia,* **56 F3**
Sarapul, *Russia,* **57 G2**
Saratov, *Russia,* **57 F3**
Saratov Reservoir, *Russia,* **57 F3**
Sardinia, *Italy,* **62 D3**
Sargodha, *Pakistan,* **48 C4**
Sarh, *Chad,* **70 C2**
Sarremaa, *Estonia,* **58 G4**
Saskatchewan, *Canada, internal admin. area,* **22 J3**
Saskatoon, *Canada,* **22 J3**
Sassari, *Italy,* **62 D3**
Satu Mare, *Romania,* **63 G2**
Saudi Arabia, *Asia, country,* **51 E7**
Sault Ste. Marie, *Canada,* **23 L4**
Saurimo, *Angola,* **72 D1**
Savannah, *U.S.A.,* **25 K4**
Savannakhet, *Laos,* **44 D4**
Sawu, *Indonesia,* **43 F6**
Sawu Sea, *Indonesia,* **43 F5**
Schwerin, *Germany,* **60 G3**
Scotland, *United Kingdom, internal admin. area,* **60 C2**
Seattle, *U.S.A.,* **24 B1**
Seeheim, *Namibia,* **72 C5**
Sefadu, *Sierra Leone,* **69 C7**
Seg, Lake, *Russia,* **58 K3**
Segou, *Mali,* **69 D6**
Seine, *France,* **60 E4**
Sekondi-Takoradi, *Ghana,* **69 E8**
Selebi-Phikwe, *Botswana,* **72 E4**
Selibabi, *Mauritania,* **69 C5**
Selvas, *Brazil,* **30 E5**
Semarang, *Indonesia,* **42 D5**
Semenov, *Russia,* **56 E2**
Semiozernoe, *Kazakhstan,* **57 J3**
Sendai, *Japan,* **47 P3**
Senegal, *Africa,* **69 C5**
Senegal, *Africa, country,* **69 B6**
Seoul, *South Korea, national capital,* **47 L3**
Serang, *Indonesia,* **42 C5**
Serbia and Montenegro, *Europe, country,* **63 G2**
Seremban, *Malaysia,* **42 B3**
Sergiyev Posad, *Russia,* **56 D2**
Serov, *Russia,* **57 J2**
Serowe, *Botswana,* **72 E4**
Serpukhov, *Russia,* **56 D3**
Serres, *Greece,* **63 G3**
Sesheke, *Zambia,* **72 D3**
Setif, *Algeria,* **68 G1**
Setubal, *Portugal,* **61 B7**
Sevastopol, *Ukraine,* **63 K2**
Severn, *United Kingdom,* **60 D3**
Severnaya Zemlya, *Russia,* **53 F2**
Severomorsk, *Russia,* **58 K1**
Sevettijarvi, *Finland,* **58 J1**
Seville, *Spain,* **61 C7**
Seward, *U.S.A.,* **22 E2**
Seward Peninsula, *U.S.A.,* **22 C2**
Seychelles, *Indian Ocean, country,* **73 J1**
Seydhisfjordhur, *Iceland,* **58 Q2**
Sfax, *Tunisia,* **66 D2**
Shalqar, *Kazakhstan,* **50 G2**
Shanghai, *China,* **47 K4**
Shannon, *Ireland,* **60 C3**
Shantou, *China,* **47 J6**
Shaoguan, *China,* **47 H6**
Sharjah, *United Arab Emirates,* **51 G6**
Sharm el Sheikh, *Egypt,* **67 H3**
Shasta, Mount, *U.S.A.,* **24 B2**
Sheffield, *United Kingdom,* **60 D3**
Shenyang, *China,* **47 K2**
Shepetivka, *Ukraine,* **59 H6**
Shetland Islands, *United Kingdom,* **60 D1**
Shieli, *Kazakhstan,* **50 J3**
Shihezi, *China,* **48 F2**
Shijiazhuang, *China,* **47 H3**
Shikoku, *Japan,* **47 M4**
Shillong, *India,* **48 G5**
Shiraz, *Iran,* **51 F6**
Shishaldin Volcano, *U.S.A.,* **23 C3**
Shiyan, *China,* **46 H4**
Shizuoka, *Japan,* **47 N3**
Shkoder, *Albania,* **63 F3**
Shreveport, *U.S.A.,* **25 H4**
Shumen, *Bulgaria,* **63 H3**
Shymkent, *Kazakhstan,* **48 B2**
Sialkot, *Pakistan,* **48 C4**
Siauliai, *Lithuania,* **59 G5**
Sibiti, *Congo,* **70 B4**
Sibiu, *Romania,* **63 H2**
Sibolga, *Indonesia,* **42 A3**
Sibu, *Malaysia,* **42 D3**
Sicily, *Italy,* **62 E4**
Sicuani, *Peru,* **30 D6**
Sidi-Bel-Abbes, *Algeria,* **68 E1**
Sidon, *Lebanon,* **50 C5**
Sidra, Gulf of, *Africa,* **66 E2**
Sierra Leone, *Africa, country,* **69 C7**
Sierra Morena, *Spain,* **61 C7**
Sierra Nevada, *Spain,* **61 D7**
Sierra Nevada, *U.S.A.,* **24 B3**
Siglufjordhur, *Iceland,* **58 P2**
Siguiri, *Guinea,* **69 D6**
Sikasso, *Mali,* **69 D6**
Sikhote Alin Range, *Russia,* **47 N1**
Siling Lake, *China,* **48 F4**
Simao, *China,* **46 F6**
Simeulue, *Indonesia,* **42 A3**
Simferopol, *Ukraine,* **63 K2**
Simpson Desert, *Australia,* **38 G4**
Sinai, *Egypt,* **67 H3**
Sinai, Mount, *Egypt,* **67 H3**
Sincelejo, *Colombia,* **30 C2**
Sines, *Portugal,* **61 B7**
Singapore, *Asia, country,* **42 B3**
Singapore, *Singapore, national capital,* **42 B3**
Sinnamary, *French Guiana,* **31 H2**
Sinuiju, *North Korea,* **47 K2**
Sioux City, *U.S.A.,* **25 G2**
Sioux Falls, *U.S.A.,* **25 G2**
Sirjan, *Iran,* **51 G6**
Sittwe, *Burma,* **44 B3**
Sivas, *Turkey,* **50 C4**
Skagen, *Denmark,* **59 D4**
Skagerrak, *Europe,* **59 C4**
Skelleftea, *Sweden,* **58 G2**
Skikda, *Algeria,* **68 G1**
Skopje, *Macedonia, national capital,* **63 G3**
Skyros, *Greece,* **63 H4**
Slavonski Brod, *Croatia,* **62 F2**
Sligo, *Ireland,* **60 B3**
Sliven, *Bulgaria,* **63 H3**
Slovakia, *Europe, country,* **59 F6**
Slovenia, *Europe, country,* **62 E2**
Slovyansk, *Ukraine,* **56 D4**
Slupsk, *Poland,* **59 F5**
Slutsk, *Belarus,* **59 H5**
Smallwood Reservoir, *Canada,* **23 N3**
Smola, *Norway,* **58 C3**
Smolensk, *Russia,* **59 J5**
Sobradinho Reservoir, *Brazil,* **31 K6**
Sobral, *Brazil,* **31 K4**
Sochi, *Russia,* **50 C3**
Society Islands, *French Polynesia,* **37 J6**
Socotra, *Yemen,* **51 F9**
Sodankyla, *Finland,* **58 H2**
Sodertalje, *Sweden,* **58 F4**
Sofia, *Bulgaria, national capital,* **63 G3**
Sohag, *Egypt,* **67 H3**
Sokhumi, *Georgia,* **50 D3**
Sokode, *Togo,* **69 F7**
Sokoto, *Nigeria,* **69 G6**
Solapur, *India,* **49 D7**
Solikamsk, *Russia,* **57 H2**
Solomon Islands, *Oceania, country,* **36 D5**
Solomon Sea, *Papua New Guinea,* **43 M5**
Solwezi, *Zambia,* **72 E2**
Somalia, *Africa, country,* **71 J2**
Somerset Island, *Canada,* **23 K1**
Songea, *Tanzania,* **71 G6**
Songo, *Mozambique,* **73 F3**
Son La, *Vietnam,* **44 D3**
Sorong, *Indonesia,* **43 H4**
Soroti, *Uganda,* **71 F3**
Soroya, *Norway,* **58 G1**
Sotra, *Norway,* **58 C3**
Souk Ahras, *Algeria,* **62 C4**
Sousse, *Tunisia,* **66 D1**
South Africa, *Africa, country,* **72 D6**
South America, 18
Southampton, *United Kingdom,* **60 D4**
Southampton Island, *Canada,* **23 L2**
South Australia, *Australia, internal admin. area,* **38 F5**
South Bend, *U.S.A.,* **25 J2**
South Carolina, *U.S.A., internal admin. area,* **25 K4**
South China Sea, *Asia,* **45 F5**
South Dakota, *U.S.A., internal admin. area,* **24 F2**
South East Cape, *Australia,* **38 J8**
Southend-on-Sea, *United Kingdom,* **60 E4**
Southern Ocean, 18
Southern Sierra Madre, *Mexico,* **26 D4**
South Georgia, *Atlantic Ocean,* **33 L10**
South Island, *New Zealand,* **39 N8**
South Korea, *Asia, country,* **47 L3**
South Orkney Islands, *Atlantic Ocean,* **33 J12**
South Sandwich Islands, *Atlantic Ocean,* **33 N10**
South Shetland Islands, *Atlantic Ocean,* **33 G12**
South West Cape, *New Zealand,* **39 N9**
Spain, *Europe, country,* **61 D7**
Split, *Croatia,* **62 F3**
Spokane, *U.S.A.,* **24 C1**
Spratly Islands, *Asia,* **45 F5**
Springfield, *Illinois, U.S.A., internal capital,* **25 J3**
Springfield, *Massachusetts, U.S.A.,* **25 M2**
Springfield, *Missouri, U.S.A.,* **25 H3**
Springs, *South Africa,* **72 E5**
Sri Jayewardenepura Kotte, *Sri Lanka, national capital,* **49 E9**
Sri Lanka, *Asia, country,* **49 E9**
Srinagar, *India,* **48 C4**
Standerton, *South Africa,* **72 E5**
Stanley, *Falkland Islands,* **33 G10**
Stara Zagora, *Bulgaria,* **63 H3**
Staryy Oskol, *Russia,* **56 D3**
Stavanger, *Norway,* **58 C4**
Stavropol, *Russia,* **50 D2**
Steinkjer, *Norway,* **58 D2**
Stellenbosch, *South Africa,* **72 C6**
Sterlitamak, *Russia,* **57 H3**
Stewart Island, *New Zealand,* **39 N9**
Stockholm, *Sweden, national capital,* **58 F4**
Stoeng Treng, *Cambodia,* **44 E5**
Stoke-on-Trent, *United Kingdom,* **60 D3**
Stora Lule Lake, *Sweden,* **58 F2**
Storavan Lake, *Sweden,* **58 F2**
Stor Lake, *Sweden,* **58 E3**
Stornoway, *United Kingdom,* **60 C2**
Stranraer, *United Kingdom,* **60 C3**
Strasbourg, *France,* **60 F4**
Sturt Stony Desert, *Australia,* **38 G5**
Stuttgart, *Germany,* **60 G4**
Subotica, *Serbia and Montenegro,* **63 F2**
Suceava, *Romania,* **63 H2**
Sucre, *Bolivia, national capital,* **32 E3**
Sudan, *Africa, country,* **67 G5**
Sudbury, *Canada,* **23 L4**
Suez, *Egypt,* **67 H3**
Suez Canal, *Egypt,* **67 H2**
Suhar, *Oman,* **51 G7**
Sukkur, *Pakistan,* **48 B5**
Sukses, *Namibia,* **72 C4**
Sula, *Norway,* **58 C3**
Sula Islands, *Indonesia,* **43 G4**
Sullana, *Peru,* **30 B4**
Sulu Archipelago, *Philippines,* **45 H6**
Sulu Sea, *Asia,* **45 G6**
Sumatra, *Indonesia,* **42 B3**
Sumba, *Indonesia,* **43 E5**
Sumbawa, *Indonesia,* **42 E5**
Sumqayit, *Azerbaijan,* **50 E3**
Sumy, *Ukraine,* **56 C3**
Sunderland, *United Kingdom,* **60 D3**
Sundsvall, *Sweden,* **58 F3**
Superior, Lake, *U.S.A.,* **25 J1**
Sur, *Oman,* **51 G7**
Surabaya, *Indonesia,* **42 D5**
Surakarta, *Indonesia,* **42 D5**
Surat, *India,* **49 C6**
Surgut, *Russia,* **52 D2**
Surigao, *Philippines,* **45 J6**
Surinam, *South America, country,* **31 G3**
Surt, *Libya,* **66 E2**
Sutherland Falls, *New Zealand,* **39 N8**
Suva, *Fiji, national capital,* **39 Q3**
Suwalki, *Poland,* **59 G5**
Suwon, *South Korea,* **47 L3**
Svalbard, *Norway,* **52 A2**
Svolvaer, *Norway,* **58 E1**
Svyetlahorsk, *Belarus,* **59 J5**
Swakopmund, *Namibia,* **72 B4**
Swan Islands, *Honduras,* **27 H4**
Swansea, *United Kingdom,* **60 D4**
Swaziland, *Africa, country,* **72 F5**
Sweden, *Europe, country,* **58 E3**
Swift Current, *Canada,* **22 J3**
Swindon, *United Kingdom,* **60 D4**
Switzerland, *Europe, country,* **62 C2**
Sydney, *Australia, internal capital,* **39 K6**
Sydney, *Canada,* **23 N4**
Syktyvkar, *Russia,* **57 G1**
Sylhet, *Bangladesh,* **49 G6**
Syracuse, *Italy,* **62 E4**
Syracuse, *U.S.A.,* **25 L2**
Syr Darya, *Asia,* **50 H2**
Syria, *Asia, country,* **50 C4**
Syrian Desert, *Asia,* **51 C5**
Syzran, *Russia,* **57 F3**
Szczecin, *Poland,* **59 E5**
Szeged, *Hungary,* **59 G7**
Szekesfehervar, *Hungary,* **59 F7**
Szombathely, *Hungary,* **59 F7**

t

Tabora, *Tanzania,* **71 F5**
Tabriz, *Iran,* **50 E4**
Tabuk, *Saudi Arabia,* **51 C6**
Tacloban, *Philippines,* **45 J5**
Tacna, *Peru,* **30 D7**
Tacoma, *U.S.A.,* **24 B1**
Tacuarembo, *Uruguay,* **32 G6**
Tademait Plateau, *Algeria,* **68 F3**
Tadmur, *Syria,* **50 C5**
Taegu, *South Korea,* **47 L3**
Taejon, *South Korea,* **47 L3**
Tagus, *Europe,* **61 B7**
Tahat, Mount, *Algeria,* **68 G4**
Tahiti, *French Polynesia,* **37 J6**
Tahoua, *Niger,* **66 C6**
Taian, *China,* **47 J3**
Taichung, *Taiwan,* **47 K6**
Tai Lake, *China,* **47 J4**
Taimyr Peninsula, *Russia,* **53 F2**
Tainan, *Taiwan,* **47 K6**
Taipei, *Taiwan, national capital,* **47 K5**
Taiping, *Malaysia,* **42 B3**
Taiwan, *Asia, country,* **47 K6**
Taiwan Strait, *Asia,* **47 J6**
Taiyuan, *China,* **46 H3**
Taizz, *Yemen,* **51 D9**
Tajikistan, *Asia, country,* **48 B3**
Taj Mahal, *India,* **48 D5**
Tajumulco, *Guatemala,* **26 F4**
Taklimakan Desert, *China,* **48 E3**
Talara, *Peru,* **30 B4**
Talaud Islands, *Indonesia,* **43 G3**
Talca, *Chile,* **33 D7**
Taldyqorghan, *Kazakhstan,* **48 D1**
Tallahassee, *U.S.A., internal capital,* **25 K4**
Tallinn, *Estonia, national capital,* **58 H4**
Taltal, *Chile,* **32 D5**
Tamale, *Ghana,* **69 E7**
Tamanrasset, *Algeria,* **68 G4**
Tambacounda, *Senegal,* **69 C6**
Tambov, *Russia,* **56 E3**
Tampa, *U.S.A.,* **25 K5**
Tampere, *Finland,* **58 G3**
Tampico, *Mexico,* **26 E3**
Tana, Lake, *Ethiopia,* **71 G1**
Tandil, *Argentina,* **33 G7**
Tanga, *Tanzania,* **71 G5**
Tanganyika, Lake, *Africa,* **70 E5**
Tangier, *Morocco,* **68 D1**
Tangshan, *China,* **47 J3**
Tanimbar Islands, *Indonesia,* **43 H5**
Tanjungkarang-Telukbetung, *Indonesia,* **42 C5**
Tanjungredeb, *Indonesia,* **42 E3**
Tanta, *Egypt,* **67 H2**
Tan-Tan, *Morocco,* **68 C3**
Tanzania, *Africa, country,* **71 F5**
Tapachula, *Mexico,* **26 F5**
Tapajos, *Brazil,* **31 G5**
Tarakan, *Indonesia,* **42 E3**
Taranto, *Italy,* **62 F3**
Taraz, *Kazakhstan,* **48 C2**
Targu Mures, *Romania,* **63 H2**
Tarija, *Bolivia,* **32 F4**
Tarim Basin, *China,* **48 E3**
Tarkwa, *Ghana,* **69 E7**
Tarnow, *Poland,* **59 G6**
Tarragona, *Spain,* **61 E6**
Tartagal, *Argentina,* **32 F4**
Tartu, *Estonia,* **58 H4**
Tartus, *Syria,* **50 C5**
Tashkent, *Uzbekistan, national capital,* **48 B2**
Tasmania, *Australia, internal admin. area,* **39 J8**
Tasman Sea, *Australasia,* **39 L7**
Tataouine, *Tunisia,* **66 D2**
Taunggyi, *Burma,* **44 C3**
Taupo, Lake, *New Zealand,* **39 Q7**
Taurus Mountains, *Turkey,* **63 J4**
Tavoy, *Burma,* **44 C5**
Tawau, *Malaysia,* **43 E3**
Taytay, *Philippines,* **45 G5**
Taza, *Morocco,* **68 E2**
Tbilisi, *Georgia, national capital,* **50 D3**
Tchibanga, *Gabon,* **70 B4**
Tebessa, *Algeria,* **68 G1**
Tegal, *Indonesia,* **42 C5**
Tegucigalpa, *Honduras, national capital,* **27 G5**
Tehran, *Iran, national capital,* **50 F4**
Tehuacan, *Mexico,* **26 E4**
Tehuantepec, Gulf of, *Mexico,* **26 E4**
Tehuantepec, Isthmus of, *Mexico,* **26 E4**
Tekirdag, *Turkey,* **63 H3**
Tel Aviv-Yafo, *Israel,* **51 B5**
Teller, *U.S.A.,* **22 C2**
Temuco, *Chile,* **33 D7**
Ten Degree Channel, *India,* **49 G9**
Tenerife, *Canary Islands,* **68 B3**
Tenkodogo, *Burkina Faso,* **69 E6**
Tennessee, *U.S.A.,* **25 J3**
Tennessee, *U.S.A., internal admin. area,* **25 J3**
Teofilo Otoni, *Brazil,* **32 K3**
Teotihuacan, *Mexico,* **26 E4**
Terceira, *Azores,* **68 K10**
Teresina, *Brazil,* **31 K4**
Ternate, *Indonesia,* **43 G3**
Terni, *Italy,* **62 E3**
Ternopil, *Ukraine,* **59 H6**
Terracotta Army, *China,* **46 G4**
Terra Firma, *South Africa,* **72 D5**
Teseney, *Eritrea,* **67 J5**
Tete, *Mozambique,* **73 F3**
Tetouan, *Morocco,* **68 D1**
Tetovo, *Macedonia,* **63 G3**
Texarkana, *U.S.A.,* **25 H4**
Texas, *U.S.A., internal admin. area,* **24 G4**
Thailand, *Asia, country,* **44 D4**
Thailand, Gulf of, *Asia,* **44 D6**
Thai Nguyen, *Vietnam,* **44 E3**
Thames, *United Kingdom,* **60 D4**
Thanh Hoa, *Vietnam,* **44 E4**
Thar Desert, *Asia,* **48 B5**
Thasos, *Greece,* **63 H3**
Thaton, *Burma,* **44 C4**
Thessaloniki, *Greece,* **63 G3**
Thies, *Senegal,* **69 B6**
Thika, *Kenya,* **71 G4**
Thimphu, *Bhutan, national capital,* **48 F5**
Thompson, *Canada,* **23 K3**
Three Points, Cape, *Africa,* **69 E8**
Thunder Bay, *Canada,* **23 L4**
Tianjin, *China,* **47 J3**
Tibesti Mountains, *Africa,* **66 E4**
Tibet, *China,* **48 F4**
Tibet, Plateau of, *China,* **48 F4**
Tidjikja, *Mauritania,* **68 C5**
Tien Shan, *Asia,* **48 D2**
Tierra del Fuego, *South America,* **33 E10**
Tighina, *Moldova,* **63 J2**
Tigris, *Asia,* **51 E5**
Tijuana, *Mexico,* **26 A1**
Tikal, *Guatemala,* **26 G4**
Tikhvin, *Russia,* **58 K4**
Tillaberi, *Niger,* **69 F6**
Timbuktu, *Mali,* **69 E5**
Timisoara, *Romania,* **63 G2**
Timor, *Asia,* **43 F5**
Timor Sea, *Asia/Australasia,* **43 G6**
Tindouf, *Algeria,* **68 D3**
Tirana, *Albania, national capital,* **63 F3**
Tiraspol, *Moldova,* **63 J2**
Tiruchchirappalli, *India,* **49 D8**
Titicaca, Lake, *South America,* **30 E7**
Tlemcen, *Algeria,* **68 E2**
Toamasina, *Madagascar,* **73 J3**
Tobago, *Trinidad and Tobabo,* **26 M5**
Toba, Lake, *Indonesia,* **42 A3**
Tobol, *Asia,* **57 K2**
Tobolsk, *Russia,* **57 K2**
Tobyl, *Kazakhstan,* **57 J3**
Tocantins, *Brazil,* **31 J4**
Togo, *Africa, country,* **69 F7**
Tokelau, *Oceania,* **36 F5**
Tokyo, *Japan, national capital,* **47 N3**
Tolanaro, *Madagascar,* **73 J5**
Toledo, *Spain,* **61 D7**
Toledo, *U.S.A.,* **25 K2**
Toledo Bend Reservoir, *U.S.A.,* **25 H4**
Toliara, *Madagascar,* **73 H4**
Tolyatti, *Russia,* **57 F3**
Tolybay, *Kazakhstan,* **57 J3**
Tomakomai, *Japan,* **47 P2**
Tombouctou, *Mali,* **69 E5**
Tomsk, *Russia,* **52 E3**
Tonga, *Oceania, country,* **36 F6**
Tongliao, *China,* **47 K2**
Tonkin, Gulf of, *Asia,* **44 E4**
Tonle Sap, *Cambodia,* **44 D5**
Toowoomba, *Australia,* **39 K5**
Topeka, *U.S.A., internal capital,* **25 G3**
Top, Lake, *Russia,* **58 K2**
Topoli, *Kazakhstan,* **57 G4**
Torghay, *Kazakhstan,* **57 J4**
Tornio, *Finland,* **58 H2**
Toronto, *Canada, internal capital,* **23 M4**
Torrens, Lake, *Australia,* **38 G6**
Torreon, *Mexico,* **26 D2**
Torres Strait, *Australasia,* **38 H2**
Tortuga Island, *Venezuela,* **30 E1**
Toubkal, *Morocco,* **68 D2**
Tougan, *Burkina Faso,* **69 E6**
Touggourt, *Algeria,* **68 G2**
Toulon, *France,* **61 F6**
Toulouse, *France,* **61 E6**
Tours, *France,* **60 E5**
Townsville, *Australia,* **38 J3**
Toyama, *Japan,* **47 N3**
Tozeur, *Tunisia,* **66 C2**
Trabzon, *Turkey,* **50 C3**
Tralee, *Ireland,* **60 B3**
Transantarctic Mountains, *Antarctica,* **77 S4**
Transylvanian Alps, *Romania,* **63 G2**
Trapani, *Italy,* **62 E4**
Trento, *Italy,* **62 D2**
Trenton, *U.S.A., internal capital,* **25 M2**
Tres Arroyos, *Argentina,* **33 F7**
Tres Marias Reservoir, *Brazil,* **32 J3**
Tres Puntas, Cape, *Argentina,* **33 E9**
Trieste, *Italy,* **62 E2**
Trincomalee, *Sri Lanka,* **49 E9**
Trinidad, *Bolivia,* **32 F2**
Trinidad, *Trinidad and Tobago,* **26 M5**
Trinidad and Tobago, *North America, country,* **26 M5**
Tripoli, *Lebanon,* **50 C5**
Tripoli, *Libya, national capital,* **66 D2**
Trivandrum, *India,* **49 D9**
Trnava, *Slovakia,* **59 F6**
Trois-Rivieres, *Canada,* **23 M4**
Tromso, *Norway,* **58 F1**
Trondheim, *Norway,* **58 D3**
Troyes, *France,* **60 F4**
Trujillo, *Peru,* **30 C5**
Tsau, *Botswana,* **72 D4**
Tses, *Namibia,* **72 C5**
Tshabong, *Botswana,* **72 D5**
Tshane, *Botswana,* **72 D4**
Tshikapa, *Democratic Republic of Congo,* **70 D5**
Tshwane, *Botswana,* **72 D4**
Tsimlyansk Reservoir, *Russia,* **56 E4**
Tsiroanomandidy, *Madagascar,* **73 J3**
Tsumeb, *Namibia,* **72 C3**
Tuamotu Archipelago, *French Polynesia,* **37 K6**
Tubmanburg, *Liberia,* **69 C7**
Tubruq, *Libya,* **66 F2**
Tubuai Islands, *French Polynesia,* **37 J7**
Tucson, *U.S.A.,* **24 D4**
Tucupita, *Venezuela,* **30 F2**
Tucurui Reservoir, *Brazil,* **31 J4**
Tugela Falls, *South Africa,* **72 E5**
Tuguegarao, *Philippines,* **45 H4**
Tula, *Russia,* **56 D3**
Tulcea, *Romania,* **63 J2**
Tulsa, *U.S.A.,* **25 G3**
Tumaco, *Colombia,* **30 C3**
Tumbes, *Peru,* **30 B4**
Tunduma, *Tanzania,* **71 F5**
Tunduru, *Tanzania,* **71 G6**
Tunis, *Tunisia, national capital,* **66 D1**
Tunisia, *Africa, country,* **66 C2**
Tunja, *Colombia,* **30 D2**
Tupelo, *U.S.A.,* **25 J4**
Tupiza, *Bolivia,* **32 E4**
Turbat, *Pakistan,* **51 H6**
Turbo, *Colombia,* **30 C2**
Turin, *Italy,* **62 C2**
Turkana, Lake, *Africa,* **71 G3**
Turkey, *Asia, country,* **50 C4**
Turkistan, *Kazakhstan,* **48 B2**
Turkmenabat, *Turkmenistan,* **50 H4**
Turkmenbasy, *Turkmenistan,* **50 F3**
Turkmenistan, *Asia, country,* **50 G4**
Turks and Caicos Islands, *North America,* **27 K3**
Turku, *Finland,* **58 G3**
Turpan, *China,* **48 F2**
Turpan Depression, *China,* **48 G2**
Tuscaloosa, *U.S.A.,* **25 J4**
Tuvalu, *Oceania, country,* **36 E5**
Tuxtla Gutierrez, *Mexico,* **26 F4**
Tuzla, *Bosnia and Herzegovina,* **63 F2**
Tuz, Lake, *Turkey,* **63 K4**
Tver, *Russia,* **56 D2**
Twin Falls, *U.S.A.,* **24 D2**
Tynda, *Russia,* **53 G3**
Tyrrhenian Sea, *Europe,* **62 D3**
Tyumen, *Russia,* **57 K2**

u

Ubangi, *Africa,* **70 C3**
Uberaba, *Brazil,* **32 J3**
Uberlandia, *Brazil,* **32 J3**
Ubon Ratchathani, *Thailand,* **44 D4**
Ucayali, *Peru,* **30 D5**
Udaipur, *India,* **49 C6**
Uddevalla, *Sweden,* **58 D4**
Udon Thani, *Thailand,* **44 D4**
Uele, *Democratic Republic of Congo,* **70 D3**
Ufa, *Russia,* **57 H3**
Uganda, *Africa, country,* **71 F3**
Uitenhage, *South Africa,* **72 E6**
Ujung Pandang, *Indonesia,* **43 E5**
Ukhta, *Russia,* **52 C2**
Ukraine, *Europe, country,* **56 C4**
Ulan Bator, *Mongolia, national capital,* **46 G1**
Ulanhot, *China,* **47 K1**
Ulan Ude, *Russia,* **53 F3**
Ulm, *Germany,* **60 G4**
Uluru, *Australia,* **38 F5**
Ulyanovsk, *Russia,* **57 F3**
Uman, *Ukraine,* **59 J6**
Ume, *Sweden,* **58 F2**
Umea, *Sweden,* **58 G3**
Umnak Island, *U.S.A.,* **23 C3**
Umtata, *South Africa,* **72 E6**
Unalaska Island, *U.S.A.,* **23 C3**
Ungava Bay, *Canada,* **23 N3**
Ungava Peninsula, *Canada,* **23 M2**
Unimak Island, *U.S.A.,* **23 C3**
United Arab Emirates, *Asia, country,* **51 F7**
United Kingdom, *Europe, country,* **60 D3**
United States of America, *North America, country,* **24 F3**
Upington, *South Africa,* **72 D5**
Uppsala, *Sweden,* **58 F4**
Ural, *Asia,* **57 G4**
Ural Mountains, *Russia,* **57 H2**
Uray, *Russia,* **57 J1**
Urganch, *Uzbekistan,* **48 A2**
Urmia, *Iran,* **50 E4**
Uruapan, *Mexico,* **26 D4**
Urucui, *Brazil,* **31 K5**
Uruguaiana, *Brazil,* **32 G5**
Uruguay, *South America, country,* **32 G6**
Urumqi, *China,* **48 F2**
Usak, *Turkey,* **63 J4**
Ushuaia, *Argentina,* **33 E10**
Uskemen, *Kazakhstan,* **52 E3**
Utah, *U.S.A., internal admin. area,* **24 D3**
Utsjoki, *Finland,* **58 H1**
Utsunomiya, *Japan,* **47 N3**
Uy, *Asia,* **57 J3**

Uyuni, *Bolivia,* **32 E4**
Uzbekistan, *Asia, country,* **52 D3**
Uzhhorod, *Ukraine,* **59 G6**

V

Vaasa, *Finland,* **58 G3**
Vadodara, *India,* **49 C6**
Vadso, *Norway,* **58 J1**
Vaduz, *Liechtenstein, national capital,* **62 D2**
Valdai Hills, *Russia,* **59 K4**
Valdes Peninsula, *Argentina,* **33 F8**
Valdivia, *Chile,* **33 D7**
Val-d'Or, *Canada,* **23 M4**
Valdosta, *U.S.A.,* **25 K4**
Valencia, *Spain,* **61 D7**
Valencia, *Venezuela,* **30 E1**
Valencia, Gulf of, *Spain,* **61 D7**
Valera, *Venezuela,* **30 D2**
Valladolid, *Spain,* **61 C6**
Vallenar, *Chile,* **32 D5**
Valletta, *Malta, national capital,* **62 E5**
Valley of the Kings, *Egypt,* **67 H3**
Valparaiso, *Chile,* **32 D6**
Van, *Turkey,* **50 D4**
Vanadzor, *Armenia,* **50 D3**
Vancouver, *Canada,* **22 G4**
Vancouver Island, *Canada,* **22 G4**
Vaner, Lake, *Sweden,* **58 E4**
Van, Lake, *Turkey,* **50 D4**
Vannes, *France,* **60 D5**
Vanua Levu, *Fiji,* **39 Q3**
Vanuatu, *Oceania, country,* **39 M3**
Varanasi, *India,* **48 E5**
Varberg, *Sweden,* **59 E4**
Varhaug, *Norway,* **58 C4**
Varkaus, *Finland,* **58 H3**
Varna, *Bulgaria,* **63 H3**
Vastervik, *Sweden,* **59 F4**
Vatican City, *Europe, country,* **62 E3**
Vatnajokull, *Iceland,* **58 P2**
Vatter, Lake, *Sweden,* **59 E4**
Vaxjo, *Sweden,* **59 E4**
Velikiye Luki, *Russia,* **59 J4**
Venado Tuerto, *Argentina,* **32 F6**
Venezuela, *South America, country,* **30 E2**
Venezuela, Gulf of, *Venezuela,* **30 D1**
Venice, *Italy,* **62 E2**
Ventspils, *Latvia,* **59 G4**
Veracruz, *Mexico,* **26 E4**
Verkhoyansk Range, *Russia,* **53 G2**
Vermont, *U.S.A., internal admin. area,* **25 M2**
Verona, *Italy,* **62 D2**
Vesteralen, *Norway,* **58 E1**
Vestfjorden, *Norway,* **58 E2**
Viborg, *Denmark,* **59 D4**
Vicenza, *Italy,* **62 D2**
Vicksburg, *U.S.A.,* **25 H4**
Victoria, *Australia, internal admin. area,* **38 H7**
Victoria, *British Columbia, Canada, internal capital,* **22 G4**
Victoria, *Chile,* **33 D7**
Victoria Falls, *Africa,* **72 E3**
Victoria Island, *Canada,* **22 J1**
Victoria, Lake, *Africa,* **71 F4**
Victoria Land, *Antarctica,* **77 L3**
Victoria, Mount, *Burma,* **44 B3**
Viedma, *Argentina,* **33 F8**
Viedma, Lake, *Argentina,* **33 D9**
Vienna, *Austria, national capital,* **62 F1**
Vientiane, *Laos, national capital,* **44 D4**
Vietnam, *Asia, country,* **44 E5**
Vigo, *Spain,* **61 B6**
Vijayawada, *India,* **49 E7**
Vikna, *Norway,* **58 D2**
Villach, *Austria,* **62 E2**
Villahermosa, *Mexico,* **26 F4**
Villa Maria, *Argentina,* **32 F6**
Villa Mercedes, *Argentina,* **32 E6**
Villarrica, *Paraguay,* **32 G5**
Vilnius, *Lithuania, national capital,* **59 H5**
Vinh, *Vietnam,* **44 E4**
Vinnytsya, *Ukraine,* **59 J6**
Vinson Massif, *Antarctica,* **77 R3**
Virginia, *U.S.A., internal admin. area,* **25 L3**
Virginia Beach, *U.S.A.,* **25 L3**
Virgin Islands (U.K.), *North America,* **26 M4**
Virgin Islands (U.S.A.), *North America,* **26 M4**
Visby, *Sweden,* **59 F4**
Viscount Melville Sound, *Canada,* **22 H1**
Vishakhapatnam, *India,* **49 E7**
Vistula, *Poland,* **59 F5**
Viti Levu, *Fiji,* **39 Q3**
Vitoria, *Brazil,* **32 K4**
Vitoria, *Spain,* **61 D6**
Vitoria da Conquista, *Brazil,* **32 K2**
Vitsyebsk, *Belarus,* **59 J5**
Vladimir, *Russia,* **56 E2**
Vladivostok, *Russia,* **47 M2**
Vlore, *Albania,* **63 F3**
Volga, *Russia,* **57 F4**
Volga Uplands, *Russia,* **57 F3**
Volgodonsk, *Russia,* **56 E4**
Volgograd, *Russia,* **56 E4**
Volgograd Reservoir, *Russia,* **57 F3**
Volkhov, *Russia,* **58 K4**
Vologda, *Russia,* **56 D2**
Volos, *Greece,* **63 G4**
Volta, Lake, *Ghana,* **69 E7**
Vorkuta, *Russia,* **52 D2**
Voronezh, *Russia,* **56 D3**
Voru, *Estonia,* **59 H4**
Votkinsk, *Russia,* **57 G2**
Vranje, *Serbia and Montenegro,* **63 G3**
Vratsa, *Bulgaria,* **63 G3**
Vyborg, *Russia,* **58 J3**
Vyg, Lake, *Russia,* **58 K3**

W

Wa, *Ghana,* **69 E6**
Waco, *U.S.A.,* **25 G4**
Wad Medani, *Sudan,* **67 H6**
Wagga Wagga, *Australia,* **38 J7**
Wainwright, *U.S.A.,* **22 C1**
Wakayama, *Japan,* **47 N4**
Wake Island, *Oceania,* **36 D3**
Walbrzych, *Poland,* **59 F6**
Wales, *United Kingdom, internal admin. area,* **60 C3**
Wallis and Futuna, *Oceania, dependency,* **36 E6**
Walvis Bay, *Namibia,* **72 B4**
Warangal, *India,* **49 D7**
Warmbad, *South Africa,* **72 E5**
Warri, *Nigeria,* **69 G7**
Warsaw, *Poland, national capital,* **59 G5**
Washington, *U.S.A., internal admin. area,* **24 B1**
Washington D.C., *U.S.A., national capital,* **25 L3**
Waskaganish, *Canada,* **23 M3**
Watampone, *Indonesia,* **43 F4**
Waterford, *Ireland,* **60 C3**
Watson Lake, *Canada,* **22 G2**
Wau, *Sudan,* **70 E2**
Weddell Sea, *Antarctica,* **77 T3**
Weifang, *China,* **47 J3**
Welkom, *South Africa,* **72 E5**
Wellesley Islands, *Australia,* **38 G3**
Wellington, *New Zealand, national capital,* **39 Q8**
Wellington Island, *Chile,* **33 C9**
Wels, *Austria,* **62 E1**
Wenchi, *Ghana,* **69 E7**
Wenzhou, *China,* **47 K5**
Werda, *Botswana,* **72 D5**
Wessel, Cape, *Australia,* **38 G2**
West Antarctica, *Antarctica,* **77 Q4**
Western Australia, *Australia, internal admin. area,* **38 D5**
Western Cordillera, *Colombia,* **30 C3**
Western Cordillera, *Peru,* **30 C6**
Western Dvina, *Europe,* **59 J4**
Western Ghats, *India,* **49 C7**
Western Isles, *United Kingdom,* **60 E2**
Western Sahara, *Africa, dependency,* **68 C3**
Western Sierra Madre, *Mexico,* **26 C2**
West Falkland, *Falkland Islands,* **33 F10**
West Siberian Plain, *Russia,* **52 D2**
West Virginia, *U.S.A., internal admin. area,* **25 K3**
Wetar, *Indonesia,* **43 G5**
Wewak, *Papua New Guinea,* **43 K4**
Whangarei, *New Zealand,* **39 P7**
Whitecourt, *Canada,* **22 H3**
Whitehorse, *Yukon, Canada, internal capital,* **22 F2**
White Lake, *Russia,* **56 D1**
White Nile, *Africa,* **67 H6**
White Sea, *Russia,* **58 K2**
White Volta, *Africa,* **69 E6**
Whitney, Mount, *U.S.A.,* **24 C3**
Wichita, *U.S.A.,* **24 G3**
Wick, *United Kingdom,* **60 D2**
Wight, Isle of, *United Kingdom,* **60 D4**
Wilhelm, Mount, *Papua New Guinea,* **43 L5**
Wilkes Land, *Antarctica,* **77 H2**
Willemstad, *Netherlands Antilles,* **27 L5**
Williams Lake, *Canada,* **22 G3**
Windhoek, *Namibia, national capital,* **72 C4**
Windsor, *Canada,* **23 L4**
Windward Islands, *North America,* **27 N5**
Windward Passage, *North America,* **27 K3**
Winnipeg, *Canada, internal capital,* **23 K3**
Winnipeg, Lake, *Canada,* **23 K3**
Winnipegosis, Lake, *Canada,* **22 J3**
Winterthur, *Switzerland,* **62 D2**
Wisconsin, *U.S.A., internal admin. area,* **25 H2**
Wloclawek, *Poland,* **59 F5**
Wollaston Lake, *Canada,* **22 J3**
Wollongong, *Australia,* **39 K6**
Wonsan, *North Korea,* **47 L3**
Woods, Lake of the, *Canada,* **23 K4**
Worcester, *South Africa,* **72 C6**
Wrangel Island, *Russia,* **53 K2**
Wroclaw, *Poland,* **59 F6**
Wuhai, *China,* **46 G3**
Wuhan, *China,* **47 H4**
Wurzburg, *Germany,* **60 G4**
Wuxi, *China,* **47 K4**
Wuzhou, *China,* **46 H6**
Wyoming, *U.S.A., internal admin. area,* **24 E2**

X

Xai-Xai, *Mozambique,* **73 F5**
Xangongo, *Angola,* **72 B3**
Xankandi, *Azerbaijan,* **50 E4**
Xiamen, *China,* **47 J6**
Xian, *China,* **46 G4**
Xiangfan, *China,* **46 H4**
Xianggang, *China,* **47 H6**
Xichang, *China,* **46 F5**
Xi Jiang, *China,* **46 H6**
Xilinhot, *China,* **47 J2**
Xingu, *Brazil,* **31 H5**
Xining, *China,* **46 F3**
Xuzhou, *China,* **47 J4**

Y

Yakutsk, *Russia,* **53 G2**
Yala, *Thailand,* **44 D6**
Yamantau, *Russia,* **57 H3**
Yamoussoukro, *Ivory Coast, national capital,* **69 D7**
Yancheng, *China,* **47 K4**
Yangtze, *China,* **47 J4**
Yanji, *China,* **47 L2**
Yantai, *China,* **47 K3**
Yaounde, *Cameroon, national capital,* **70 B3**
Yapen, *Indonesia,* **43 J4**
Yaren, *Nauru, national capital,* **36 D5**
Yarmouth, *Canada,* **23 N4**
Yaroslavl, *Russia,* **56 D2**
Yazd, *Iran,* **51 F5**
Yekaterinburg, *Russia,* **57 J2**
Yelets, *Russia,* **56 D3**
Yellow, *China,* **47 J3**
Yellowknife, *Canada, internal capital,* **22 H2**
Yellow Sea, *Asia,* **47 K3**
Yellowstone, *U.S.A.,* **24 E1**
Yellowstone Lake, *U.S.A.,* **24 D2**
Yemen, *Asia, country,* **51 E8**
Yenisey, *Russia,* **52 E2**
Yerevan, *Armenia, national capital,* **50 D3**
Yevpatoriya, *Ukraine,* **63 K2**
Yichang, *China,* **46 H4**
Yichun, *China,* **47 L1**
Yinchuan, *China,* **46 G3**
Yining, *China,* **48 E2**
Yogyakarta, *Indonesia,* **42 D5**
Yongan, *China,* **47 J5**
York, Cape, *Australia,* **38 H2**
Yosemite Falls, *U.S.A.,* **24 C3**
Yoshkar-Ola, *Russia,* **57 F2**
Youth, Isle of, *Cuba,* **27 H3**
Yucatan Peninsula, *Mexico,* **26 G3**
Yukon, *North America,* **22 D2**
Yukon Territory, *Canada, internal admin. area,* **22 F2**
Yulin, *China,* **46 H6**
Yumen, *China,* **46 E3**
Yurimaguas, *Peru,* **30 C5**
Yu Shan, *Taiwan,* **47 K6**
Yushu, *China,* **46 E4**
Yuzhno Sakhalinsk, *Russia,* **53 H3**
Yuzhnoukrayinsk, *Ukraine,* **56 C4**

Z

Zabol, *Iran,* **51 H5**
Zadar, *Croatia,* **62 E2**
Zagreb, *Croatia, national capital,* **62 F2**
Zagros Mountains, *Iran,* **50 E5**
Zahedan, *Iran,* **51 H6**
Zalaegerszeg, *Hungary,* **59 F7**
Zambezi, *Africa,* **73 F3**
Zambia, *Africa, country,* **72 E2**
Zamboanga, *Philippines,* **45 H6**
Zamora, *Spain,* **61 C6**
Zamosc, *Poland,* **59 G6**
Zanjan, *Iran,* **50 E4**
Zanzibar, *Tanzania,* **71 G5**
Zanzibar Island, *Tanzania,* **71 G5**
Zapala, *Argentina,* **33 E7**
Zaporizhzhya, *Ukraine,* **56 D4**
Zaragoza, *Spain,* **61 D6**
Zaraza, *Venezuela,* **30 E2**
Zaria, *Nigeria,* **69 G6**
Zaysan, Lake, *Kazakhstan,* **48 E1**
Zealand, *Denmark,* **59 D5**
Zeil, Mount, *Australia,* **38 F4**
Zelenogorsk, *Russia,* **58 J3**
Zelenograd, *Russia,* **56 D2**
Zenica, *Bosnia and Herzegovina,* **62 F2**
Zhangjiakou, *China,* **47 H2**
Zhanibek, *Kazakhstan,* **57 F4**
Zhanjiang, *China,* **46 H6**
Zhayylma, *Kazakhstan,* **57 J3**
Zhengzhou, *China,* **47 H4**
Zhetiqara, *Kazakhstan,* **57 J3**
Zhlobin, *Belarus,* **59 J5**
Zhodzina, *Belarus,* **59 J5**
Zhuzhou, *China,* **47 H5**
Zhytomyr, *Ukraine,* **59 J6**
Zibo, *China,* **47 J3**
Zielona Gora, *Poland,* **59 E6**
Ziguinchor, *Senegal,* **69 B6**
Zilina, *Slovakia,* **59 F6**
Zimba, *Zambia,* **72 E3**
Zimbabwe, *Africa, country,* **72 E3**
Zinder, *Niger,* **66 C6**
Zlatoust, *Russia,* **57 H2**
Zlin, *Czech Republic,* **62 F1**
Zomba, *Malawi,* **73 G3**
Zonguldak, *Turkey,* **63 J3**
Zorzor, *Liberia,* **69 D7**
Zouerat, *Mauritania,* **68 C4**
Zumba, *Ecuador,* **30 C4**
Zumbo, *Mozambique,* **72 F3**
Zunyi, *China,* **46 G5**
Zurich, *Switzerland,* **62 D2**
Zvishavane, *Zimbabwe,* **72 F4**

GENERAL INDEX

Africa 12, 13, 16–17, 18–19, 64–73
Antarctica 8, 16–17, 18–19, 76–77
Arctic 8, 12, 13, 16–17, 18–19, 74–75
Asia 12, 13, 17, 19, 40–53, 74
Australasia and Oceania 12, 13, 17, 19, 34–39
cartography 10–11
climate 13
earthquakes 79
Equator 8, 9, 13, 79
Europe 12, 13, 16–17, 18–19, 54–63, 74
flags 82–95
floods 79
governments 81
Greenwich Mean Time 80
grid references 9
International Date Line 80
key to maps 15
lakes 78
latitude 8–9, 15
longitude 8–9, 15
map projections 10–11
minerals 12
mountains 78
natural disasters 79
natural fuels 12
North America 12, 13, 16, 18, 20–27, 74
physical maps 6, 18–19
political maps 6, 14, 16–17
population 13
Prime Meridian Line 8, 9, 80
rivers 78
satellite photographs 6, 7, 10, 74, 76
satellites 7
scale 7
South America 12, 13, 16, 18, 28–33
space 79
storms 79
thematic maps 12–13
time zones 80
United Nations (U.N.) 95
volcanic eruptions 79
waterfalls 78
world maps 16–19
world records 78–79

Acknowledgements

Every effort has been made to trace the copyright holders of the material in this book. If any rights have been omitted, the publishers offer to rectify this in any subsequent edition, following notification. The publishers are grateful to the following organizations and individuals for their contributions and permission to reproduce material (t=top, m=middle, b=bottom, l=left, r=right):

© **AFP Photos** 95bm (Henry Ray Abrams). © **Agripicture** 55br (Peter Dean). © **Craig Asquith** 11 projections, 12b, 13, 80. © **Corbis** 8tr (Dan Guravich), 9tr (W. Perry Conway), 10 (Christopher Cormack), 12tr (Bill Ross), 20bl (Richard Cummins), 21br (W. Perry Conway), 28b (Galen Rowell), 29tr (Eye Ubiquitous), 35br (Bates Littlehales), 40–41b (Michael S. Yamashita), 41br (Keren Su), 64–65b (Tom Brakefield), 65br (Gallo Images), 74bl (Galen Rowell), 76b (Wolfgang Kaehler). © **Digital Vision** cover globe, 1, 2–3, 4–5 background, 7tr Earth, 14 background, 54–55 background, 74br, 82–95 background, 96–97b, 97tr. © **European Map Graphics Ltd** 7bm & br, 9bl, 14–19, 20–21 map, 22–27, 28–29 map, 30–33, 34–35 map, 36–39, 40–41 map, 42–53, 54–55 map, 56–63, 64–65 map, 66–73, 75, 77. © **Flag Enterprises Ltd** 82–95 all flags except Afghanistan, Bahrain, Comoros, East Timor, Rwanda, Turkmenistan. © **Stephen Moncrieff** 6mr, 8bl globes, 11 globes. © **NASA** cover background, endpapers (data by Marc Imhoff, NASA GSFC, & Christopher Elvidge, NOAA NGDC; image by Craig Mayhew & Robert Simmon, NASA GSFC), 7tr satellite (JPL). © **Science Photo Library** 4tr (Geospace), 6bl (CNES, 1988 Distribution SPOT image), 74tr (Worldsat International), 76mr (NASA). © **Shipmate Flags, Vlaardingen, The Netherlands** 82 Afghanistan & Bahrain flags, 84 Comoros flag, 85 East Timor flag, 92 Rwanda flag, 94 Turkmenistan flag. © **Still Pictures** 34–35t (Pascal Kobeh).

Managing editor: Gillian Doherty Managing designer: Mary Cartwright Cover design by Zöe Wray

Usborne Publishing is not responsible and does not accept liability for the availability or content of any website other than its own, or for any exposure to harmful, offensive, or inaccurate material which may appear on the Web. Usborne Publishing will have no liability for any damage or loss caused by viruses that may be downloaded as a result of browsing the sites it recommends.

First published in 2004 by Usborne Publishing Ltd, 83–85 Saffron Hill, London EC1N 8RT, England. www.usborne.com Copyright © 2004, 2002, 2001 Usborne Publishing Ltd. The name Usborne and the devices are Trade Marks of Usborne Publishing Ltd. All rights reserved. No part of this publication may be reproduced, stored in a retrieval system, or transmitted in any form or by any means, electronic, mechanical, photocopying, recording or otherwise, without the prior permission of the publisher. UE. First published in America in 2004. Printed in Italy.